WITHDRAWN
HARVARD LIBRARY
WITHDRAWN

Theism and Explanation

Routledge Studies in the Philosophy of Religion

PETER BYRNE, MARCEL SAROT AND MARK WYNN, *Series Editors*

1. God and Goodness
A Natural Theological Perspective
Mark Wynn

2. Divinity and Maximal Greatness
Daniel Hill

3. Providence, Evil, and the Openness of God
William Hasker

4. Consciousness and the Existence of God
A Theistic Argument
J.P. Moreland

5. The Metaphysics of Perfect Beings
Michael J. Almeida

6. Theism and Explanation
Gregory W. Dawes

Theism and Explanation

Gregory W. Dawes

Routledge
Taylor & Francis Group
New York London

First published 2009
by Routledge
270 Madison Ave, New York, NY 10016

Simultaneously published in the UK
by Routledge
2 Park Square, Milton Park, Abingdon, Oxon OX14 4RN

Routledge is an imprint of the Taylor & Francis Group, an informa business

© 2009 Taylor & Francis

Typeset in Sabon by IBT Global.
Printed and bound in the United States of America on acid-free paper by IBT Global.

All rights reserved. No part of this book may be reprinted or reproduced or utilised in any form or by any electronic, mechanical, or other means, now known or hereafter invented, including photocopying and recording, or in any information storage or retrieval system, without permission in writing from the publishers.

Trademark Notice: Product or corporate names may be trademarks or registered trademarks, and are used only for identification and explanation without intent to infringe.

Library of Congress Cataloging in Publication Data
Dawes, Gregory W.
  Theism and explanation / by Gregory W. Dawes.
    p. cm.—(Routledge studies in the philosophy of religion ; 6)
  Includes bibliographical references and index.
  1. Theism. 2. Religion—Philosophy. I. Title.
  BD555.D38 2009
  211'.3—dc22
                                        2008053329

ISBN10: 0-415-99738-0 (hbk)
ISBN10: 0-203-87612-1 (ebk)

ISBN13: 978-0-415-99738-6 (hbk)
ISBN13: 978-0-203-87612-1 (ebk)

*To Anna
who never tires of asking "why?"*

Contents

Acknowledgements ix

1 Against Religious Explanations   1

2 On Explanations in General   19

3 What are Theistic Explanations?   33

4 What Would They Explain?   59

5 Potential Theistic Explanations   77

6 Inference to the Best Explanation   101

7 Successful Theistic Explanations   115

8 Conclusion   143

Appendix: Intentional Explanations   147
Notes   167
Bibliography   191
Index   203

Acknowledgements

My thanks are due first of all to Alan Musgrave, who oversaw the writing of this work. Alan has been a model supervisor, mentor and friend, whose unfailing encouragement helped me to make the transition from biblical studies to philosophy. I am grateful, too, to my colleagues Heather Dyke and James Maclaurin, who commented on earlier versions of the work, and to the two anonymous referees whose suggestions contributed to its improvement. Erica Wetter, my editor at Routledge, has been both patient and helpful. Last, but certainly not least, my thanks are due to Kristin, *sine qua non*.

1 Against Religious Explanations

> 'Tis a pious account, cried my father, but not philosophical—
> there is more religion in it than sound science.
>
> Tristram Shandy

Sometime in the nineteenth century, God disappeared. He did not, of course, disappear from the wider culture, where belief in God remains influential, in some contexts more than ever. But he did disappear from the professional writings of those who were coming to be known as scientists.[1] It is not that all scientists ceased to be believers. They did not. And for those who remained believers, even a world without miracles, a world of "fixed and invariable laws,"[2] could be seen as bearing witness to a Creator.[3] But no matter how religious scientists may have been as individuals, God was banished from their scientific discourse, as the sciences came to be exclusively concerned with natural rather than supernatural causes.

This development is particularly noteworthy in the life sciences, which had provided rich pickings for the natural theologians of an earlier age. As late as 1830, the geologist Charles Lyell did not try to explain how species emerged; he merely described the circumstances of their emergence.[4] And the "creative energy" to which Lyell attributed their emergence has a strongly providentialist flavour. It ensured that species appeared in places where they could flourish and gain a foothold on the earth.[5] But with the publication in 1859 of Charles Darwin's work *On the Origin of Species*, even such quasi-religious explanations come to an end.[6] After Darwin, no religious explanation of a feature of the natural world would be taken seriously, at least by scientists. Even if scientists could discover no natural cause of the phenomenon in question, they would assume that one exists.[7] This exclusion of divine agency has become a taken-for-granted feature of scientific endeavour. The attitude it expresses is often described as the "naturalism" of the modern sciences.

1.1 THE NATURALISM OF THE SCIENCES

In the pages that follow I explore an alternative to this naturalistic stance. I explore the possibility of offering a non-natural explanation of some observable state of affairs, one which invokes a divine agent. My question is: Could an explanation that invokes a divine agent be a good explanation?

2 Theism and Explanation

Could it meet our general criteria of explanatory adequacy, whether or not we choose to call it "scientific"? But before I address this question, it may be useful to reflect on the naturalistic stance of the modern sciences. What is this position, which in recent years has given rise to so much debate? And how might it be defended?

1.1.1 Two Kinds of Naturalism

The problem here is that the term *naturalism* is ambiguous. One could define naturalism in such a way that it would not, in principle, exclude appeal to supernatural agents. We see this in the definition adopted by W. V. Quine. For Quine, naturalism entails "the recognition that it is within science itself, and not in some prior philosophy, that reality is to be identified and described."[8] More precisely, it is the view that "the *most* we can reasonably seek in support of an inventory and description of reality is testability of its observable consequences."[9] Naturalism in this sense is a view of how we gain epistemic access to reality, and there is nothing about this view that is inconsistent with theism. Nor is it inconsistent with the offering of a theistic explanation. Indeed Quine himself notes that if positing the existence of God were to offer some "indirect explanatory benefit," he would embrace this posited deity without in any way abandoning his naturalism.[10]

Naturalism in this broad, Quinean sense is a widely-held position among contemporary philosophers. Many would agree that (in the words of Susan Haack) "the only means we have of figuring out what the world is like, is our experience of the world and our explanatory theorizing about it."[11] Like all philosophical positions, a Quinean naturalism of this kind may be controversial, but it is a different controversy from that with which I began. The controversy with which I began my discussion has to do with a stronger sense of "naturalism," which represents an ontological rather than an epistemological claim.[12] It may be described as the view "that there is nothing besides nature, nothing in addition to nature, nothing outside or beyond nature."[13] The natural world, according to this view, is all that there is. It follows that we should not even consider proposed explanations that posit non-natural entities.

This is a common-sense but crude description of the naturalism I am discussing. Can we produce something more precise? It is not easy to do so. As it stands, my crude definition is less than informative, since it merely raises a new question: What do we mean when we speak of *nature*? If we take "nature" to be equivalent to "the physical universe," then naturalism can be thought of as equivalent to physicalism. But again this merely shifts the question, which now becomes: What do we mean by the *physical* universe? On the assumption that the physical is what is studied by the physicist, a naturalist could argue that only those entities exist that are posited by contemporary physics. But any attempt to spell out what this means would merely give hostages to fortune, for it is all but certain that the theories of contemporary physics will be revised.[14] So a more tenable version of naturalism might insist that all that exists are the *kinds* of entities posited by contemporary physics.[15] What kinds of entities are these? They are, in van Inwagen's words, entities having "non-mental, non-teleological, numerical quantifiable properties" and "composite objects that have these properties as their ultimate parts."[16]

That's one definition of naturalism. It is, perhaps, a little narrow. There are many things the existence of which a naturalist might wish to concede that do not fall into this category. He may, for instance, recognise the existence of "dreams, joys, plans, aspirations"[17] and other mental states, such as beliefs and desires. And even if he is sceptical about mental properties, he may grant some kind of reality to predators, genomes, or inflation rates, none of which fall under van Inwagen's description.[18] So it might be better to speak of "the existential and causal primacy" of physical properties.[19] What would this primacy entail? There are a number of options here. It could be argued that there are, in fact, no non-physical properties, or that such properties exist but are in some sense identical with, supervene on, or are realised by physical properties.[20] And while van Inwagen's definition equates naturalism with physicalism, the latter term may be misleading. *Physicalism* was originally used of a distinct thesis, namely that "all meaningful sentences can be translated into sentences of a universal physical language"[21] or—more modestly—that all scientific theories could, in principle, be reduced to those of physics, in the same way as thermodynamics was reduced to mechanics. I would argue that one can be a naturalist without accepting either of those theses.[22] Finally, like many such definitions, van Inwagen's assumes that there is some "fundamental" level of reality? But what if there is not? What if the world turns out to be "infinitely decomposable"? Could one still make sense of the naturalist thesis?[23]

These are interesting and important issues, but I shall make no attempt to address them. The point I wish to make is a more straightforward, less controversial one. However you define a naturalism of this kind, there is no doubt that it excludes any reference to a supernatural agent,[24] that is to say, an agent who is not part of the natural world but who can interact causally with it.[25] A methodological naturalist will insist that we must proceed *as if* there were no supernatural agents, while an ontological naturalist will insist that there *are* no such agents. The two are united in their view that, in the words of Richard Lewontin, "our explanations of material phenomena exclude any role for supernatural demons, witches, and spirits of every kind, including any of the various gods from Adonai to Zeus."[26] It is this feature of naturalism, and this feature alone, which is the starting point of my investigation. What interests me is the point made in my opening remarks, namely that this view is shared by "nearly every present-day scientist,"[27] the only exceptions being those who are professed creationists.[28] The origins of this attitude are a question for the historian. What the philosopher can ask is: Is it warranted?

4 *Theism and Explanation*

While I hope that my study will shed light on this issue, it will do so indirectly, for the question I wish to address is a broader one. I am interested not merely in those explanations that we customarily describe as scientific; I am interested in explanations in general (1.2.2).[29] The question I am addressing can be variously described. Could any account of divine action have explanatory force? Could the existence and action of a divine agent be the primary causal factor in a satisfactory explanation? Or, to put it crudely, even if all this talk about God were true, could it *explain* anything? If the answer to these questions is "no," then it is not only scientists who have good reason to be methodological naturalists. We all do.

1.1.2 Methodological and Ontological Naturalism

I have suggested that the naturalism in which I am interested is an ontological rather than an epistemological position. It is this fact that enables us to distinguish it from Quinean naturalism, which would not (in principle) exclude the supernatural. (Quinean naturalism could, perhaps, exclude the supernatural *in practice*, on the grounds that science has shown physicalism to be at least probably true, but that's another issue.[30]) But defenders of the naturalism of the modern sciences often insist that theirs is not, in fact, an ontological commitment. What they are defending, they argue, is nothing more than a *methodological* naturalism. An ontological naturalism, writes Robert Pennock, "makes substantive claims about what exists in nature and then adds a closure clause stating 'and that is all there is.'"[31] By way of contrast, methodological naturalism is an epistemological position. It specifies how we should seek to attain knowledge: typically, by using the methods of the natural sciences.[32] It does not, at least in the first place, specify the content of our knowledge.

Is this a workable distinction? Could you be a methodological naturalist without committing yourself to any particular ontology? More precisely, could you be a methodological naturalist while continuing to believe in God? There are many who think you can: philosopher Michael Ruse is perhaps the best-known defender of this position.[33] Phillip Johnson, on the other hand, argues that such people are deceiving themselves, that a methodological naturalism leads naturally and inevitably to a stronger, metaphysical commitment.

> The problem, very briefly stated, is this: if employing MN [methodological naturalism] is the only way to reach true conclusions about the history of the universe, and if the attempt to provide a naturalistic view of the universe has continually gone from success to success, and if even theists concede that trying to do science on theistic premises always leads nowhere or into error (the embarrassing "God of the gaps"), then the likely explanation of this state of affairs is that naturalism is true and theism is false.[34]

I shall be critical of Johnson's work shortly, but in this case he is surely right. It is true that he would not grant the premise of his own argument. He would deny that the naturalistic programme of the sciences has been as successful as its advocates urge. (Johnson is a leading opponent of evolutionary theory and advocate of "intelligent design.") But if he is wrong, if the naturalistic research programme of the sciences has been overwhelmingly successful, then one could argue that the best explanation of its success *is* the truth of ontological naturalism.[35]

Indeed I would go further. I would argue that for the purpose of offering explanations, methodological naturalism is practically indistinguishable from its ontological sibling. It is true that *in itself* methodological naturalism entails no particular metaphysics. But this is only because it entails nothing at all, since it is a procedural matter, a rule rather than a proposition. What does that rule specify? If it specified nothing more than a particular method of enquiry, as Pennock suggests, it would be less controversial. As Quine notes, we could not assume that adherence to such a method would exclude the supernatural. But those who defend the methodological naturalism of the sciences apparently mean something more than this. They wish to exclude any possible appeal to a divine agent.

So it seems more plausible to interpret the phrase "methodological naturalism" in a second way. It tells us that in our quest for knowledge we should proceed *as if* ontological naturalism were true. If you accept this definition, then at least in practice methodological and ontological naturalism are indistinguishable. It scarcely matters if you hold to naturalism as a procedural rule or as an ontological commitment. In both cases it will guide your enquiry, determining what kinds of entities or forces you will posit when offering explanations.

1.1.3 An *A Priori* Commitment?

So yes, one can distinguish between methodological and ontological naturalism. But if the former means acting as if the latter were true, the distinction has little practical significance. Many opponents of scientific naturalism, such as Phillip Johnson, would readily agree. What conclusion do they draw? Well, Johnson argues that what presents itself as a modest methodological naturalism is, in fact, nothing more than an *a priori*, dogmatic commitment to a materialist world view. It is not the case, he argues, that science has shown naturalism to be justified, by demonstrating the truth of its assumptions. Rather, he suggests, a prior commitment to naturalism has determined the kinds of answers that will be considered "scientific" and thus acceptable. As he writes of his particular *bête noir*, namely the theory of evolution by natural selection,

> Darwinism became unchallengeable scientific orthodoxy not because the creative power of the mutation/selection mechanism was

experimentally demonstrated, but because the scientific community adopted standards of evaluation that made something very much like Darwinism inevitable.[36]

In an article in *First Things*, Johnson develops this idea. "For scientific materialists," he writes, "*the materialism comes first; the science comes thereafter.* We might more accurately describe them as 'materialists employing science.'"[37] In support of this view, Johnson cites the following, extraordinary passage from an essay by the evolutionary biologist Richard Lewontin.

> We take the side of science *in spite of* the patent absurdity of some of its constructs, *in spite of* its failure to fulfill many of its extravagant promises of health and life, *in spite of* the tolerance of the scientific community for unsubstantiated just-so stories, because we have a prior commitment, a commitment to materialism. It is not that the methods and institutions of science somehow compel us to accept a material explanation of the phenomenal world, but, on the contrary, that we are forced by our *a priori* adherence to material causes to create an apparatus of investigation and a set of concepts that produce material explanations, no matter how counter-intuitive, no matter how mystifying to the uninitiated. Moreover, that materialism is absolute, for we cannot allow a Divine Foot in the door.[38]

One might argue that Lewontin's attitude was not typical of those who pioneered an exclusive reliance on natural explanations, many of whom (as I noted earlier) were themselves Christians.[39] One might also argue that Darwin himself was anxious to establish, on *empirical* grounds, the superiority of his theory to that of "special creation."[40] His theory was able to account for facts, such as the existence of vestigial organs, that were puzzling on any creationist view.[41] But these are questions for the historian, not for the philosopher.[42] What the philosopher wants to know is whether the kind of naturalism employed by the sciences is justified. Is it, as Johnson suggests, merely a matter of atheistic prejudice? Or are there good reasons for adopting this stance?

What kinds of reasons might these be? The first point to be made is that they need not be *a priori* reasons, in the sense of reasons that are prior to empirical enquiry. As Johnson himself concedes, one could argue for the exclusion of supernatural agency on *a posteriori* grounds, by appealing to the success of the naturalistic research programme of the modern sciences. I shall be offering such an argument myself in due course (7.3). The second point to be made is that not all *a priori* reasons need be matters of simple prejudice. There might be *a priori* considerations, drawn from the very nature of proposed religious explanations, which lead us to reject them. It may be, for instance, that proposed religious explanations by their very

Against Religious Explanations 7

nature lack explanatory force. Whether this is the case is a question that Johnson fails to address; it will be a central question of the present enquiry. And even if there could, in principle, exist a respectable religious explanation, natural explanations might still be preferable. They might exhibit certain explanatory virtues that religious explanations lack, virtues such as a high degree of testability, simplicity, economy, and precision. Such considerations would be *a priori*, but could hardly be regarded as a matter of mere atheistic prejudice.

1.2 RELIGION, EXPLANATION, AND REVELATION

In the debate regarding scientific naturalism—a debate which I shall argue in a moment is largely misconceived—both sides assume that religions are in the business of offering explanations. If the task of the sciences is also that of explanation,[43] then religion and science can be in competition only if religious beliefs have some intended explanatory function. But is this true? What role, if any, do proposed religious explanations play in the lives of our religious traditions? How are alleged religious and scientific explanations related? And what kinds of objections might be raised to proposed religious explanations?

1.2.1 Religion and Explanation

When I speak of "religious explanations," I am not making any claim about the *origin* of religion. In particular, I am not implying that religions arose as quasi-scientific attempts to explain empirical data. There are those who have defended such "intellectualist" explanations of religion—one thinks of E. B. Tylor or, in our own day, Robin Horton—but nothing of that kind is being defended here. Nor do I wish to suggest that religious believers customarily *embrace* their faith because it explains empirical facts. I suspect that in practice such an attitude is rare. As Alvin Plantinga writes, can anyone imagine that a Christian would reason as follows?

> What is the best explanation for all that organized complexity in the natural world and the characteristic features of human life and all the rest of what we see about us? Well, let's see, perhaps there is an omniscient, omnipotent, wholly good being, who created the world. Yes, that's it; and perhaps this being is one of three persons, the other two being his divine son, and a third person proceeding from the first two (or maybe just the first), yet there are not three gods but one; the second person became incarnate, suffered, was crucified, and died, thus atoning for our sins and making it possible for us to have life and have it more abundantly. Right; that's got to be it; that's a dandy explanation of the facts.[44]

Plantinga's point is well made. But of course there is nothing to prevent the theistic philosopher from formulating *some* of her core beliefs as explanatory hypotheses. Indeed, from the days of Thomas Aquinas (1225–74)—or perhaps the medieval Muslim philosophers, such as Abu Nasr al-Farabi (872–950),[45] from whom Aquinas borrowed his arguments[46]—this has been the customary way of arguing for the existence of God. There is some fact about the world, such thinkers argue, that can be explained only by positing God's existence. As we shall see shortly, some contemporary theistic philosophers take this idea further. They argue that not only do the facts require a religious explanation, but that the religious explanation they offer meets the standards that we expect of explanations in other fields.[47]

1.2.2 A Misconceived Debate

Now such thinkers may be wrong. It may be that religious explanations are not, in fact, and could never be adequate explanations. But this needs to be demonstrated rather than assumed. Until it is demonstrated, we should not assume that all theories that posit a supernatural agent *ipso facto* fail to meet our general standards of explanatory adequacy.

I say "our general standards of explanatory adequacy," because much of the current debate regarding scientific naturalism has been misconceived.[48] This is particularly the case in discussions regarding creation science and its successor, intelligent design. For legal and constitutional reasons, particularly in the United States, opponents have focused on the claim that such theories cannot be described as scientific. And one of the reasons, it is argued, why they cannot be regarded as scientific is that they posit, or at least entail the existence of, a supernatural agent. In the legal arena, those arguments have been remarkably successful. In a series of trials, beginning in 1968, American courts have consistently ruled that creationist theories are religious, not scientific. It follows, they argue, that such theories should not be taught in public schools. The most recent of such decisions was given in December 2005, against the Dover Area School Board in Pennsylvania, which had sought to introduce "intelligent design" (ID) into schools. On that occasion, Judge John E. Jones argued that intelligent design fails to qualify as scientific

> on three different levels, *any one of which is sufficient to preclude a determination that ID is science.* They are: (1) ID violates the centuries-old ground rules of science by invoking and permitting supernatural causation; (2) the argument of irreducible complexity, central to ID, employs the same flawed and illogical contrived dualism that doomed creation science in the 1980s [the idea "that to the extent evolutionary theory is discredited, ID is confirmed"]; and (3) ID's negative attacks on evolution have been refuted by the scientific community.[49]

What is interesting is that, according to Judge Jones, any explanation that "invokes" or even merely "permits" supernatural causation *ipso facto* ceases to be scientific. This ruling defines science in such a way as to exclude supernatural agency, which hands an easy victory to the opponents of ID. But it would be a Pyrrhic victory if it resulted in the exclusion of what is, in fact, the best explanation of some phenomenon.

In any case, the important philosophical question is not whether these proposed religious explanations are scientific; it is whether they are any good, as explanations. After all, what we choose to count as "scientific" is, to some extent, a mere matter of definition.[50] Richard Swinburne, for instance, thinks that what he calls "personal" (and I call "intentional") explanations—those that appeal to the purposes of an agent—are not, and cannot be reduced to, scientific explanations.[51] I myself would argue that since such explanations yield testable predictions, they *can* be regarded as scientific, even if they rarely rise above the level of a "folk science." But little of substance rests on this debate. The more important question is whether they are adequate explanations, and on the answer to this question Swinburne and I would probably agree.

1.2.3 Religion and Revelation

There are at least two ways in which one might argue against proposed religious explanations. Let me begin with a work in which the two are confused, namely a recent article by Matthew Brauer, Barbara Forrest, and Steven Gey. What Brauer, Forrest, and Gey are concerned with is, once again, the teaching of intelligent design in American schools. But in the course of their discussion they offer a defence of the methodological naturalism of the sciences. What they fail to notice is that they are offering two, quite distinct defences. At times they appear to be arguing that naturalism is a defeasible position, justified in a *de facto* manner by its explanatory success. "MN [methodological naturalism]," they write, is simply

> science's universal *procedural* protocol requiring natural explanations for natural phenomena. . . . This protocol is not arbitrary, and contrary to ID proponents' accusations, requires no a priori *metaphysical* commitments. The only commitment is to an empirical methodology, which scientists use with good reason: it works. Natural explanations are scientifically successful; supernatural ones are not. The commitment to MN is thus pragmatic and provisional, not ideological.[52]

So far, so good. It appears that there exist proposed "supernatural explanations" and that they have been shown to fail. We do not have sufficient reason to regard them as true. I, for one, would have no quarrel with that conclusion, which I shall describe shortly as a *de facto* objection to religious explanations (1.3.1). But Brauer, Forrest, and Gey immediately introduce another, quite distinct reason.

> If a better methodology were devised, science would adopt it and adjust the definition of science to reflect its use, but humans have no recognized cognitive faculties for knowing the supernatural. Consequently, despite other ways in which people claim to know things (intuition, revelation, etc.), naturalistic methodology is the only *intersubjective*, *public* way of knowing nature.[53]

This is what I shall shortly call an *in principle* objection (1.3.2). It suggests that what is wrong with claims about the supernatural is that they are based on "intuition," "revelation," or some other alleged cognitive mechanism that is not intersubjectively testable.[54] The same *in principle* objection is to be found in another passage.

> Science simply uses any methodology that affords explanatory and predictive success, and only MN does this. MN's epistemological reach is coextensive only with human sensory faculties and inferences derived from empirical data. It need not, nor does it, assume a priori that MN is the *only* source of truth and that claims purportedly derived from intuition and revelation are false, but neither is there any known methodology for intersubjectively calling upon intuition and revelation to explain the natural world.[55]

It is true that religious beliefs are often based upon claims to divine revelation which are not intersubjectively testable. Indeed some theologians insist on this fact, arguing that Christian beliefs cannot be tested empirically or otherwise demonstrated, but are "known" to be true only by those to whom God has revealed them.[56] In making such extraordinary claims (which amount to, "How do I know this is true? Because God told me") they are in distinguished company, for perhaps the most influential of twentieth-century theologians, Karl Barth, held a similar view.[57] I have elsewhere criticised appeals to "faith" for precisely this reason,[58] and have argued that a theology that rests on such appeals has no place in the secular academy.[59]

But it may be that claims originally based on faith could be defended by argument, by offering an explanation that has one or more of these claims as its *explanans*. If this is true, then a religious claim cannot be discredited merely on the grounds it arises from an assumed divine revelation. To object to religious claims because they arise from an alleged revelation is to confuse the context of discovery and the context of justification,[60] or—if you prefer—to commit the genetic fallacy. According to some reports, the mathematician Srinivasa Ramanujan claimed to receive formulas from the goddess of Namakkal while asleep.[61] If this *is* what he believed, it cannot be used to discredit his mathematical work *if* he could support those formulas with proofs. The same is true of any religious claim. The important question is not, "Where did it come from?," but, "Can it be defended? Can it function as the *explanans* of a successful explanation?"

Interestingly, Brauer, Forrest, and Gey concede that there are circumstances in which propositions about the supernatural *would* be acceptable.

> Doubts about the supernatural as a scientific explanation would vanish were [ID advocates] to produce (1) an epistemology for intersubjective knowledge of the supernatural and (2) a workable methodology for producing original data and constructing explanations of it.[62]

But if we had such an epistemology or methodology—if claims about the supernatural were intersubjectively testable—then the sole serious objection to such explanations would be the pragmatic, *de facto* one, that they have failed the test and no longer merit our acceptance.

1.3 OBJECTIONS TO RELIGIOUS EXPLANATIONS

What emerges from this discussion? We can see that there are two kinds of objections to proposed religious explanations, which I shall refer to as *de facto* and *in principle* objections. The weakness of, for instance, Brauer, Forrest, and Gey's article is that it fails to distinguish these. So let's see what the distinction involves.

1.3.1 A *De Facto* Objection

A first kind of objection maintains that while propositions about divine agency might once have been apparently successful explanations, they have been superseded. Across the sciences, we now have competing natural theories that are more successful than the old, theological ones. In other words, religious explanations represent a failed research tradition. They need be taken no more seriously than accounts of planetary movements derived from Ptolemaic astronomy. There was a time when Ptolemy's view of the cosmos was the best explanation we had of the movements of the heavenly bodies, but that time has passed. Ptolemaic astronomy has now been superseded by a more successful explanation, one capable of explaining phenomena that Ptolemaic astronomy could not. In the same way, the atheist could concede that religious accounts of the origins of living beings do have some explanatory force, while arguing that they have been superseded. We now have natural accounts, such as that offered by Charles Darwin, which we have more reason to accept. I shall refer to this as the *de facto* objection to religious explanations. According to this view, religious explanations are acceptable *in principle*—they could have explanatory force—but *in fact* we have insufficient reason to accept them.

As we have seen (1.2.3), there are hints of this *de facto* objection in the work of Brauer, Forrest, and Gey. But let me illustrate it in more detail by reference to Philip Kitcher's comments on creationism. Kitcher is not at all impressed with the work of contemporary creationists, which, he argues, fails to meet the standards of an adequate theory. Contemporary creationism has no detailed solutions, no clear strategies for advancing our knowledge, and is saved from refutation only by its vagueness.[63] But Kitcher argues that eighteenth- and nineteenth-century creationists—men such as William Buckland, Adam Sedgwick, and Louis Agassiz—offered something more substantial, which *was* worthy of the name "science."

> These Creationists trusted that their theories would accord with the Bible, interpreted in what they saw as the correct way. However, that fact does not affect the scientific status of those theories. Even postulating an unobserved Creator need be no more unscientific than postulating unobservable particles. . . . The great scientific Creationists of the eighteenth and nineteenth centuries offered problem-solving strategies for many of the questions addressed by evolutionary theory. They struggled hard to explain the observed distribution of fossils. Sedgwick, Buckland, and others practiced genuine science. They stuck their necks out and volunteered information about the catastrophes that they invoked to explain biological and geological findings.[64]

The fact that such thinkers offered "definite proposals" meant that their theories were refutable and (of course) eventually refuted. Many of them recognised this, a fact which Kitcher illustrates by reference to Adam Sedgwick's public retraction of his own brand of creationist theory in 1831.

As it happens, Kitcher's view is questionable, historically. Many nineteenth-century geologists did abandon geological theories that corresponded, to some degree, to the Genesis account of creation. They recognised that these theories had been falsified. But it could be argued that the theories they abandoned were *geological* theories, logically distinguishable from a religious explanation of the same facts. They may have corresponded, to some degree, to the pattern of the biblical account, and they may have left room for divine agency, but they did not themselves invoke God as an agent. If this is correct, the example Kitcher chooses does not (in itself) show that theistic explanations are falsifiable. But let me leave this objection aside. All I am doing here is illustrating a particular position, namely the *de facto* objection to religious explanations. Kitcher's comments illustrate that position. He apparently has no objection to religious explanations *in principle*; he simply believes they have been superseded.

A clearer example of a *de facto* objection is to be found in a recent book by Niall Shanks. Shanks rejects the Johnsonian idea that the naturalism of the sciences represents a dogmatic, *a priori* commitment. On what, then, is it based? It is based, he argues, on the success of naturalistic science and the failure to find any evidence in support of alternative views.

Methodological naturalism, as it appears in science, is based on an inductive generalization derived from 300 to 400 years of scientific experience. Time and time again, scientists have considered hypotheses about occult entities ranging from souls, to spirits, to occult magical powers, to astrological influences, to psychic powers, ESP, and so on. Time and time again such hypotheses have been rejected, not because of philosophical bias, but because when examined carefully there was not a shred of good evidence to support them. Scientists are allowed, like anyone else, to learn from experience.... The experience is straightforward. We keep smacking into nature, whereas the denizens of the supernatural and paranormal realms somehow manage to elude careful analysis of data.[65]

Once again, this is a *de facto* rather than an *in principle* objection. Indeed Shanks is apparently prepared to concede the possibility of what he calls "supernatural science."[66] The explanations it offers might be prompted by faith, but they would be supported by evidence.[67] He illustrates this possibility by discussing the (largely inconclusive) "prayer trials"—clinical trials of the efficacy of intercessory prayer in medicine—to which I myself shall make reference later (4.2.2).

This *de facto* objection to religious explanations is a modest position, which is not difficult to defend. There is no doubt that across a variety of fields, religious explanations have been replaced by those invoking only natural causes (7.3). But to many opponents of religious explanations, the *de facto* objection seems inadequate. Applied to the debate about scientific naturalism, it justifies a provisional exclusion of religious explanations from the sciences, but it cannot guarantee that this exclusion will be permanent. It cannot prevent people from offering religious explanations and insisting that we take them seriously. So some opponents of religious explanations have adopted a more uncompromising position. In John Earman's words, they have tried to find a "silver bullet" which will "put a merciful end to all the nonsense."[68] The most promising candidate for a silver bullet would be a demonstration that even if a proposition about divine action were true, it would fail to explain. It would fail to meet some condition that must be met by any successful explanation. I shall refer to this as the *in principle* objection to religious explanations.

1.3.2 An *In Principle* Objection

We find hints of an *in principle* objection to religious explanations in the published work of Charles Darwin. At one point in the *Origin of Species*, for instance, Darwin suggests that to appeal to a divine plan—to what today would be called "intelligent design"—does not in fact explain anything. In speaking of "the plan of creation," we may think we are giving an explanation, but in reality we are only restating the fact to be explained.[69] But in his unpublished writings, Darwin is more forthright. As early as 1838, he writes that

> the explanation of types of structure in classes—as resulting from the *will* of the deity, to create animals on certain plans,—is no explanation—*it has not the character of a physical law* & is therefore utterly useless.—it foretells nothing because we know nothing of the will of the Deity, how it acts & whether constant or inconstant like that of man.—the cause given we know not the effect.[70]

This objection raises some important issues. Whether it is true that, given a divine cause, "we know not the effect" will be one of the central questions of the present study (5.1–5.2). And a key issue here is whether all explanations must depend on laws (Appendix 3.3).

Some of Darwin's followers took up his *in principle* objections. In a review of Darwin's *Origin of Species*, Thomas Henry Huxley summarises the explanatory advantages of Darwin's theory over that of the special creation of individual species. But he goes on to add the following qualification.

> Suppose for a moment we admit the explanation [special creation], and then seriously ask ourselves how much the wiser are we; what does the explanation explain? Is it any more than a grandiloquent way of announcing the fact, that we really know nothing about the matter? A phaenomenon is explained when it is shown to be a case of some general law of Nature; but the supernatural interposition of the Creator can, by the nature of the case, exemplify no law, and if species really have arisen in this way, it is absurd to attempt to discuss their origin.[71]

More recent advocates of *in principle* objections are not difficult to find. Richard Dawkins, for instance, writes that to explain the machinery of life "by invoking a supernatural Designer is to explain precisely nothing."[72] Why? Because it "leaves unexplained the origin of the Designer."[73] A more sophisticated argument is offered by E. Thomas Lawson and Robert N. McCauley. They argue that propositions about God are "semantically anomalous" insofar as they are open to an indefinite number of interpretations.[74] This flexibility allows them to appear to explain any possible state of affairs. But this is a philosophical vice rather than a virtue. As they write,

> religious models remain undefeated in the face of any contrary experience. Consequently, they explain nothing at all, since the theory that explains everything explains nothing. However, because they are incapable of defeat, they are also consistent with any possible state of affairs, and this certainly leads to the appearance that they have an

explanation for everything. But . . . when explanation is complete, science (and genuine explanation) is dead.[75]

A similar view of religious explanations has been put forward by Robert Pennock. Pennock argues that religious explanations are "immune from disconfirmation," since they "give no guidance about what follows or does not follow from their supernatural components."[76] For Pennock, this is a consequence of the fact that the agent whom they invoke is capable of working miracles. For this reason, "nothing definite can be said about the processes that would connect a given effect with the will of the supernatural agent—God might simply say the word and zap anything in or out of existence."[77]

1.3.3 Deciding the Issue

So the key question for opponents of religious explanations is: Are such explanations flawed in principle, or merely superseded in practice? From the atheist's point of view, a "flawed in principle" answer would be preferable, since it would "put a merciful end to all the nonsense." But is it true? There are two ways in which I could attempt to answer that question. One option would be to survey the *in principle* objections that have been offered to such explanations, perhaps from Darwin onwards, to see if such objections are well founded. But this would not necessarily settle the issue, for there may be other objections that have not yet been raised. And in any case, many of these objections appear misguided. It may be possible to formulate better ones.

Some of the *in principle* objections to which I have referred hark back to the accusation that religious propositions are meaningless, or at least unscientific, because they are unfalsifiable.[78] There is, however, an ambiguity here. When philosophers argue that a theory is "unfalsifiable," they may mean that there are no possible observations that would demonstrate its falsity. If this were true, the theory *would* be unfalsifiable, in the strict sense of the term. But they may mean something quite different, namely that the proponents of the theory adopt all manner of *ad hoc* strategies to avoid admitting that their theory *has* been falsified.[79] This latter does not necessarily indicate a weakness in their theory, although it does represent a moral failure on the part of its proponents.

Now it may be the case that many religious believers are guilty of this failure: they refuse to admit there are facts that demonstrate their beliefs to be false. But that does not mean their beliefs are unfalsifiable in the strict sense. On the contrary, it assumes that there are facts—such as the existence of gratuitous evils—that constitute evidence against religious explanations.[80] And while it is true that some proposed religious explanations do appear to be unfalsifiable, because they lack empirical content (3.2.3), they can often be made falsifiable by a more careful formulation. That

God created the world may (or may not) be an unfalsifiable proposition, but that he did so on Sunday October 23, 4004 BC, surely *is* falsifiable.[81] Indeed, as all but young-earth creationists would agree, it has been shown to be false.

Similar questions may be raised about the *in principle* objection made by Dawkins: the idea that religious explanations are unacceptable because they leave unexplained the existence of their *explanans* (God). Dawkins apparently assumes that every successful explanation should also explain its own *explanans*. But this is an unreasonable demand. Many of our most successful explanations raise new puzzles and present us with new questions to be answered. As Peter Lipton remarks, "a drought may explain a poor crop, even if we don't understand why there was a drought; . . . the big bang explains the background radiation, even if the big bang is itself inexplicable."[82] I shall discuss later the further objection, raised by Pennock, that religious explanations invoke an agent who can work miracles (4.4), arguing that this objection, too, is not decisive. The fact that a divine agent can work miracles does not necessarily mean that we cannot predict his behaviour.

So at least these *in principle* objections do not seem adequate. But rather than trying to find others, I shall adopt a different strategy. Rather than surveying the possible *in principle* objections to religious explanations, I shall start from scratch. I shall begin with the very idea of a religious explanation and examine its implications. Critics of religious explanations have objected to them on a variety of grounds. But before we can evaluate their arguments, we need to get some fundamental issues clear. Those fundamental issues have to do with both the form and the content of proposed religious explanations. What kind of explanations are these? What kind of an agent do they invoke? Under what conditions, if any, would invoking such an agent be explanatory? It is these questions which I shall be addressing.

Let me briefly anticipate the answer I shall give. We cannot, I shall argue, assume that a proposed religious explanation is flawed *in principle*. We can reconstruct religious explanations in a form that resembles the kinds of explanations we accept in other fields. A religious explanation would be yet another theoretical explanation, positing the existence of yet another unobservable entity. By formulating its claim regarding divine action with sufficient care, we could even ensure that it was testable. But of course it remains an open question whether it passes the test, whether any proposed religious explanation is successful *in practice*. It may be that none of the particular religious explanations that have been proposed has explanatory force. And it may be that even if some do have explanatory force, there is no case in which a proposed religious explanation represents the *best* available explanation of any phenomenon. But this, I shall argue, is not a question that can be decided in advance: it can be decided only on a case-by-case basis.

Does this conclusion support the methodological naturalism which I discussed at the beginning of this chapter, the idea that we can exclude, from the outset, proposed religious explanations? No, it does not. It leaves open the bare possibility that there might exist a successful religious explanation, one that would warrant our acceptance. What I hope this study will do is to spell out the conditions that a successful religious explanation would have to meet. Once one has examined these conditions, one may come to suspect that it is *unlikely* that any proposed religious explanation would be successful.[83] This suggests that religious explanations should be, at best, explanations of last resort.[84] But whether or not any proposed religious explanation will ever be shown to be successful remains an open question. If the world really is as advocates of naturalism believe, we have nothing to fear from allowing that question to be openly addressed.

2 On Explanations in General

> "Explain all that," said the Mock Turtle.
> "No, no! The adventures first," said the Gryphon in an impatient tone: "explanations take such a dreadful time."
>
> Lewis Carroll

My initial discussion of religious explanations suffered from the ambiguity of the phrase "religious explanation." In fact, ambiguities surround both the term "religious" and the term "explanation." I have already discussed one possible ambiguity (1.2.2). Is the focus of my enquiry those explanations that we customarily describe as "scientific"? Or is it explanations in general? My answer is that I am interested in explanations in general. Whether we choose to call some of these explanations "scientific" is a relatively unimportant matter. What I shall argue is that there are certain features that all adequate explanations will share, and it is those features that I wish to reflect on here. To spell out what those features are will involve a certain amount of philosophical spade-work, preparing the ground for what is to come. But spade-work is important, and at the end of the day there is no substitute for rolling up one's sleeves and getting on with it.

2.1 INITIAL CLARIFICATIONS

Let me begin with the term "religious," before moving on to what I mean by an "explanation."

2.1.1 Religious and Theistic Explanations

In the course of my introductory remarks, I have generally used the phrase *religious explanations*. But what I am interested in here are more accurately described as *theistic explanations*. They posit the existence, not just of any supernatural agent, but of the traditional God of Jews, Christians, and Muslims. In these traditions, God is thought to be "a person, without a body (i.e., a spirit) who necessarily is eternal, perfectly free, omnipotent, omniscient, perfectly good, and the creator of all things."[1] He is believed to be, not just a great being, but the "*greatest possible being*, the being than which none greater exists or can even be conceived to exist."[2] It is important to make this point because there exist religious explanations that are not theistic, in this sense. After all, most religions posit deities to whose action particular events are attributed.[3] But many of these deities are thought of in strikingly anthropomorphic ways. They have limited knowledge and power and are sometimes far from benevolent.

In practice, even those who are theists—in the sense of Christian theism—sometimes think of God in strikingly anthropomorphic ways. Within the Jewish and Christian Scriptures, there are passages which suggest that the God of whom they speak is merely one divine being among others, or that he is far from unambiguously good. And there is some evidence that, even today, the *working concept* of God employed by many Jews and Christians is similarly anthropomorphic. It is true that such believers will produce a "theologically correct" description of God if asked to do so. But when asked to make rapid inferences about divine action, the conception of God which they employ is very different from that which they have been taught.[4] However, we can set those issues aside here. It is the God of the philosophers and theologians with which I am concerned here.

One group of thinkers might at first sight seem to escape this net. Ironically, it is precisely those who most vigorously protest the methodological naturalism of the sciences, namely the advocates of intelligent design (ID). What is striking about such thinkers is that they generally avoid identifying their alleged designer. To the extent that they do this, their theory (if it warrants that name[5]) falls short of being a religious explanation. At best, it represents a first step towards a religious explanation. But it is clear from the other writings of intelligent design theorists—such as Stephen Meyer[6]—that their arguments are intended to lend support to a religious explanation. And the religious explanation in question is theistic. It is the God of Jewish, Christian, and Islamic theism whose agency they are wanting to invoke.[7]

2.1.2 Proposed, Potential, and Actual Explanations

A second clarification has to do with the appropriateness of the phrase "theistic explanation." The problem here is that "explanation" can be thought of as a success term. As such, it would properly be used only of theories that have been shown to be true, or at least worthy of our provisional acceptance. On this view, propositions about divine agency would become pseudo-explanations *by virtue of* having been superseded. If they are not true, or if they no longer deserve our acceptance, they are simply not explanations.

There is something to be said for this understanding of the term "explanation." But at first sight it seems to undermine the very project I am undertaking. For it would apparently undercut the distinction I made earlier between *de facto* and *in principle* objections to theistic explanations. The *de facto* objection, you will recall, holds that some accounts of divine action are indeed explanations—they have some explanatory force—but that we no longer have sufficient reason to regard them as true (or worthy of our acceptance). But if "explanation" is a success term, an account that we no longer accept is not an explanation at all. The most it could be is a *proposed* explanation. A proposed explanation is nothing more than a proposition that someone (as a matter of fact) *considers* to be explanatory. The problem I am highlighting here is that if "explanation" is a success term, properly applied only to true accounts, it would make no sense to speak of a "false explanation."

How can I respond to this objection? First of all, I am happy to accept that "explanation" is best thought of as a success term. In the pages that follow I shall be using it in precisely this sense. Sometimes, it is true, I shall use the phrase "theistic explanation" without qualification. But this will be merely a shorthand way of saying "*proposed* theistic explanation."[8] (I hope the context will make this clear.) Under what conditions such an explanation would be an *actual* explanation is the central question of this study. However, there are occasions when we do want to speak of "false explanations." And I do not wish to abandon my distinction between *de facto* and *in principle* objections, which seems to me an important one. Fortunately, this problem can be resolved by using another phrase. The phrase in question is one I have already had reason to use, namely "potential explanation."[9]

What do I mean by a potential explanation? I shall argue later (6.2) that the best way of defending a theistic explanation would be by way of *abductive reasoning*. According to C. S. Peirce, who coined this term, the typical form of an abductive argument is as follows.

(1) The surprising fact, C, is observed.
(2) But if A were true, C would be a matter of course.
(3) Hence, there is reason to suspect that A is true.[10]

The A and C here are confusing, so let's make the schema clearer. Let's replace C with E (which here stands for the *explanandum*—the fact to be explained) and let's replace A with H (for "hypothesis"—i.e. the proposed *explanans*). Peirce's schema now reads as follows.

(1) The surprising fact, E, is observed.
(2) But if H were true, E would be a matter of course,
(3) Hence, there is reason to suspect that H is true.

For the moment, I shall make use of just the second premise of this formulation. Any proposition H that satisfies the second premise of this schema is what I shall call a *potential* explanation of E. A potential explanation is one which, if it were true, would make the fact to be explained (the *explanandum*) intelligible. It would make the *explanandum* what we would expect to observe, in these circumstances. An *actual* explanation, by way of contrast, has another feature, namely that it is true (or, at least, that we have sufficient reason to accept it [2.1.3.2]).[11] Under what conditions, then, should we regard something as the actual explanation of some fact about the world? It must fulfil two conditions. It must be a potential explanation of that fact and it must be a potential explanation that we have sufficient reason to accept.

Peter Lipton offers an objection to this apparently simple distinction. He argues that to think of truth as what distinguishes an actual from a potential explanation entails that all true potential explanations are actual explanations. But if the explanation in question is a causal explanation, this is simply false, since "a potential cause may exist yet not be an actual cause, say because some other cause preempted it."[12] It is tempting to ward off preempting causes by invoking a *ceteris paribus* ("other things being equal") clause, or to argue that no divine action could be preempted. But such expedients may not be necessary, for on closer examination the objection evaporates. Let's take an example of causal preemption.

> Suppose that two men, Mr White and Mr Pink, independently of each other, are set on killing Mr Smith. Unbeknown to them, they make very similar arrangements. They are positioned close to Mr Smith at about the same time and they have him on target. Mr White fires his own shotgun; the bullet takes its course and strikes Mr Smith on the head. Mr Smith dies soon after. Mr Pink was ready to shoot his shotgun, and had he fired it, given his position, his shooting skills, and so on, the bullet would have also struck Mr Smith in the head, leading to his death. But Mr White's shot scares off Mr Pink, who then flees the scene.[13]

In this situation, there does exist a potential explanation of Mr. Smith's death, namely Mr. Pink's firing his shotgun. But it is not a *true* potential explanation: the event it posits, which would have caused Mr. Smith's death, did not occur. So causal preemption, if it were to occur, would

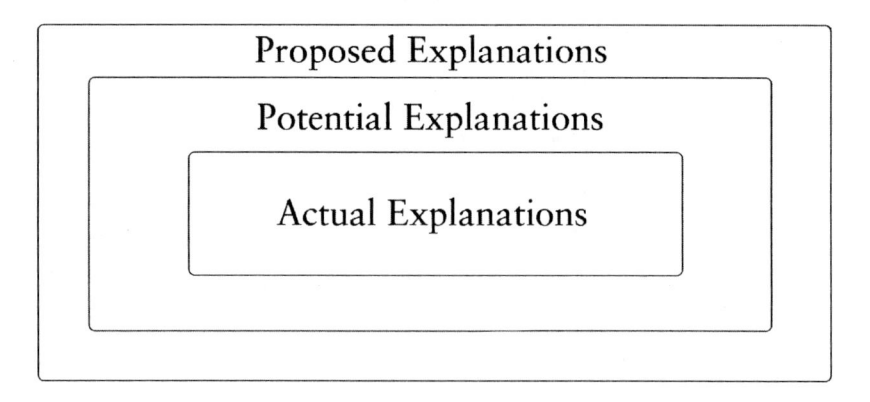

Figure 2.1 The relation between proposed, potential, and actual explanations.

merely indicate that one of the potential explanations was not, in fact, the true one. So it seems my distinction can survive this apparent objection.[14]

One final clarification of terms may be in order. My phrase "proposed explanation" covers both hypotheses and theories. These two terms are used in various ways by different authors. For the purpose of this enquiry, I am assuming that hypotheses and theories lie on a continuum, a theory being a more complex explanatory posit. (It may include a number of distinct hypotheses.) But I am also assuming that for many purposes, the two terms can be used interchangeably. There are those who would make a sharper distinction. In a response to creationist claims that evolution is "only a theory," the U.S. National Academy of Sciences defines a theory as "a well-substantiated explanation of the natural world that can incorporate facts, laws, inferences, and tested hypotheses."[15] By way of contrast, a hypothesis is merely "a tentative statement about the natural world leading to deductions that can be tested."[16] There is nothing wrong with such a distinction; it is simply not the one I am using. I shall not be assuming that "theories" are well substantiated. Some theories enjoy a high degree of what I shall call corroboration (evolution is surely among them); some do not. Nor will I be assuming that "hypotheses" are, in fact, testable. That a particular hypothesis *is* testable is something that needs to be established.

2.1.3 Accepting an Explanation

I have made use of Peirce's schema, as a way of explicating my distinction between potential and actual explanations. But as it stands, this schema lacks precision. I have said, for instance, that we can regard H as a potential explanation of E if it is the case that if H were true, E "would be a matter of course"? But what does this entail? In what sense would we "expect" to observe E if H were true? I have also argued that we can regard H as the actual explanation of E if we have sufficient grounds to consider that H is true (or at least to accept it). But what kinds of grounds would be required? Let me see if I can sharpen up some of these claims a little.

2.1.3.1 Confirmation Theory

At the risk of putting the cart before the horse, I shall begin with the second of those questions. Given that H is a potential explanation of E (which must, of course, be demonstrated), what grounds would we require in order to consider H to be true? There are two ways in which this question has traditionally been answered. Some theistic philosophers—such as Richard Swinburne and Robin Collins[17]—employ confirmation theory in support of what I shall call a "justificationist" view. What characterizes justificationism is the belief that the considerations that lead us to accept a theory must be such that they show the theory to be at least probably true.[18] What does this mean, in practice? It means that we are justified in accepting a

24 *Theism and Explanation*

potential explanation only if it is confirmed in the absolute sense, that is to say, if the evidence in its favour makes it more probable than not, and if it has no more probable competitor.[19] More formally, where E is the evidence, H is a potential explanation of E, and K our background knowledge, then we can regard H as a successful explanation if

$$\Pr(H|E \mathbin{\&} K) > 0.5$$

and there exists no competing hypothesis whose probability given E and K is higher.[20] The probability of H given E and K (its posterior probability) can be discovered by estimating the prior probability of H and the likelihood of E given H and then applying Bayes's theorem. In its simplest form, this states that the posterior probability of a hypothesis, given some piece of evidence (E), is discovered by multiplying the prior probability of H by the likelihood of E given H, and dividing the result by the prior probability of E.

$$\Pr(H|E) = \frac{\Pr(E|H) \times \Pr(H)}{\Pr(E)}$$

As we shall see (6.1.2), this is precisely how Swinburne argues.

There are practical difficulties with a justificationist view, particularly one that appeals to Bayes's theorem. There is, first of all, the difficulty, which Swinburne readily acknowledges,[21] of assigning precise numerical values to the probability estimates required.[22] But there are also difficulties in spelling out the required conception of probability. Swinburne, for instance, identifies three broad categories of probability, which he refers to as "physical," "statistical," and "inductive." Physical probability has to do with the propensities that are actually at work in the universe. As Swinburne puts it, it is "a measure of the extent to which some particular outcome is predetermined by its causes at some earlier time."[23] In a fully deterministic universe, every actual event would have a physical probability of 1.0. Statistical probability, on the other hand, is a measure of the proportion of the members of a class who possess a certain property.[24] But what really interests Swinburne—and what he employs in *The Existence of God*—is what he calls "inductive probability." This is, as Swinburne writes, "a measure of the extent to which one proposition r makes another one q likely to be true."[25]

What about explanations? Does it make sense to speak of the probability of an explanatory hypothesis? Swinburne assumes that since both hypotheses and bodies of evidence are expressed in propositions, inductive probability can also be applied to explanations. The inductive probability of a hypothesis, on this view, is a measure of how likely it is to be true, given

```
┌─────────────────────────────────────────────────┐
│  ┌──────────────────┐    ┌──────────────────┐   │
│  │    Physical      │    │    Statistical   │   │
│  └──────────────────┘    └──────────────────┘   │
│  ┌───────────────────────────────────────────┐  │
│  │                                           │  │
│  │               Inductive                   │  │
│  │          subjective or logical            │  │
│  │                                           │  │
│  └───────────────────────────────────────────┘  │
└─────────────────────────────────────────────────┘
```

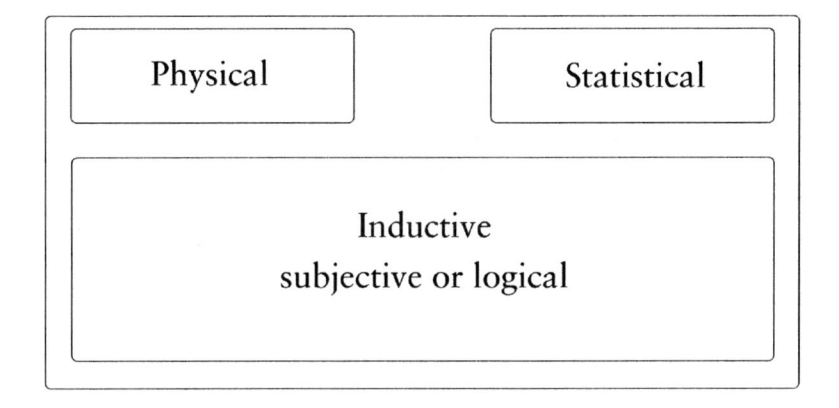

Figure 2.2 Swinburne's conceptions of probability.

a certain body of evidence. Swinburne advocates an objective, normative view of inductive probability, rejecting what he calls "subjective probability." Subjective probability, he writes, is simply "the force that the evidence has for someone with a certain way of assessing that evidence, and a certain ability to do so."[26] It does not assume that his way of assessing the evidence is correct. The probability estimates in which Swinburne is interested are estimates of what he calls "logical" probability. In Swinburne's words, the logical probability of a hypothesis is "that measure of inductive support that would be reached by a logically omniscient being (that is, one who knows what are all the relevant logical possibilities and knows what they entail, and has correct inductive criteria)."[27]

One might argue that this is not very useful, since we are not omniscient beings. The only probability measure of which we could possibly make use—the only measure that is, in Wesley Salmon's terms, "ascertainable"[28]—is what Swinburne calls "epistemic probability." This measures the degree of support that the evidence lends to the hypothesis, when that is assessed by subjects with correct rules of reasoning but limited knowledge.[29] (Subjective probability, as we saw a moment ago, does not assume that subjects are using the correct rules of reasoning.[30]) But if, in practice, epistemic probability is the best we can achieve, Swinburne implies that it is logical probability at which we should aim.[31] What are the criteria of logical probability? Swinburne argues that we can assess the logical probability of a hypothesis by reference to its explanatory power, its narrowness of scope, its fit with background knowledge, and its simplicity.[32]

There are philosophers who would take issue with each of these claims. Karl Popper famously denied what is, in effect, Swinburne's opening assumption: that one can speak of the "probability" of a hypothesis (that is to say, of inductive probability). Popper argues that this is an indefensible carry-over from the statistical use of the term.[33] Howard Sobel rejects Swinburne's idea of logical probability, arguing that the only probabilities one can speak of in this context are measures of the degree to which actual individuals are confident about their beliefs.[34] And Timothy McGrew argues that Swinburne's definition of logical probability merely plays into the hands of the sceptic, by setting our standards for justified belief impossibly high.[35]

So there are difficulties facing the use of confirmation theory in the context of a proposed theistic explanation. But while I believe they are serious difficulties, I do not intend to pursue them here. In Chapter 7, I shall be outlining my own criteria of theory choice, which include degree of testability, simplicity, economy, and fit with background knowledge. But my preferred notion of simplicity (7.4) differs from Swinburne's, and I shall not be using these criteria in order to estimate probabilities. For reasons that will become clear in a moment (2.1.3.2), my reconstruction of proposed religious explanations will make no use of confirmation theory. And in discussing the work of those theists who do appeal to probability arguments, I shall simply assume that they have some answer to these objections. After all, these are not objections to religious explanations in particular; they are objections to a particular way of defending explanations in general. But as I hope to show, it is not the only way in which explanations could be defended.

2.1.3.2 *Explanationism*

One of the factors that makes me reluctant to embrace confirmation theory in this context is that it simply sets the bar too high. It uses a higher standard for the acceptance of a theistic hypothesis than is actually applied within the sciences. There are a number of senses in which scientists can be said to "accept" theories,[36] but let me take a relatively strong sense of this term. Let me say that a scientist *accepts* a theory when he begins working within the framework it provides and abandons alternative approaches. There are occasions when scientists have accepted a theory (in this sense) when that theory has not yet been shown to be even probably true.[37] Yet we may judge that they were acting rationally in doing so.

Let me take as an example Darwin's theory, at the moment of its introduction in 1859. If it was worthy of acceptance (and we can be grateful some people considered it so), was it because its posterior probability had been shown to be greater than 0.5? John Earman, at least, thinks not. He argues that given the difficulties facing the theory at the time of its introduction,[38] it had a low posterior probability.[39] Darwin himself was very aware of the difficulties facing his theory. At times he seems to be arguing for a relatively modest position—not that his theory of natural selection was probably true, but that it was what Barry Gale calls "the least objectionable theory" on offer.[40] Huxley appears to have offered a similar defence at the famous British Association meeting at Oxford in 1860.[41] So if Darwin's theory was worthy of acceptance in 1859, it was not so much because of its overall probability given the evidence, but because it displayed some highly desirable features. It was capable of explaining a range of hitherto puzzling phenomena. It posited a mechanism (natural selection) for which there existed a familiar analogy (artificial selection). And it was potentially fruitful, suggesting new lines of research. In Philip Kitcher's felicitous phrase, Darwin's theory "gave a structure to our ignorance."[42]

So given the actual practice of scientists, who do accept theories they have not yet shown to be (probably) true, it would seem unreasonable to make such a demand of the theist. We need not expect him to demonstrate the truth, or even the probable truth, of his theistic hypothesis. He could be acting rationally in accepting a proposed theistic explanation, in treating it as though it were true (albeit in a provisional manner), even if he cannot show that its overall probability exceeds 0.5. What we *can* legitimately require of such a proposed explanation is that it both be a potential explanation of the facts in question and that it possess—to a greater degree than any competitor—the features we value in a successful theory. What those features are, why we should value them, and how they relate to the confirmation theorist's probability calculations is a question to which I shall return (6.2). I shall describe this alternative, somewhat broader view of theory acceptance as "explanationist."

As Quine remarks, "names of philosophical positions are a necessary evil,"[43] and the term "explanationism" is no exception. It was apparently first used by Keith Lehrer for the view that "a belief is justified by its explanatory role in a system of beliefs."[44] But I am using it in a more precise sense, as a position that is distinct from (and opposed to) justificationism. Explanationism, in this context, is the view that we are justified in accepting a potential explanation when it displays, to a greater degree than any competitor, certain explanatory virtues, *even if we cannot demonstrate it to be probably true*. It is the last claim that is the important one in this context. It assumes, in William Lycan's words, that "explanatory inference can do its justifying intrinsically, that is, without being *derived* from some other form of ampliative inference, such as probability theory, taken as more basic."[45]

2.1.4 Explanation and Arguments

As a description of what constitutes a successful explanation—one we are justified in accepting—that will do for the moment. I shall be expanding on it later. But as I mentioned a moment ago, in approaching the topic in this way I am putting the cart before the horse. For we can only accept an explanation as the actual or best explanation if we are already convinced that it is a potential explanation of the fact in question. And I still have not clarified what I mean by a *potential* explanation. Let me begin by returning for a moment to Peirce's schema.

(1) The surprising fact, E, is observed.
(2) But if H were true, E would be a matter of course,
(3) Hence, there is reason to suspect that H is true.

I have argued that a potential explanation is an account that satisfies the second premise (line 2) of Peirce's schema. Now Peirce's schema as a whole tells us what might warrant our acceptance of a proposed explanation. But it tells us nothing about the shape of the explanation itself. It does not tell us just what it means to say that "if H were true, E would be a matter of course" (line 2).

There are two ways in which this question has commonly been answered. The first is to argue that H entails E, the explanation in question taking the form of a deductive argument. I shall refer to this as a "deductivist" approach to explanation. The second is to argue that H renders E more likely than it would be otherwise. More precisely, this approach argues that truth of H makes E more likely than it would be if H were not true:

$Pr(E|H) > Pr(E|H)$.

I shall refer to this as a "probabilistic" approach to explanation. Among proponents of theistic explanations, Richard Swinburne adopts the probabilistic approach. While recognising that theistic explanations are intentional explanations,[46] his arguments assume that the existence of a divine agent would render the *explanandum* more likely that it would be otherwise. I shall examine Swinburne's arguments in more detail later (6.1.2).

All I want to note here is that I shall be adopting the first, deductivist view. This is not because I believe that all explanations can be reduced to deductive arguments. (Perhaps they can; perhaps they can't. I'm not sure.) It is because proposed theistic explanations are a species of intentional explanation and intentional explanations, I shall argue (Appendix 2.1), are best reconstructed as deductive arguments. From a deductivist point of view, if one can deduce a description of the explanandum from the hypothesis, then one's hypothesis corresponds to the second premise (line 2) of Peirce's schema. It will show why, given the truth of H, we would expect to observe E.

Note that, assuming that one can make sense of the relevant notion of probability (2.1.3.1), a deductivist approach to explanation does not necessarily exclude probability calculations. It is true that, on this view, the explanation *itself* would not be probabilistic, in the sense of assigning a certain probability to the *explanandum* (perhaps in the light of a statistical law). If the deductive argument it embodies is sound, then the likelihood of the *explanandum*, given the hypothesis, is 1.0. If one wanted to speak of "confirmation" in this context (perhaps adopting Hempel's entailment condition[47]), then the confirmation in question would be "an all-or-nothing affair."[48] But if the prior probability of H is less than 1.0, then the posterior probability of H, given the evidence, could still be low.[49] The mere fact that the truth of our *explanans* would not assign some degree of likelihood to the *explanandum* does not mean that we cannot assign some degree of probability to our *explanans*. Once again, my own reconstruction of theistic explanations adopts a different strategy (2.1.3.2), but this would be a consistent way for a theist to argue.

2.2 THE OBJECTIONS RESTATED

It has been a long journey back to my starting point. But with these clarifications in mind, let's now return to the two positions I identified earlier. The *de facto* objection to proposed theistic explanations accepts that a theistic explanation may be a potential explanation of some fact about the world. But it denies that any theistic explanation meets the other criteria that would warrant our regarding it as true. As we shall see, these criteria are often used comparatively. They have to do with how a particular explanation fares when ranked alongside its competitors. If no theistic explanation meets these criteria, it means that no theistic explanation deserves to be regarded as an actual explanation. What about the *in principle* objection? Its proponents would agree that no theistic explanation is an *actual* explanation. But they would go further. They would argue that no proposed theistic explanation could be even a *potential* explanation. If H is a proposition about divine agency, then even if H were true, it would not lead us to expect E, whatever E may be.

2.2.1 Alternative Views

It is this distinction that I shall employ in the discussion that follows. I concede that this way of presenting the initial distinction—that between *de facto* and *in principle* objections—is my own. The *in principle* objection I am articulating here is not the only form of *in principle* objection one could formulate. Let me illustrate this point. As we have seen (1.3.2), some authors argue that propositions about divine agency fail to be explanatory because they exclude no possible state of affairs. Let's say that someone offers as an explanation of event E the proposition "God willed E." The problem, such authors argue, is that any event, let's say E^*, could be substituted for E. The same formula ("God wills E^*") could be used to "explain" E^* as well. The objection is that this counts against regarding "God wills E" as an explanation of E. A formula that can "explain" anything, it is argued, explains nothing.

This objection may or may not be well founded. I shall come back to it shortly when discussing what Philip Kitcher calls "spurious unification"

(3.2.3.1). For the moment, I wish merely to ask what kind of an objection it is. If we employ the distinction I have just outlined, this argument counts as a *de facto* objection to theistic explanations. For even if any event could be substituted for *E*—which, incidentally, I don't believe to be true (3.2.3.1)—*H* would still be a potential explanation of *E*. One could use *H* to construct an argument that corresponds to the second premise of Peirce's schema, albeit in an almost trivial fashion.

(1) God wills *E*.
(2) Whatever God wills comes about.
(3) Therefore *E*.

But, of course, "God wills *E*" will still fail to count as an actual explanation. Why? Because it would have practically no empirical content (3.2.3) and would not be independently testable (7.1).

The point I am making here is that, on my terms, the above objection is a *de facto* objection, not an *in principle* one. This may seem odd. I can imagine someone else regarding it as an *in principle* objection; some of the authors cited above seem to have done so. But the problem here is largely terminological. My distinction is not the only one that could be adopted in such discussions. But I have to start somewhere, and this is the distinction I shall use in the discussion that follows.

2.2.2 The Way Ahead

The distinctions I have made will determine the shape of the discussion to come. Chapters 3 and 4 are largely descriptive, setting out as clearly as possible just what I mean by a proposed theistic explanation. Chapter 3 will take as its starting point the *explanans* of such a proposed explanation. It will argue that a theistic explanation is a theoretical explanation, positing a particular divine intention, and embodying a causal claim. In the course of the discussion, I shall examine two initial objections to the very idea of such an explanation. The first is that the idea of a divine agent is internally inconsistent. The second is the related claim that the will of God cannot be described as a cause. Neither objection, I shall argue, is necessarily fatal, although both imply that the theist has some work to do.

Chapter 4 will continue my description of theistic explanations, but from the point of view of their *explananda*. I shall argue that theistic explanations cover both events and states of affairs and that they embody both singular and general causal claims. I shall then examine the relationship between theistic and secular explanations, highlighting the fact that the two forms of explanation can, on occasions, be complementary. This will bring me to a third objection to such proposed explanations, which has to do with miracles. At least some theistic explanations posit miracles. And all theistic explanations posit an agent capable of working miracles. But could appeal to such an agent be explanatory? I shall argue that it could (in principle), if it employs the rationality principle that lies at the heart of all intentional explanations.

Chapter 5 takes us into the heart of my discussion. It addresses the issue of what would constitute a *potential* theistic explanation. A key requirement it that the theistic hypothesis ought to have independently specifiable consequences. If we attribute to God a particular intention, we need to be able to specify how he is likely to act in order to achieve his goals. And we need to be able to do this without drawing on our knowledge of what is actually the case. If we cannot do this, then any proposed theistic explanation will be without content. Once again, the rationality principle offers the theist a way ahead. But it has a flip side. When applied to an agent who is omnipotent, omniscient, and morally perfect, the rationality principle entails what I shall call an "optimality condition." We will be warranted in regarding a proposed theistic explanation as a potential explanation of any fact only if we cannot conceive of any better way in which that divine intention could have been realised. And whatever else "better" may mean in this context, it surely means "entailing less suffering."

Chapters 6 and 7 apply to proposed theistic explanations the procedure known as "inference to the best explanation." If we assume, for the sake of the argument, that an account of divine action is a potential explanation of some fact, then how could one show that we have sufficient reason to accept it? Under what conditions should we regard it as the *actual* explanation of the fact in question. It is here that I discuss the explanatory virtues against which the adequacy of a proposed explanation can be measured. These virtues will include its degree of testability, its coherence with the rest of our knowledge, the previous success of the research tradition to which it belongs, and whether it enjoys the features of simplicity, ontological economy, and informativeness.

The issue is complicated, in this case, by the fact that a proposed theistic explanation is often the *only* explanation on offer: sometimes there are no competing natural hypotheses. Given that most commentators regard testability as a key explanatory virtue, we need to ask: Can a solitary potential explanation be tested? I shall argue that it can, and that it can be judged by the same criteria as are used for the assessment of competing theories. If we do apply these criteria, we find that a proposed theistic explanation will inevitably score poorly. Other things being equal, we will have good reason to prefer a non-theistic, natural account, if one is available, or to seek one, if it is not. Nonetheless, a proposed theistic explanation might still have some degree of explanatory force. In the absence of a natural explanation we could, conceivably, have reason to accept it. But given its inherent limitations, a proposed theistic explanation would always be an explanation of last resort.[50]

The Appendix defends the view of intentional explanations I have presented in the body of the work. Since none of this material relates specifically to theistic explanations, I have chosen to deal with it separately. Here I shall expand on my view that an intentional explanation can be thought of as a practical syllogism and that it relies on a presumption of rationality. I shall also discuss how an intentional explanation might be tested. I shall argue that, although they suffer from a certain lack of precision, intentional explanations are no less testable than the non-intentional explanations employed in the sciences.

3 What are Theistic Explanations?

> In magic and religion the individual does not reason,
> or if he does his reasoning is unconscious . . .
> We are sometimes able to retrace the secret pathway of his ideas,
> but he himself is usually incapable of it.
>
> Marcel Mauss

Throughout this study, I shall be working with a particular understanding of what constitutes a theistic explanation. A theistic explanation, I shall assume, is one that posits the existence and action of God, in an attempt to account for some fact about the world. There are three features of such proposed explanations that will shape my discussion. First of all, theistic explanations are theoretical explanations, in the sense that they posit an agent whose existence cannot be directly verified by observation. If the existence of this agent is to be demonstrated, it will need to be by an inference from what can be observed. Secondly, theistic explanations are intentional explanations: the agent whose existence and activity they posit is one who has beliefs and desires (or at least mental states analogous to human beliefs and desires). Thirdly, such explanations can be defended as instances of abductive reasoning, one form of which is inference to the best explanation (IBE). The positing of an unobservable agent could be defended by arguing that this represents the best available explanation, not merely of the particular fact under consideration (the *explanandum*), but of a range of phenomena.

This chapter and the next one will expand on each of these points. They will set out as clearly as possible what a successful theistic explanation would look like. In keeping with a long-standing philosophical tradition, what I shall be offering is a *rational reconstruction* of theistic explanations.[1] I shall take as my starting point the kinds of explanations that theists actually offer. But I shall also seek to develop and improve them, setting out the reasoning involved in as systematic and consistent a manner as possible. Whether or not this corresponds to the way in which any theist actually does reason, it corresponds to how (in my judgement) she ought to reason. Note, too, that when I speak of theistic explanations, I mean nothing more than proposed explanations (2.1.2). I am not assuming they are potential explanations or that they warrant our acceptance. What I am arguing is that if any religious explanation were to be successful, it would resemble the kind of explanations I shall examine in the following pages.

3.1 THEORETICAL EXPLANATIONS

Let's start with the least controversial of my preliminary claims. Any proposed theistic explanation is a theoretical explanation. The believer posits the existence and action of an unobservable agent, namely God, in much the same manner as the physicist posits the existence of unobservable entities, in order to explain some observable fact about the world. Such explanations are common in the sciences. A striking example is J. J. Thomson's 1897 paper on cathode rays.[2] The paper sets out to decide between two hypotheses as to the nature of these rays. According to the first, they represent a wave motion in the aether. According to the second, they represent streams of electrically-charged particles, particles which in due course would come to be called "electrons."[3] As I shall argue later (6.2.1), at least some of Thomson's arguments in support of the electron hypothesis are classic instances of abductive reasoning. For the moment, I wish only to note that the particles whose existence he was positing were inaccessible to observation, even with the aid of instruments. If we accept the legitimacy of Thomson's reasoning, one possible objection to proposed theistic explanations may be dismissed immediately. Whatever else may be said about such proposed explanations, they are not illegitimate merely because the being whose existence they posit cannot be observed.

3.1.1 The Legitimacy of Theoretical Explanations

The existence of theoretical explanations is not a matter of dispute. Scientists apparently feel no qualms about positing the existence of unobserved entities, in order to explain some phenomena. And some such explanations have been stunningly successful.[4] As J. J. Thomson's discovery reminds us, they have been widespread within the fields of physics and chemistry, where scientists posit the existence of atoms and subatomic particles. But an historical science, such as evolutionary biology, must also posit unobserved entities and causal processes. It is true that these are unobserved rather than unobservable. If an observer were to live for long enough, she would presumably witness natural selection at work. But the particular processes that gave rise to the living beings we see around us occurred so long ago, and over such an extended period of time, that they are in practice inaccessible to observation.

So there is no dispute about the existence or the success of theoretical explanations. They are widely used by scientists and they work. What is a matter of dispute, at least among philosophers, is the ontological status of the unobserved (or unobservable) entities which these explanations posit. On the one hand, there are contemporary philosophers who defend a realist understanding of theoretical explanations.[5] Following in the footsteps of Thomson, they believe that atoms, molecules, and electrons actually exist. More precisely, they believe that the success of the explanations that invoke such entities gives us sufficient reason to believe they exist.[6] A realism of this kind is not restricted to philosophers. It is also, I would suggest, the taken-for-granted view of many, if not most, scientists.

Writing in the 1930s, the philosopher Hans Reichenbach—at one time associated with the Vienna Circle—offers a striking illustration of a cautiously realist view. Reichenbach refers to theoretical entities as *illata*, "inferred things."[7] He argues that our position vis-à-vis such entities is comparable to that of people who are imprisoned within a cube of white cloth, which is translucent (but not transparent) and illuminated by the sun. If birds were to fly past the cube, their shadows would be cast on the cloth, that is to say, on the ceiling and on the walls of the cube. For a start, the people inside will not be aware of the existence of the birds; they will assume that the shadows *are* the reality. "They will develop a cosmology in which the world has the shape of a cube; outside the cube is nothing, but on the walls of the cube are dark spots running about."[8] But then "some Copernicus" will come along, will demonstrate that the movements of shadows on the ceiling and the wall are correlated, and will posit the existence of an outside world inhabited by bird-like beings. Reichenbach argues that this conclusion—that there exist birds outside his cubical world—will be at best probable,[9] but it will be rational and defensible.

That is a particular version of scientific realism. But such realism with regard to unobserved entities is not universally shared. There have been scientists and philosophers who, following in the footsteps of David Hume, have doubted our ability to know the "secret powers" of nature.[10] When Albert Einstein visited Ernst Mach, one of the last physicists to deny the existence of atoms, he tried to get Mach to retract his view.

> He asked Mach what his position would be if it proved possible to predict a property of a gas by assuming the existence of atoms—some property that could not be predicted without the assumption of atoms and yet one that could be observed. . . . Could Mach accept the hypothesis of atoms under the circumstances Einstein had stated, even if it meant very complicated computations? Einstein told me how delighted he was when Mach replied affirmatively.[11]

If Mach, whose instrumentalist view of scientific theories was well known, did make this admission, he soon repented of it, distancing himself from the atomic hypothesis a short time later.[12]

Mach was primarily a scientist. But there were also some early twentieth-century philosophers who were reluctant to admit inferences to unobservable entities. A. J. Ayer, for instance, expressly distanced himself from the uncompromising positivism of Mach, believing this to be untenable. He argued that a proposition which included terms such as "atom," "molecule," or "electron" was not to be condemned simply because such terms could not be *directly* correlated with sense data. Such a proposition, he argued, was meaningful and legitimate insofar as it could be *indirectly* correlated with sense data, that is to say, insofar as there existed "empirical observations" which are "relevant to its truth or falsehood."[13] But Ayer argued that such terms refer only to "entities of reason," which are "postulated as a means of describing and predicting the course of sensible phenomena."[14] We are not entitled to draw any conclusion regarding their actual existence. For "it is impossible, by any valid process of inference, to make a transition from what is observed to anything that is conceived as being, in principle, unobservable."[15]

The foremost contemporary defender of an instrumentalist—or, to use his own phrase, a "constructive empiricist"—view of science is Bas van Fraassen. In particular, van Fraassen addresses the particular type of abductive reasoning known as inference to the best explanation (IBE). He argues against the idea that the success of an explanation entails its truth. A particular explanation may be the best explanation on offer, but its truth is another matter. The inference from success to truth would be defensible only if we already knew that the true explanation were among the candidate explanations under consideration. But of course we do not know this. As van Fraassen writes, "we can watch no contest of the theories we have so painfully struggled to formulate, with those no one has proposed. So our selection may well be the best of a bad lot."[16] What follows? According to van Fraassen, even if a particular explanation is the best available, we cannot infer it is true. We cannot infer that the theoretical entities of which it speaks actually exist.

3.1.2 Theism and Realism

We might expect to encounter corresponding arguments among theological antirealists. Surprisingly, we do not. Theological antirealists (instrumentalists or positivists) certainly exist. The best known—and the most explicit about his antirealism—is Don Cupitt.[17] But while theological antirealists believe that talk about God has a range of important functions (often ethical), these functions rarely if ever include explanation. Indeed one school of theological antirealists, the Wittgensteinians,[18] argue that religion represents an entirely different "language-game" from that of science. Religious propositions, they argue, should not be regarded as explanatory hypotheses.[19] Many, if not most, theistic philosophers disagree. They do offer theistic explanations, and they do so precisely as theological realists. Such explanations are most commonly offered in support of belief in the existence of God. They suggest that the existence of God is the best explanation, or perhaps the only explanation, of some observable state of affairs. And by the existence of God such thinkers mean the existence of a being who is independent of our theories about him.[20]

I would like, if possible, to defend this realist assumption. I would like to say that the success of scientific explanations gives us good reason to believe in the existence of the entities they posit. And I would like to say that if we had a series of successful theistic explanations, this would give us reason to believe in the existence of a divine agent. But to defend this view is no easy task, for on the face if it van Fraassen is surely right. The fact that some hypothesis is our best available explanation does not entail that it is (even probably) true. The following argument is invalid.

(1) F is a fact.
(2) Hypothesis H is a potential explanation of F.
(3) No other potential explanation would explain F as well as H does.
(4) Therefore H is true.[21]

But whatever difficulties this poses for the realist, it is not a fatal objection to IBE, for there is another way of presenting its logic. It holds merely that we are *acting rationally* in *accepting* the best explanation on offer. On this basis we can construct a valid argument.

(1) It is reasonable to accept the best available potential explanation of any fact.
(2) F is a fact.
(3) Hypothesis H is a potential explanation of F.
(4) No available competing hypothesis would explain F better than H does.
(5) Therefore it is reasonable to accept H.[22]

I shall discuss a variant form of this argument later (6.2.1). For the moment, let me note that the debate regarding realism will centre on how we understand the term "accept" in both the first premise and the conclusion. I have already argued that there are occasions when scientists accept theories, even though they cannot demonstrate that the theories in question are even probably true (2.1.3.2). To accept some proposition p

> is to have a policy of deeming, positing, or postulating that p—that is, of going along with that proposition (either for the long term or for immediate purposes only) as a premiss in some or all contexts for one's own and other's proofs, argumentation, inferences, deliberations, etc.[23]

Acceptance can be a voluntary act, whereas belief typically lies beyond our immediate control.[24] And while acceptance may sometimes go hand-in-hand with belief, there are other occasions when it does not. Indeed, there may be occasions when it is appropriate that we accept a theory without necessarily believing it. This would be the case if, for instance, a theory shows great potential, even though we cannot (yet) demonstrate it to be even probably true. (I suggested in a previous chapter that this was the case with Darwin's theory at the time of its publication [2.1.3.2].) One might argue that even the acceptance of a theory entails a certain belief. And so it does. But what it entails is not necessarily belief in the theory; it can be belief in some fact about the theory (such as its fruitfulness).[25] Under what circumstances (if any) IBE would warrant belief (*simpliciter*) is an important question, but it is not one I need address here.

All that IBE needs to support, for my purposes, is the kind of commitment discussed by John Bishop, who has offered a defence of what he calls (rather misleadingly) religious "belief." In fact, what Bishop is arguing is that a religious commitment can sometimes be what he describes as a "subdoxastic venture." A subdoxastic venture is one in which we take a proposition to be true in our practical reasoning, without actually considering it true, since we realise that it is not adequately supported by the total available evidence.[26] Bishop offers a William James-style defence of the conditions under which this might be defensible, on which I shall offer no comment. But what I am suggesting is that a similar (subdoxastic) attitude might be defensible if it could be shown that a proposed theistic explanation was indeed the best explanation on offer of some puzzling phenomenon. I suspect that Bishop would share my pessimism about the likely success of such a project, but it is its mere possibility that I wish to argue for here.

3.1.3 Physics and Theology

What I have been arguing is that proposed theistic explanations resemble some explanations in the natural sciences insofar as they posit an unobservable entity. But the opponent of proposed theistic explanation might argue that while this is true, the parallel does not take us very far. The fact that scientists also posit unobservable entities offers little support to proposed theistic explanations, for the being whose existence is posited in a theistic explanation is very different from the entities whose existence is posited, say, in physics. It may be true that God resembles an electron insofar as he is generally regarded as inaccessible to observation.[27] But in other respects, the two are hardly comparable. An electron, however inaccessible it may be to observation, is at least part of the same physical universe as other, observable entities. It obeys the same kinds of laws as other entities. And we have well-established theories about how electrons interact with things we can observe. The presence of an electron can be traced in a more direct manner than the presence of God. (It might, for instance, leave a track in a cloud chamber.) And of course, as we shall see in a moment, an electron is an impersonal entity, whereas God is supposed to be a personal being, one who has something analogous to human beliefs and desires. Yet unlike all the personal agents with whom we are familiar, he is an unembodied agent. How, then, can he interact with the material world?

This is a serious objection. If we are to regard God as a theoretical entity, comparable in this respect to an electron, we shall have to take into account just how peculiar this posited being would be. In particular, we shall have to take into account the deep divide between the impersonal theoretical entities whose existence is posited by the sciences and the (unembodied) personal entities whose existence is posited by a proposed theistic explanation.[28] But these differences do not, by themselves, undermine the parallel I am drawing. Theistic explanations can still be regarded as a type of theoretical explanation. The place to discuss these differences will be in Chapter 7, when I examine the criteria against which we should assess a proposed theistic explanation. Here, I shall argue, a key question will be whether the posited entity resembles the kinds of entities posited by our established scientific theories (7.2). If it does not, this does not, by itself, disqualify the explanation being offered. The existence of spiritual beings may simply be a surprising fact about the world. But it will count against its acceptance.

3.2 INTENTIONAL EXPLANATIONS

The second feature of proposed theistic explanations I wish to highlight is that they are intentional explanations. They invite us to see the fact to be explained (the *explanandum*) as the outcome of an intentional action on the part of an agent having particular beliefs and desires. They suggest that what we observe is what we would expect to observe, given such an agent. Intentional explanations are, of course, very common in everyday life. They are also employed in interpretative sciences such as history and anthropology. The resources on which they draw are those of our everyday knowledge of human psychology, often referred to as "folk psychology." What sets proposed theistic explanations apart from other intentional explanations is not their intentional character, but the nature of the agent whose actions they posit.

3.2.1 The Legitimacy of Intentional Explanations

For some decades the status of intentional explanations has been a hotly contested issue among philosophers and (more recently) psychologists.[29] There is no doubt that we employ such explanations in everyday life. But it does not follow that they are defensible, in the sense of having any significant degree of explanatory utility. Nor can we assume that they are testable, a feature which we would normally consider at least a *desideratum* of any proposed explanation (7.1). Some philosophers would argue that the folk-psychological concepts such proposed explanations employ—such as "belief," "desire," and "intention"—are fatally imprecise. They will eventually turn out to be inconsistent with the findings of a more scientific psychology. Indeed the more radical critics of intentional explanations argue for the elimination of such terms, at least in formal discourse, and their replacement by more technical concepts, such as those referring to brain states.[30]

Similar questions could be raised about theistic explanations, for the simple reason that they are a subset of intentional explanations. If all intentional explanations are fatally flawed, then theistic explanations are fatally flawed as well. They will suffer from just the same defects and they could be dismissed for just the same reasons. No further discussion would be required. If, on the other hand, intentional explanations are acceptable in principle, then theistic explanations cannot be rejected on these grounds alone. If the proposed explanations that invoke God as an agent are to be regarded as pseudo-explanations, some further argumentation will be required. It follows that anyone who wishes to defend theistic explanations will also need, as a first step, to defend intentional explanations.

As it happens, I believe intentional explanations can be defended, that despite their imprecision they do have explanatory force. It follows that while proposed theistic explanations may suffer various other, perhaps fatal flaws, the mere fact that they are intentional explanations is not sufficient reason to reject them. As I mentioned earlier (2.2.2), I have relegated my defence of intentional explanations to an appendix. No aspect of that discussion relates to theistic explanations, except insofar as these are a species of intentional explanation, and I was anxious to spare the reader a tedious digression. At this point, let me merely state my conclusions. If you believe that intentional explanations require further defence, or you disagree with my conclusions, you may wish to consult that discussion.

An intentional explanation, as I suggested earlier (2.1.4), is best regarded as an argument. It is very particular kind of argument, namely a practical syllogism. This syllogism begins by positing an agent possessing a certain intention, along with a set of beliefs relevant to its attainment, and has as its conclusion a description of the *explanandum*. Such an explanation does not depend on laws describing a regular association of intentions and actions. (There may be rough and ready laws of this sort, but an intentional explanation does not need to cite them.) What an intentional explanation relies on is another kind of generalisation, namely a rationality principle. It presumes that the agent will act rationally in order to attain her intended goal. Like the legal presumption of innocence, this presumption of rationality is defeasible. Admittedly, it is not easily defeated. But if it were, if we were forced to conclude that the agent is acting irrationally, some other form of explanation would be required. I shall also argue that proposed intentional explanations are testable, insofar as they allow us to make predictions. If a prediction turns out to be correct, our explanation is corroborated. But if we continually fail to make successful predictions, we should consider abandoning our intentional hypothesis. Only a persistent failure to corroborate a range of proposed intentional explanations would warrant the conclusion that the agent is, in fact, acting irrationally.

3.2.2 Positing a Divine Agent

A first point to make here is that an intentional explanation is itself a particular kind of theoretical explanation. For it posits unobservable mental states—such as intentions or an agent's beliefs and desires—in order to explain some observable event, namely her behaviour. So the same criteria of explanatory adequacy and explanatory success can be applied to intentional explanations as are applied to other forms of theoretical explanation.

Could one defend a realist interpretation of intentional explanations (3.1.2)? If we accept the legitimacy of intentional explanations, and if such explanations speak of an agent's beliefs, desires, and intentions, is the realist committed to the idea that there exist mental states to which such terms refer? Once again, this is a difficult question, and I shall comment on just one aspect of it. A realist is surely not committed to the idea that these terms—"belief," "desire," "intention," and so on—pick out natural kinds.[31] It may be that a mature scientific psychology would replace these terms with others, which more accurately describe the workings of the mind. But this does not entail that there are no beliefs, desires, and intentions. The term "sea creature" does not pick out a natural kind—it embraces, for instance, both fish and marine mammals—but this does not mean there are no sea creatures.[32]

What I do want to highlight here is a particular feature of proposed theistic explanation. It is the fact that such proposed explanations do not posit merely the existence of a certain *intention* on the part of the agent. They have a further theoretical dimension. They posit the very existence of the *agent* to whom this intention is being attributed. In everyday life we are generally in no doubt that the agent to whom we are attributing the *explanandum* exists. (We may end up wondering if she is, on this occasion, acting in a rational manner, but that she exists is generally taken for granted.) And often, although not always, we are in no doubt that the fact to be explained *is* the result of her action.[33] We know these things on the basis of observation, or perhaps on the basis of testimony. What we are trying to understand is *why* this agent acted as she did. What makes a proposed theistic explanation different is that the existence of the agent is itself contested. It is not a matter on which proponents and opponents of such explanations already agree. It is true that we could have other reasons to believe that there is a God who is responsible for the event to be explained. But if those other reasons take the form of other explanatory claims, then the problem is deferred rather than resolved.

Let me approach this point another way. In general, any fact can be explained only under a certain description, which picks out its relevant features.[34] Now in order to offer an intentional explanation of an event, we must describe it, or at least understand it, as an action.[35] What the atheist contests is the theist's very description of the *explanandum* as the

42   *Theism and Explanation*

action of an agent (4.3.3.1). It follows that the proposed explanation must give him sufficient reason to accept it. So, at least on a realist construal of theistic explanations, the theist faces a double burden. In offering a theistic explanation, she must both posit the existence of an unobservable agent and show that the *explanandum* is best understood as the work of that agent. And this means that there must be something about the event to be explained that would be less puzzling if it were described as an intentional action. I shall try to sharpen up what this means later (4.3.3).

This double burden certainly makes the theist's task more difficult. Does it make it impossible? In principle, no. As Richard Swinburne argues, we can at least conceive of explanations that are parallel to that offered by the theist, in which we posit both the existence and the activity of an agent. Swinburne's favoured example is that of a hypothetical poltergeist.

> It is possible that we might find certain otherwise inexplicable phenomena that could be explained by the action of a non-embodied agent, such as a ghost or poltergeist. The phenomena to be explained may be that books, chairs, inkwells, etc. start flying about my room. We postulate a poltergeist *P* with certain intentions, beliefs, and powers to be responsible. Clearly we have to suppose *P* to be very unlike other rational agents known to us both in his powers and in his ways of acquiring beliefs. . . . But we can suppose *P* to have beliefs influenced as are ours by how things are, and to have intentions of the kind that we have . . . For example, we can suppose *P* to have previously been a certain embodied person who had been greatly injured by *X* and who had greatly loved *Y*, *X* and *Y* being still alive . . . The supposition will be rendered probable if it has high explanatory power. It would have this, for example, if the books, chairs, inkwells, etc. hit *X*, or form themselves into words that warn *Y* of impending danger; and so on. We would expect this kind of thing to happen if *P* is as we have supposed, far more than we would ordinarily expect it to happen.[36]

Swinburne is surely right. If the objects do not fly around at random, but are clearly directed towards *X*, and particularly if they were to spell out a message, it might be reasonable to explain this by positing the existence and action of an unobservable agent. There are, of course, alternative, natural explanations, such as the existence of some kind of elaborate hoax, using technology with which we are currently unfamiliar. But let's assume that we have somehow excluded this possibility. (Swinburne's scenario becomes less likely if we impose this condition, but it is still not inconceivable.) We can imagine circumstances in which we are forced to posit both the existence and the action of an (unembodied) agent to explain such an event.

Note that Swinburne's example illustrates another feature of proposed theistic explanations. It is that in offering such an explanation, we do not first posit the existence of a poltergeist and then attribute certain intentions to him. I have distinguished these two tasks for the sake of clarity, for they are distinct. But in practice they may be undertaken simultaneously. What we posit is the existence of an agent having certain beliefs and desires. Both claims stand or fall together.

You may feel some unease about Swinburne's illustration. I do myself. But this unease is not warranted by the structure of the explanation, which seems to be legitimate. My unease, at least, arises from the nature of the agent whose existence is being posited. For he is, *ex hypothesi*, an unembodied personal agent, and we know of no other agents of this kind. This fact will make us at least hesitate before we accept the proposed explanation. Swinburne recognises the force of this objection; he simply attempts to find a way around it, when it comes to theism (7.2.2). But Swinburne is surely right when he insists that the lack of an existing analogy does not, by itself, rule out the proposed explanation. For the existence of an unembodied agent may be simply a surprising fact about the world. (Given the strangeness of, for example, quantum mechanics, it would not be the first surprising fact about the world we have had to stomach.) To what degree, if at all, background knowledge impacts on our assessment of proposed theistic explanations is a question to which I shall return (7.2).

3.2.3 Positing a Divine Intention

In the previous section, I argued that the theist has a double burden. He must successfully posit both the existence of God and the existence of a particular divine intention. Merely positing the existence of God is a *necessary* but not *sufficient* condition of a proposed theistic explanation, at least if that explanation is to have any degree of content. If the proposed explanation is to have any significant degree of empirical content, then something else is required, namely that we posit a particular divine intention.

3.2.3.1 *Spurious Unification*

Let me develop this idea for a moment, taking as my starting point a remark made by Philip Kitcher. Kitcher defends the idea that successful explanations unify our knowledge, bringing disparate facts under the same pattern of explanation. But he also speaks of the danger of what he calls "spurious unification." The apparent unification of our knowledge is spurious when a pattern of explanation is offered that could embrace any state of affairs. One of Kitcher's examples is a proposed explanation that has what he calls a theological pattern, which may be expressed as follows:[37]

(1) God wants it to be the case that *a*.
(2) What God wants to be the case is the case.
(3) Therefore *a*

44 *Theism and Explanation*

If the phrase "God wants it to be the case" imposes no restrictions on what can be substituted for *a*, if (in other words) *a* could be any actual state of affairs, then the unification achieved by this pattern is spurious. The explanation in question would lack empirical content, since—as Karl Popper pointed out—the empirical content of a theory is measured by the possible states of affairs it excludes.[38] It is only by excluding possible states of affairs that a theory can single out what *is* the case from what *might have been* the case.

What kind of an objection is this? I have already argued (2.2.1) that it is a *de facto* objection. It is conceivable that a proposed explanation of this form might count as a *potential* explanation of fact *a*. It all depends on what *a* is. If we could show that *a* is the kind of fact that we could plausibly expect God to will, then the above argument would satisfy the second premise of Peirce's abductive schema (2.1.2). If the premises of the argument were true, then one could deduce a description of the *explanandum*. Kitcher's objection is that one could deduce from an argument of the same form (and almost identical premises) a description of any *explanandum* at all. Any fact at all could be substituted for *a*. If this is true, then (he argues) the proposed explanation is spurious.

But is Kitcher correct? Is it true that any state of affairs at all could be substituted for *a*? I don't think it is. I shall argue later (5.3.3) that there *are* possible states of affairs which any proposed theistic explanation must exclude; this would be true of even a bare-bones proposed explanation of the form Kitcher cites. If the God in question is omnipotent and morally perfect, we would not expect him to bring about, for instance, states of gratuitous suffering. If *a* were an instance of gratuitous suffering, then the theistic hypothesis "God wants it to be the case that *a*" would not constitute even a *potential* explanation of *a*. The state of affairs which *a* designates is not the kind of thing that God could plausibly be said to want.

This is, of course, the heart of the atheist's argument from evil, the force of which most theists recognise. (They may argue that the instances of suffering the atheist cites are not gratuitous, or at least that we cannot know they are gratuitous. But to say this is to accept the force of the atheist's argument.) So *pace* Kitcher, it is simply not true that one could substitute any state of affairs for *a*. It follows that even a very minimal proposed theistic explanation of the kind Kitcher cites has *some* empirical content. There are possible states of affairs that it excludes.

3.2.3.2 A Legitimate Objection

But even if this is correct, this does not mean that Kitcher's warning is unnecessary. I have just argued that even a bare-bones proposed theistic explanation of the kind he cites cannot cover *any* possible state of affairs. But it may still cover *too many* possible states of affairs. Its empirical content may not be zero, but it may be unhelpfully low. And the point I want to make here is that it would be unhelpfully low if it "explained" the *explanandum* merely by attributing it to God. It may be true that "God willed *a*," but this tells us little more than that *a* occurred. Why is this? Well, if God exists, then he is, *ex hypothesi*, the cause of every event that occurs and of every actual state of affairs. His causation of events may be indirect, but the theist cannot accept that there exists any event for which God is not responsible,[39] even (as Aquinas notes) morally evil actions.[40] It follows that simply to attribute an event or state of affairs to God is not yet to say anything distinctive about it. Within the range of events that can plausibly be attributed to God, merely to attribute an event to divine agency is not yet to explain it. For it would not tell us why this event occurred rather than some other.

To illustrate this point, let me go back to Swinburne's poltergeist scenario, modifying it a little. Let's posit the existence of a poltergeist who is responsible for both the existence and the behaviour of *every* object in the room. We can then ask, "Why did the inkwell fly across the room?" On this scenario, it would be true that "the poltergeist did it." But this proposition lacks empirical content. It constitutes nothing more than the beginning of an answer to our question. For if the inkwell had simply fallen to the floor, the same answer could be given. And if the inkwell had not moved at all, the poltergeist would also be responsible, for he would have chosen to maintain it in existence in its current position. I concede that "the poltergeist did it" would still be an interesting and informative claim. It would be of some interest to know that there *exists* an unembodied, personal agent in control of the room. But this fact alone would not constitute an adequate explanation, since it would not single out the event to be explained from any other event. "Why did the inkwell fly across the room?" "The poltergeist did it." "OK, but why did he do that?" That's the question that needs to be answered.

If a proposed theistic explanation is to have any significant degree of empirical content, it must answer the same question with regard to God: "OK, but why did God do that?" It is not enough to attribute the event to the action of God, for this would tell us very little. A proposed theistic explanation should tell us not merely *that* God willed the fact-to-be-explained *E*; it should tell us *why* God willed *E*. It must, in other words, posit a particular divine goal to which (it is suggested) his willing the *explanandum* contributes. This is an important point, and I shall come back to it repeatedly. Is there any other way in which a proposed theistic explanation could be given a significant degree of empirical content? I don't know. But given the nature of intentional explanations, this seems the obvious solution. What I shall suggest later is that few real-life proposed theistic explanations meet this requirement (7.1.1).

There may be one exception to this rule, namely the cosmological argument for the existence of God. The conventional starting point of this argument is Leibniz's famous question, "Why is there something rather than nothing?" If we understand this as a question regarding the universe,[41] then it could be argued that "because God willed it" is all the answer we need. But I'm not so sure. Even in response to Leibniz's question, this answer does not seem to have much content. After all, what we are asking is, why does the universe exist? Or, as the theist might put it, why is it not the case that God alone exists? Keep in mind that if there were no universe, then given God's existence, he would have willed this state of affairs, too.[42] If God was free either to create or not to create, what we want to know is *why* he created.[43] So even in response to Leibniz's question, a proposed theistic explanation needs to say something more than "because God willed it." It must spell out *why* he willed what he did.

3.3 THE COHERENCE OF THEISM

I have been speaking of God's "reasons," his "purposes," his "goals" in acting as he has. This reminds us of another feature of proposed theistic explanations. They assume that we can apply the language of intentional explanations to God, that we can intelligibly speak of God as having beliefs and desires. Such language seems essential to the theistic hypothesis, which draws on a kind of "folk theology" similar to the folk psychology upon which everyday intentional explanations draw. But it is by no means clear that such language is applicable to God. In what sense could God have such mental states? Do such terms have any intelligible meaning when applied to God?

3.3.1 Theism and Analogy

It could be argued that such terms *are* applicable to God, but that some of them are applicable only in some extended, analogous sense. God could not have "desires" in our ordinary sense of this term, but he could have attitudes which in some pertinent way resemble human desires. Perhaps God could have what Donald Davidson calls "pro attitudes,"[44] even if they do not include the affective element that we find in beings such as ourselves. A more precise theology would make this clear. It would, for example, agree that when the folk speak of God as "angry" they are right to do so. This word does capture something of the mind of God. But the theologian would also insist that divine anger is very different from human anger.

The problem here is highlighted by another common theistic doctrine, that of divine simplicity. As found in Aquinas, this doctrine denies that there is any real distinction between the instances of the divine properties.[45] God's omnipotence, for instance, is identical with his omniscience, and his mercy identical with his justice. When applied to God, all these names signify just one divine reality.[46] In Hume's *Dialogues*, the figure of Demea offers what Gerard Hughes calls "a pretty fair summary of Aquinas's view."[47] "All true theists," Demea notes, ascribe to God "perfect immutability and simplicity."[48]

> By the same act, say they, he sees past, present, and future: His love and his hatred, his mercy and his justice are one individual operation: He is entire in every point of space; and complete in every instance of duration. No succession, no change, no acquisition, no diminution. What he is implies in it not any shadow of distinction or diversity. And what he is, this moment, has ever been, and ever will be, without any new judgment, sentiment, or operation. He stands fixed in one, simple, perfect state; nor can you ever say, with any propriety, that this act of his is different from that other, or that this judgment or idea has been lately formed, and will give place, by succession, to any different judgement or idea.[49]

The difficulty this poses for the theist, as Cleanthes argues, is that such a doctrine of God is practically indistinguishable from atheism. It certainly seems incompatible with the idea that God is a personal being, an agent with beliefs, desires, and intentions. As Cleanthes writes,

> a mind, whose acts and sentiments are not distinct and successive; one, that is wholly simple and wholly immutable; is a mind which has no thought, no reason, no will, no sentiment, no love, no hatred; or in a word, is no mind at all. It is an abuse of terms to give it that appellation; and we may as well speak of limited extension without figure, or of number without composition.[50]

Hume is not alone in expressing such doubts. At least one modern theist philosopher, Alvin Plantinga, rejects the traditional doctrine of divine simplicity. And one reason why he does so is that it apparently makes it impossible to think of God as a person.[51]

These discussions raise complex theological and metaphysical issues, which would lie far beyond the scope of this study. And even if you reject the doctrine of divine simplicity, there will be something deeply mysterious about the mental states that the theist attributes to God. The underlying question here is whether we can predicate any terms of God in their literal sense. It is not only "liberal Protestant theologians" who deny this, as William Alston suggests.[52] There is a long-standing theological tradition that does so, extending from Pseudo-Dionysius (in the fifth century) to Richard Swinburne (3.3.3). It is not without its exceptions. Edward Schoen, for instance, argues that we *can*, in fact, predicate terms of God univocally.[53] But it is safe to say that Schoen's position is a minority one. No less a figure than Thomas Aquinas denies that "what is said of God and creatures is said of them univocally."[54] To use terms univocally of God and creatures, Aquinas argues, would imply that "they stood in the same rank."[55] But this is manifestly untrue, since "the divine substance, by its immensity, transcends every form that our intellect can realise."[56] If we can say anything positive about God, it is only because effects necessarily resemble their causes.[57]

So there must be some respect in which creatures resemble their creator. But while this means that at least some of the language used of creatures is applicable to God, it also means that it is applicable only when used in an extended or analogical sense.

This traditional doctrine regarding theological language requires some explication. It is not the case that *all* our language about God is analogical. For, as Aquinas's own words suggest, we can use certain negative predicates of God in their literal sense. As William Alston writes, God is literally "incorporeal," "immutable," and "not-identical-with-Richard-Nixon."[58] And one could argue that there are "extrinsic" predicates (such as "thought of now by me") that can also be predicated of God in a literal way.[59] So presumably what Aquinas is referring to are "intrinsic" predicates: those that tell us something about "the nature and operations of the subject."[60] As Aquinas suggests, if we cannot predicate these of God in any literal way, it is presumably because we cannot form precise concepts of the divine properties to which they refer.[61] It follows that we can apply intrinsic predicates to God only by using language in a metaphorical or analogical manner.

If I were to pursue this line of thought, I would need to identify the different ways in which we can speak of things analogically,[62] and decide which of these would allow us to speak of God.[63] Once again, however, such a discussion would take me far beyond the scope of my study. The only issue I wish to address here is whether this common theological doctrine—the idea that we can speak of God only by analogy—undermines the force of a proposed theistic explanation.

A moment's reflection suggests that it does not, for we already have apparently successful explanations that use analogical terms. In explaining the behaviour of non-human animals we often use terms such as "belief" and "desire," while recognising that the referents of those terms must be very different from the beliefs and desires with which we are familiar.[64] When my cat wanders into the kitchen and sits by the fridge, it seems reasonable to explain his action by saying that he "desires" a saucer of milk and "believes" that it is to be found in the fridge. Yet we know the feline mental states corresponding to these terms must be very different from the corresponding mental states in human beings.[65] A more sophisticated feline psychology would perhaps use different terms (3.2.2); to say that the cat "desires" milk is to use a human folk-psychological term in reference to a cats. But the mere fact that language is being used analogically does not undermine its explanatory use. Such language can still be informative and could, in principle, form the basis of a successful explanation.

3.3.2 The Concept of God

The more serious issue here has to do with the internal coherence or consistency of the theistic conception of God. Could the various attributes which theists attribute to God co-exist in the one being? Could he be an intentional

What are Theistic Explanations? 49

agent *and* be omniscient, omnipotent, and so on? Take, for instance, the view, widespread among medieval philosophers, that God is an atemporal being, that he exists outside of time. Or take the related doctrine that God is immutable, that he cannot change. Is either of these doctrines compatible with the idea that God is an intentional agent, that he acts for a purpose? Many contemporary theist philosophers have thought not. They have argued, for instance, that a being who wills certain states of affairs undergoes intrinsic changes, and so cannot be immutable. And if he wills some temporal state of affairs, then he exists in interaction with it. So he, too, must exist in time.[66] But if you abandon the view that God's existence is atemporal, does this, in turn, create difficulties for the traditional doctrine of divine omniscience?[67] For one might argue that a deity existing within time cannot know of future states of affairs and so cannot be said to be fully in control of events.[68]

Once again, I cannot hope to resolve any of these questions here. I wish only to note that there exists a difficulty. At least some of the traditional divine attributes constitute *prima facie* evidence against the idea that God could be an intentional agent. Insofar as a theistic explanation posits the existence of an agent having these attributes, it may turn out to be an incoherent hypothesis. Of course, it may not. Perhaps such objections can be shown to be baseless. Or perhaps we can rework our conception of God, to overcome them. But one could argue that these are questions that at some point need to be resolved, if a theistic hypothesis is to prove itself worthy of acceptance.

The issue is not limited to the question of whether God could have beliefs and desires. There are other respects in which the theist's concept of God may turn out to be incoherent. Is it, for instance, conceivable that a morally perfect being should be omniscient, that an omniscient being should be free, or that an unembodied agent should be omniscient? Given that there are good *prima facie* reasons for answering "no" to each of these questions,[69] this constitutes a *prima facie* argument against proposed theistic explanations.

3.3.3 Direct and Indirect Proofs

How could the theist respond to such objections? Well, he might be tempted to argue from *esse* to *posse* (as it were), from fact to possibility. If some state of affairs is actual, then it must also be possible. If I have sufficient reason to attribute beliefs and desires to my cat, then clearly I have sufficient reason to think that cats can have beliefs and desires. Similarly, if I have sufficient reason to think there exists a God having certain intentions, then clearly God is capable of having such intentions. This is precisely the route taken by Richard Swinburne, and it will be worth examining it briefly, to see if it could vindicate the theist's conception of God.

Swinburne concedes that there is a *prima facie* objection here. Theists make claims about God that make little sense if their words are taken

50 *Theism and Explanation*

literally. They say, for instance, that God is a "person" who "knows" things and can "bring about" states of affairs.[70] If such propositions are in fact coherent, it can only be because such language is being used analogically. But precisely because such language is being used analogically, we cannot directly demonstrate its internal coherence, since we cannot specify exactly what it does and does not mean. This might appear to constitute a fatal objection to a theistic hypothesis: if we cannot demonstrate its coherence, why should we accept it? Swinburne's response is that we can establish the coherence of theism *indirectly*, by showing that there is good reason to believe that there exists a God who has these apparently incompatible properties.[71] And, of course, Swinburne has devoted much of his life to arguing for the existence of the Christian God.

Does this offer the theist a way out? Well, perhaps the charge of incoherence is not fatal (3.3.4), but Swinburne underestimates its seriousness. I shall argue later that Swinburne's arguments for the existence of God are best thought of as abductive arguments (6.1.3). But if someone is offering an abductive argument, then it seems vital that his hypothesis be consistent. The reason is simple, and will become clear if we call to mind Peirce's schema for abductive reasoning (2.1.2).

(1) The surprising fact, E, is observed.
(2) But if H were true, E would be a matter of course,
(3) Hence, there is reason to suspect that H is true.

A potential explanation, I argued, is one that satisfies the second premise of this schema. The key question in each case is: What would follow, if H were true? But it is a well-known principle of at least classical logic that from a contradiction anything follows: *ex contradictione quodlibet*, in its traditional Latin formulation.[72] Let's say, for the sake of the argument, that the theistic hypothesis (H) does embody a contradiction. (If this were true, we could easily be unaware of it, especially if the language we are using is being used analogically.) Let's say, for instance, that God simply could not be both perfectly just and perfectly merciful, but that our theistic hypothesis attributes both qualities to him. Then whatever the *explanandum* is, we could derive from H a proposition describing it. For the same reason, we could apparently corroborate H by appealing to any fact whatever.[73] But this is equivalent to saying that a self-contradictory hypothesis could never be an acceptable explanation. While we have reason to doubt the consistency of the theistic hypothesis, we have reason to treat it with some suspicion.

3.3.4 The Consistency Requirement

It follows that we should not underestimate the seriousness of the charge of internal incoherence. But neither should we overestimate it, for it may not be a fatal objection. Are there circumstances in which we would be acting rationally in accepting an apparently inconsistent hypothesis? Most philosophers would hold that we are not entitled to *believe* such a theory, which would be equivalent to believing a contradiction.[74] But perhaps we can *accept* an apparently inconsistent hypothesis, even if we do not believe it (2.1.3). If it enjoys other explanatory virtues—such as a high degree of testability, simplicity, ontological economy, and informativeness—we might accept it in the sense of continuing to work on it, to see if the apparent inconsistencies can be resolved. As Alan Musgrave remarks, "unless we are allowed to work with logically inconsistent theories, how will they ever get turned into consistent ones?"[75] (This might entail abandoning the principle that *ex contradictione quodlibet*, but a number of logicians have advocated precisely this move.) So from this point of view, Swinburne's proposal is not as objectionable as it might appear at first sight. We could legitimately adopt a theistic hypothesis, in some provisional, heuristic way, even if there were some *prima facie* evidence that it was internally incoherent. We could do so if it possessed other explanatory virtues. How likely is it that a theistic hypothesis would possess those explanatory virtues? Once again that's a question I shall address later.

3.4 CAUSAL EXPLANATIONS

I have been arguing that a proposed theistic explanation is an intentional explanation. But theistic explanations are also, it appears, causal explanations. The God whose existence and action they posit is a creator God, who brings things into existence by an act of the divine will. But can these two things be combined? Are intentional explanations causal explanations? And can we make any sense of the idea that the will of God has causal efficacy? Is the idea of a creator God a coherent one?

3.4.1 Intentional and Causal Explanations

A first objection rests on the very character of intentional explanations. It suggests that a theistic explanation could not be both intentional and causal, since these represent distinct and mutually exclusive forms of explanation. No intentional explanation is a causal explanation. But I believe this claim to be wrong, for reasons I shall outline later (Appendix 1.1). I have no argument with the idea, defended by Donald Davidson, that intentions are causes and that intentional explanations are also causal explanations.[76] There *is* one issue that needs to be clarified here. I have suggested that intentional explanations are not nomological (3.2.1). They do, if you like, depend on something resembling a law, namely the rationality principle. But they do not depend on law-like generalisations linking particular intentions and particular actions. Does this mean that they cannot be regarded as causal explanations? Only if you believe that the citing of causal laws is

52 *Theism and Explanation*

a necessary condition of a causal explanation. But I shall argue later that it is not (Appendix 3.3.1), that causal explanations do not necessarily involve causal laws.[77] If this is true, then there is no difficulty with the idea that an intentional explanation is also a causal explanation.

3.4.2 Intermediate Causal Mechanisms

But a different objection may be raised, one that suggests that even if intentional explanations in general can be causal explanations, proposed *theistic* explanations cannot. They fail to be causal explanations—or, at least, adequate causal explanations—because they say nothing about the mechanism of divine action. Adolf Grünbaum articulates this objection, arguing that

> the hypothesis of divine creation does not even envision, let alone specify an appropriate *intermediate* causal *process* that would *link* the presence of the supposed divine (causal) agency to the effects that are attributed to it. Nor, it seems is there any prospect at all that the chronic inscrutability of the putative causal linkage will be removed by new theoretical developments.[78]

It is difficult to know what to make of this objection. It is of the essence of the theistic hypothesis that God can bring about events and states of affairs directly, without any intermediate causal process. *Ex hypothesi*, God could (if he chose) bring about any effect merely by willing it, as a basic action.[79] Indeed given the traditional concept of God, the divine will is unfailingly efficacious. We cannot conceive of a situation in which God wills some state of affairs and it fails to come about. Of course, one might argue that positing the existence of such a being—one possessed of "magical" powers—is extravagant, in the sense that it is not warranted by the evidence. One might also point out that we know of no other causal process of this type (7.2). But it is no objection to the *idea* of divine action, the idea that the will of God could bring about some state of affairs.

In fact, taken at face value, Grünbaum's argument leads to an infinite regress of causal attributions. What it appears to be saying is that if we claim that A causes B, we must be able to specify an "intermediate causal process" that links A and B. Let's call this intermediate causal process A_1.

$$A \to A_1 \to B$$

But is A_1 itself a cause? Then its causal relationship to B (for example) requires a further intermediate causal mechanism, namely A_2.

$$A \to A_1 \to A_2 \to B$$

And then A_2 must be linked to B by an intermediate causal process, A_3, and so *ad infinitum*. How can this be avoided? Well, if the "intermediate causal process" (A_1) is not a distinct cause, then it is presumably nothing more than a specification of how cause A operates. In this case, what is being affirmed is a direct causal link between A and B.

$$A \rightarrow B$$

And there is nothing incoherent about the idea that the divine will could be a direct cause of this type.[80]

3.4.3 God and Causation

But behind these misplaced objections lurks a more serious difficulty. It is the difficulty of finding a conception of causation that is applicable to the posited divine agent. It might be tempting, for instance, for a theist to adopt the counterfactual analysis of causation.[81] Applied to theistic explanations, such an analysis implies merely that if God had not willed the *explanandum*, then some other state of affairs would prevail. It may be that this is not an adequate analysis of what we mean by "cause."[82] Mackie, for instance, feels compelled to supplement it with the idea of causal priority.[83] But if one could defend a counterfactual analysis of causation, its theistic use might, at first sight, seem unexceptionable.[84]

On closer analysis, however, this impression would be misleading. There may be difficulties with regarding the action of God as a cause, even in the counterfactual sense. Quentin Smith, for instance, argues that the very idea that God could be the cause of some state of affairs is incoherent. His particular target is the idea that God could be the cause of the universe, and in particular the cause of the "big bang," the event thought by many to be the beginning of the universe.[85] Smith concedes that his is a minority position, that "virtually all contemporary theists, agnostics, and atheists" believe that there are no logical problems with the idea that God could be the cause of the universe.[86] But of course a minority position may still be correct. And if it is, then proposed theistic explanations are entirely without content. So let me examine Smith's arguments, to see if the theist has at least a *prima facie* case to answer.

3.4.3.1 A De Facto *Argument*

Smith offers two arguments against the idea of divine causation. The first is a *de facto* argument, which rests on the claim that there is no *existing* sense of the word "cause" that is applicable to God. Smith begins with Hume's influential definition of causality, with its three conditions of temporal priority, spatial contiguity, and law-like conjunction. Smith argues that the temporal priority condition could, conceivably, apply to God, on the assumption that both God's willing the *explanandum* and the *explanandum* itself exist in time. (Where the big bang is the *explanandum*, the temporal priority condition would entail that the big bang was not, as commonly believed,[87] the beginning of time. As Smith writes, this is at least a "logical possibility."[88]) But the other two conditions—those of spatial contiguity and law-like conjunction—do not apply to God.[89] What about "singularist" definitions of causality, which reject the nomological requirement? Well, at least the best known of such definitions, that of C. J. Ducasse,[90] still requires spatial contiguity.[91] Another option consists of "transference" definitions of a cause, which claim that what is essential to causation is a transfer of some mark or property from cause to effect. This, too, Smith argues, fails in application to God. For what could it be that is transferred between a non-physical cause and a physical effect?

There remains the counterfactual analysis of causation to which I referred a moment ago. If the theist could answer the various objections that have been offered to the counterfactual analysis, could the theist not think of divine action as "causal" in this sense? No, Smith argues, he cannot. When applied to God, a counterfactual analysis of causation runs into a new problem. The problem was already identified in the work of David Lewis. Lewis points out an objection to his own counterfactual analysis of causation, namely that it leads to what he calls a "spurious causal dependence" of the cause on its effect. To see what he means, let's designate the cause as c and the effect as e. And let's imagine a situation in which—given the particular laws and circumstances involved—"c could not have failed to cause e."[92] Then, as Lewis writes, "it seems to follow that if the effect e had not occurred, then its cause c would not have occurred."[93] But on a counterfactual analysis, this would make e the cause of c, which is an unacceptable conclusion. Something like Mackie's added condition of causal priority seems to be needed (3.4.3).

Lewis's way out of this objection is to deny the counterfactual in question, to deny that if e had not occurred then c would not have occurred either. Rather, he insists,

> c would have occurred just as it did but would have failed to cause e. It is less of a departure from actuality to get rid of e by holding c fixed and giving up some or other of the laws and circumstances in virtue of which c could not have failed to produce e, rather than to hold those laws and circumstances fixed and get rid of e by going back and abolishing its cause c.[94]

What Lewis seems to be doing here is retracting his original stipulation, namely that here is a situation in which "c could not have failed to cause e." And one can read this as a denial that there could ever be an unfailingly efficacious cause. But of course to deny that there could be an unfailingly efficacious cause is to reject the theistic hypothesis. For as we have seen, God's willing of an event or state of affairs cannot be other than unfailingly efficacious. It is unthinkable that God would will *e* and that *e* would not occur. And it is unthinkable that God, the divine cause, could be dependent, even counterfactually, on what he himself creates. It follows that the counterfactual analysis of causation is not applicable to God. It cannot avoid the "spurious causal dependence" problem identified by Lewis.

3.4.3.2 *An* In Principle *Argument*

These reflections bring Smith to his second, *in principle*, argument against the idea of divine causation. It relies on the idea that if an event or state, x, is a logically sufficient condition of another event or state, y, then x cannot also be the cause of y. To take Smith's example, "a body's being in motion is logically sufficient condition of the body occupying space."[95] So far, so good, although this surely needs rewording. If the condition in question *is* logical, it seems better to express it as a relationship between propositions. The truth of the proposition "the body is in motion" is a logically sufficient condition of the truth of the proposition "the body occupies space." For if a body is in motion, it must also be in space, and we could understand this from an analysis of both concepts. Nonetheless, Smith argues, "the body's being in motion is not the cause of the body's occupation of space."[96] This, too, seems correct. Intuitively, at least, we would not speak of this as a cause. This gives us, in Smith's view, a distinction between logically sufficient conditions and causes.

Into which category does the action of God fall? Smith argues that God's willing y is a logically sufficient condition of y. Again, we might more accurately express this in terms of propositions. Where y is any event, the truth of "God wills y" is a logically sufficient condition of "y occurs." For if an omnipotent being wills y and y does not occur, then the agent in question is not an omnipotent being. But this is a contradiction. Given the principle that a logically sufficient condition cannot be a cause, it follows that God's willing y cannot be a cause of y. Smith speaks of a cause of the universe, but it seems it would be true whatever we substitute for y.

If this argument is sound, it is a fatal objection to the very idea of a theistic explanation. For it entails that any argument which suggests that x—let's say the universe—has a cause is also an argument against the idea that its cause is a divine state. And on the assumption that all explanations are causal explanations, then there could never be a successful theistic explanation. How might the defender of theistic explanations respond?

Are all explanations causal? One response would be to deny the assumption: the idea that all explanations are causal explanations. The theist might argue that while all *scientific* explanations might be causal explanations, when science runs out, theology takes over. And what theology offers is a

56 *Theism and Explanation*

non-causal explanation. One problem with this response is that it undermines the apparent parallel between scientific and proposed theistic explanations, and for many theists it is this parallel that can be used to lend support to theism (3.1). It would also require a radical rethink of what we mean by a theistic explanation, my own reconstruction of which assumes that such explanations *are* causal explanations. So is there another way out?

A case of fallacious reasoning? A second response would cast doubt on the cogency of Smith's argument. If God exists, his willing is unfailingly efficacious. Necessarily, if God wills some event, then it occurs. But does it follow that if God wills that event, it necessarily occurs? Apparently not. We can see this by representing God's act of willing as *G*, and the *explanandum* as *E*. The following argument, where the symbol □ means "necessarily," represents a fallacy.

(1) □ (G ⊃ E)
(2) G
∴ (3) □ E.[97]

If this argument were valid, then every truth would be a necessary truth.[98] For one could substitute for *G* and *E* any fact *A*.

(1) □ (A ⊃ A)
(2) A
∴ (3) □ A.

But this is an unacceptable conclusion.

A category mistake? A third response would be to suggest that Smith's argument rests on a kind of category mistake, confusing logical and metaphysical issues. There is a sense in which God's willing *E* "necessitates" the occurrence of *E*. But the necessity here is not in the first place logical, but metaphysical. It is true that when it is expressed in propositions, there exists a logical relationship between those propositions. As we've just seen, one could set out this relationship in terms of a deductive argument.

(1) All events willed by God occur.
(2) *E* is willed by God.
(3) Therefore *E* occurs.

But the truth of the premises is not itself a mere matter of logic. If God exists, then his willing *E* is unfailingly efficacious because of the kind of being God is.

Smith all but acknowledges this point when responding to an objection. His original argument was that the propositions "an omnipotent agent wills the big bang" and "the big bang does not occur" contradict one another. But, the objection goes, one can avoid this contradiction simply by rewording the proposition about divine agency. "There occurs a willing that has as its aim the actualization of the big bang, but the big bang is not actualized" is not self-contradictory.[99] So if the two events are appropriately described, their relationship could be thought of as causal. But, Smith counters, even given this redescription, it may still be true that "the divine volition necessarily possess[es] the relational property of being conjoined with the occurrence of the big bang."[100] Fair enough. It may still be impossible that the act of will should occur and that its intended effect should not. But the possession of a property of this kind is a metaphysical, not a logical fact.

All-in-all, then, I am far from convinced by Smith's second, *in principle* argument. If we do reject it, but acknowledge the force of his first, *de facto* argument, then we must—sadly for the atheist—settle for a more modest conclusion. It is a conclusion which does not rule out the possibility of a successful theistic explanation. It is true that if none of our existing accounts of causation are applicable to God, then the onus is on theists to come up with another. And given the difficulties philosophers have had making sense of our everyday use of "cause," we cannot expect this will be an easy task. But the failure of our existing ideas of cause to make sense of theistic claims does not necessarily mean those claims are incoherent. It may suggest merely that there is more work for a theistic philosopher to do.

3.4.4 The Ubiquity of Divine Causation

Here's a final observation before I leave this topic of God and causation. We have seen that on the theistic hypothesis, God is a causal factor in every event which occurs (3.2.3). He may not cause events directly, but he certainly does so indirectly. His willing event E is a necessary condition of the occurrence of E: if he did not will E, then E would not occur. As Swinburne writes, "if there is a God, he is omnipresent and all causal processes operate only because he sustains them."[101] This means that, from the theist's point of view, no explanation is complete without reference to God.[102] If God exists, then any complete explanation of any fact must at some point make reference to divine action.

The question this raises for the theist is, at first sight, a surprising one. It is whether, given the truth of theism, there can exist a *natural* explanation of any fact. If God is causally involved in every event, does it make sense to speak of a *non-theistic* explanation of that event? If we assert that God is the cause of E, then does that assertion not occupy all the explanatory space, as it were? What else could possibly remain to be said? It is perhaps this idea that gave rise to the theological position I shall examine shortly ("occasionalism"), which denies the reality of "secondary" or created causes (4.3.1). Does the explanatory logic of theism compel a theist to be an occasionalist, to deny the force of any natural explanation?

No, it does not. Given the truth of theism, we can still speak of a natural explanation of some event. Or at least, we can still do so if we admit that not every explanation need be a complete explanation.[103] I anticipated this suggestion when I argued that Richard Dawkins's objection to theistic explanations was unsound (1.3.3). *Pace* Dawkins,[104] it is not a necessary condition of a successful explanation that it can explain its *explanans*.[105] If we follow my earlier suggestion and assume that explanations are arguments (2.1.4), then an explanation is an argument which has the *explanandum* as its conclusion. To explain an explosion, for instance, all we need is a description of a leak of gas, coupled with a description of its causal field, and some low-level laws regarding the behaviour of gases. One might argue that a complete explanation would need to cite further laws, which would explain the lower-level laws.[106] Of course, this leads to a regress of explanations, which may or may not have an end.[107] But that doesn't matter, since it is not obligatory. We do not need to have a complete explanation in order to have an explanation.

In speaking of a natural explanation of some phenomenon, where might a theist draw the line? Well, assuming that there exist created causes—what are traditionally called "secondary causes"—God could act in two ways. He could bring about an effect immediately, merely by willing it. We could then describe the outcome as a "miracle." But God could also act by way of secondary causes, using them as his instrument. Of a miracle, there is, by definition, no natural explanation. But if an event is not thought of as a miracle, a theist could concede that there exists a natural explanation of that event. A natural explanation would cite those secondary causes which were responsible for bringing about the effect, without prejudice to the idea that they, in turn, depend on God. How might the theist reconcile these two forms of explanation? The following chapter will seek to answer that question.

4 What Would They Explain?

> It's a nervous tick of analytic philosophy to be forever wishing to clarify distinctions that nobody is actually confused about.
>
> Jerry Fodor

The previous chapter highlighted some key features of proposed theistic explanations, by approaching the issue from the point of view of the *explanans*. To complete this descriptive part of my task, let me now turn to the *explananda* of theistic explanations, the facts that theists claim to be able to explain. There are three features of proposed theistic explanations that I wish to discuss under this heading. The first is that they cover both events and states of affairs (4.1). The second is that proposed theistic explanations are generally, but not always, singular explanations (4.2). The third has to do with the relationship of theistic and natural explanations. On some occasions, proposed theistic explanations cover facts that admit of a natural explanation, which the theist accepts; on other occasions they claim to be the only explanations on offer (4.3). The chapter will end with a discussion of the problem of miracles. If an account of divine action invokes an agent capable of working miracles, does this undermine its explanatory force (4.4)?

4.1 EVENTS AND STATES OF AFFAIRS

My first point is that proposed theistic explanations cover both events and states of affairs. The distinction between events and states of affairs is one we employ in everyday life, although it is metaphysically controversial. Jaegwon Kim, for instance, has suggested that the facts we refer to as "events" and those we refer to as "states" could be subsumed under a common definition. They are both *"exemplifications by substances of properties at a time."*[1] This suggestion is not without its relevance to discussions of causation. In many cases, at least, it is some *property* of the *explanans* which we regard as responsible for the effect. (If I say, "he broke the chair," what I mean is that his excessive weight broke the chair.[2]) However, I will not enter into these metaphysical discussions here; for my present purposes the everyday distinction will do. Proposed theistic explanations cover the two classes of facts that we customarily distinguish with the aid of these terms.

4.1.1 States of Affairs

Let me begin with states of affairs. The *explanandum* of a theistic explanation is not always an event, in the sense of something closely bounded in space and time. It is sometimes a state of affairs, one which exists over time and may be distributed in space. It may even be a state of affairs coextensive with time itself, as in the case of the existence of the universe. As I noted earlier, one way of construing the cosmological argument is to see it as a response to Leibniz's question, "Why is there something rather than nothing?" Here we have a state of affairs—the existence of something rather than nothing—without which there could be no other state of affairs (other than the existence of God himself). A similar comment may be made about Richard Swinburne's teleological argument, which suggests that positing the existence of God explains the very existence of laws of nature.[3] Here, too, we have a state of affairs in a very broad sense of the term. In fact, this state of affairs may turn out to be identical with the first, since it is hard to see how one could have a universe which did not include regular, law-like processes.[4]

4.1.2 Events

Alongside theistic explanations of states of affairs we also find explanations of particular events. These are the explanations of *narrow scope* to which Philip Clayton refers ("Yahweh caused the Flood to punish the people's sinfulness; God allowed the flat tire to teach me patience").[5] A striking, real-life example of such an explanation came to light as I was writing this chapter. Shortly after the Indian Ocean tsunami of December 26, 2004, the chief Sephardic rabbi of Israel "explained" the catastrophe by attributing it to God's anger at our neglect of his commandments.[6] One might regard this suggestion as morally abhorrent, but it at least takes seriously the logic of classical theism. If there is a God, then he was responsible for the event, and must have had some reason to bring it about.[7] And in offering such an explanation, the rabbi stands in a long tradition. Theistic explanations of particular events, particularly catastrophes, have been enormously influential. Indeed much of the Bible consists of a series of such explanations.

As a general rule, theistic philosophers favour theistic explanations of *states of affairs* over explanations of particular *events*. (To sophisticated believers, the latter can appear a little naïve.) Indeed from the theist's point of view, the more fundamental the state of affairs, the better. A hypothesis of the broadest possible scope—one that covers the existence of the universe or the existence of laws of nature—is unlikely to have a competing, natural explanation. In fact, in some cases, a natural explanation may be simply inconceivable. (What would it mean to offer a natural explanation of the existence of laws of nature?) I shall come back to this idea shortly (4.3.2).

4.2 SINGULAR AND GENERAL EXPLANATIONS

A closely related point is that proposed theistic explanations are generally, but not always, singular explanations. If we understand the term "event" broadly, to cover all the *explananda* of proposed theistic explanations, we may say that these *explananda* are generally event-tokens rather than event-types.[8] Or, to put it another way, the causal claim they embody is normally of the form "C caused E." They are rarely causal generalizations, of the form "C-events cause E-events."[9] So when the chief rabbi declares the Indian Ocean tsunami to have been brought about by God in order to punish human sinfulness, he is speaking of a particular tsunami, not tsunamis in general. He is not intending to formulate a causal law.

Could one not argue that even this proposed explanation embodies a law, that is to say, a causal correlation between event-types rather than event-tokens? The law in question would simply be at a higher level than one covering tsunamis. It would state, for instance, that God always punishes sin, leaving open the particular means by which he punishes. But if this were the case, what class of events would such a law cover? The class of divine punishments? But this is more than a description of the *explanandum*; to describe an event *as* a divine punishment is already to explain it. Perhaps such a law could be taken to cover any event with unpleasant consequences for some group of subjects. Well, perhaps it could. But theists certainly don't explain *all* unpleasant events as divine punishments, any more than they explain all tsunamis in this way. (There are other proposed theistic explanations of unpleasant events, namely that they are tests of our faith or unavoidable consequences of some greater good.) So my own interpretation seems more plausible. When someone describes the Indian Ocean tsunami as a punishment for sin, he is not citing any law of divine action. Rather, he is attempting to explain this particular event as the result of a particular divine intention. This is, I propose, a singular explanation.

4.2.1 The Status of Singular Explanations

This suggestion, however, raises some broader questions. For there exists a long-standing philosophical debate about what are thought to be singular explanations. Does it make sense to speak of a singular causal explanation? There are, in fact, two issues to be discussed here, which need to be distinguished (Appendix 3.3.1).[10] The first is a metaphysical question regarding causation. The second is an epistemic issue, regarding explanation. On the metaphysical question, a broadly Humean position is that something is a cause only if it is regularly associated with an effect, the *relata* here being event-types. (This may not be a sufficient condition, but it is a necessary one.) According to this view, causation is invariably a matter of law-like association. To say that A causes B is to say that events of type A are regularly followed by events of type B. On the epistemic question, one might argue that any causal explanation must reflect this law-like association. It will be a nomological explanation, one that cites one or more causal laws, which cover the *explanandum*.

One author who tries to keep these two issues distinct is Donald Davidson. Davidson argues that intentional explanations are law-less (or "anomalous"), while holding to the broadly Humean view that causation always involves law-like regularities. Reconciling these two claims is not a simple matter, for on the face of it, the two issues are closely related. If a proposed explanation is a causal explanation, and if the causation to which it refers is a matter of law-like regularities, then one would expect the explanation to reflect this. As we shall see, Davidson's solution is to distinguish two levels of explanation. Intentional explanations do not cite laws, but facts to which they refer could also be explained using the language of the natural sciences, and such language would cite causal laws.

This is an important question, to which I shall return (Appendix 3.3.1). Like Davidson, I wish to argue that intentional explanations need not cite causal laws. But in this context, Davidson's arguments do not leave us any further ahead. For the question of whether an explanation must cite a causal law is not quite the same as the question of whether there exist singular causal explanations, that is to say, explanations relating event-tokens rather than event-types. The claim that there exist singular explanations is not merely a claim about the structure of our explanations; it involves a metaphysical claim, about causation. My own view is that unless one holds that causation is *nothing other* than a regular association of events, then there is no reason to deny the possibility of singular causation. As C. J. Ducasse put it, an event "could be unique in the history of the universe, and yet be, and be known to be, a case of causation."[11] But this is not a position I can defend here.

All I can do here is to ask: What would follow if my suggestion is wrong? What if it turns out that there are no singular explanations, that all causal explanations must relate event-types? What implications would this have for the theist? Well, it would eliminate a whole class of proposed theistic explanations, namely those that do not claim to relate event-types. (The chief rabbi's suggestion, if I have understood it correctly, could be discredited immediately, which may be a good thing.) But it would not eliminate *all* proposed theistic explanations. For while most proposed explanations of this kind do not take the form of general causal propositions, some do. There exist proposed theistic explanations that *do* purport to express law-like regularities, that relate event-types rather than event-tokens.

Edward Schoen offers us an instance of a proposed theistic explanation of this kind. It has to do with a believer named Fred, an intellectually sophisticated believer, who "hopes to introduce God as an explanatory entity to account for certain regular patterns he has noticed in his own life."[12] What are those "regular patterns"? Well, at times when he has little financial support Fred finds that his daily needs (for food, clothing, and shelter) are regularly supplied, often in unexpected ways. Fred attributes this regular (and presumably predictable) pattern to divine action. Another example of a general causal explanation is implicit in the biblical injunction regarding prayer—"Whatever you ask for in my name, I will do it" (John 14:13)—which may be regarded as embodying a generalised causal claim. And there are believers who appeal to the efficacy of petitionary prayer by claiming that prayers of this type regularly produce their effect.

4.2.2 Testing a Proposed Explanation

This distinction—between singular and general explanations—has at least one important implication. It is that the kind of explanation being offered will determine the manner in which it can be tested. In particular, if the theist is offering a singular explanation, we cannot test it by replicating condition C and seeing if event E is observed. But this does not mean it is untestable; we can, I shall argue, test it in other ways (Appendix 3.3.2). And of course those theistic explanations that do embody general causal claims *could* be tested by way of replication. In fact, there have been a number of studies which have attempted to do this: they have tested religious claims regarding the efficacy of petitionary prayer by means of controlled trials. What results have they produced? Well, for the most part the results have failed to lend support to theism.[13] In fact, the most recent trial suggests that if there is any effect, it is actually harmful to the patient,[14] a conclusion that offers little comfort to the theist. It is worth noting, too, that the very fact of undertaking such studies has been controversial, both theologically and scientifically.[15] But whatever one may think of this way of "putting God to the test," it simply cannot be done in the case of singular proposed explanations.

4.3 THEISTIC AND SECULAR EXPLANATIONS

Another way of approaching the question of the *explananda* of theistic explanations is to ask: How are such explanations related to their secular counterparts? Are the two classes of explanation in competition, so that it is a matter of choosing between them? Or are they complementary, so that they can legitimately co-exist? This, too, is an important question, which has implications for how we view the relationship between religion and science. Unfortunately, no simple answer can be given, for the answer will depend on the kind of event that the theist is attempting to explain.

4.3.1 Occasionalism and Causation

A key question here is a theological one, which has to do with how one conceives of God's relationship to the world. One view, known as

64 *Theism and Explanation*

"occasionalism," denies that there exist any created causes; the only agent with the power to bring about effects is God. The occasionalist doctrine is helpfully summarised by Steven Nadler. It is the belief that

> God is directly, immediately, and solely responsible for bringing about all phenomena. When a needle pricks the skin, the physical event is merely an occasion for God to cause the appropriate mental event, a pain; a volition in the soul to raise an arm or to think of something is only an occasion for God to cause the arm to rise or the appropriate idea to become present to the mind; and the impact of one billiard ball upon another is an occasion for God to put the first ball at rest and move the second ball. In all three contexts—mind-body, body-mind, and mind alone—God's ubiquitous causal activity proceeds in accordance with certain general laws, and (except in the case of miracles) he acts only when the required requisite material or psychic conditions obtain.[16]

Occasionalism was a popular view among medieval Muslim philosophers.[17] While it has been a minority view in the West, even there it has had its followers, the best known of whom was Nicolas Malebranche (1638–1715).

Given the logic of theism, it is perhaps surprising that occasionalism was not more popular. If the divine will is both a necessary and sufficient condition of the production of some effect, then why attribute the effect to any other cause? For a consistent theist, it might be argued, talk of natural causes is redundant (3.4.4). Occasionalism also takes a widely accepted theistic principle—that God preserves all beings in existence—to its logical conclusion. If a chair *exists* only because God wills it to exist (a principle all theists accept), then surely it continues to exist and exists *here* rather than *there* only because God wills it. And if it *moves* from here to there, this, too, must be because God wills it.[18] But then why bother with secondary causes? And from the theist's point of view invoking secondary causes is dangerous. For the existence of secondary causes might appear to make talk of divine action redundant. Once you accept that there exist secondary causes, it might appear that they can do all the explanatory work.[19] Indeed, it is tempting to argue, with Ludwig Feuerbach, that belief in secondary causes represents a failure of nerve: it is a compromise struck between "the unbelieving intellect" and "the still believing heart."[20]

If a theist does adopt an occasionalist view, what happens to his understanding of explanation? It is true that he can still offer natural explanations, in the sense of explanations that make no immediate reference to God. In this respect, the adoption of an occasionalist view leaves much of the scientist's work unchanged.[21] There can still exist a "natural philosophy." As Malebranche himself wrote,

> recourse to God as the universal cause should not be had when the explanation of particular effects is sought. For it would be ridiculous

were we to say, for example, that it is God who dries the roads or who freezes the water of rivers. We should say that the air dries the earth because it stirs and raises with it the water that soaks the earth, and that the air or subtle matter freezes the river because in this season it ceases to communicate enough motion to the parts of which water is composed to make it fluid.[22]

But it remains the case that such natural explanations are not *causal* explanations, at least not in any strong sense of that term.[23] The most they can do is to spell out the regularities which we can discover in the occasions of divine action. They can draw our attention to the fact that event A is regularly followed by event B. And since such regularities are lawlike, this could form the basis of a nomological explanation.[24] If to explain B is to subsume it under some law ("all As are followed by Bs"), then the occasionalist can explain B. But unless he were to define causation as *nothing other than* a regular succession of events, the occasionalist could not say that A causes B.[25] Given the truth of the occasionalist doctrine, all causal explanations would have to be theistic explanations.

From the theist's point of view, there is much to be said for occasionalism. Nonetheless, the following discussion will be based on the alternative theistic view, which holds that created beings do have their own causal powers. This view certainly holds that God is the primary cause of all that occurs. But it argues that for the most part he works through secondary causes, which have a degree of relative autonomy. Such secondary causes are real causes, even though they are dependent ones. I shall be taking this view for granted, not only because it was the view with which I was brought up (as a Roman Catholic), but also because it represents the more common position, at least among Christian theists. Thomas Aquinas, for example, argues at some length for the existence of secondary causes. He claims that it is fitting to the dignity and nature of God that the things he creates should have a power of acting that is proper to them.[26] It remains true that they are subservient causes, executing the divine will in the same way as the ministers of a king execute his will.[27] And they can execute the divine will so only because their existence and activity is sustained by God.[28] But this does not make their actions any less their own.

This second view of divine action undoubtedly has its difficulties, some of which I have already highlighted and to which I shall return (4.3.3.1). But many of these are difficulties for the philosophical theologian, which need not detain us here. The question to be addressed here is: If we adopt (as a hypothesis) this view of God's relationship to the world, what is the relationship between theistic and secular explanations? This question brings us back to the *explananda* of proposed theistic explanations, but from a new point of view. Our question now is: Do the facts that the theist wishes to explain by reference to God *also* have a natural explanation?

4.3.2 Facts Lacking a Natural Explanation

Some of the phenomena that the theist is attempting to explain do not have a natural explanation. But there are two senses in which something may lack a natural explanation. It may lack a natural explanation *in practice*, as a contingent matter of fact. It is not so much naturally inexplicable as currently unexplained. Or it may lack a natural explanation *in principle*. It is a fact of which we cannot even conceive that a natural explanation could be given. This gives us two classes of facts that lack natural explanations.

4.3.2.1 Naturally Unexplained Facts

Let's start with the first of these classes. These are facts of which we can conceive of a natural explanation being given; it is just that we don't (yet) have one. Such facts may be naturally unexplained in one of two senses. We may not have even a *potential* natural explanation of such facts. We just have no idea how the *explanandum* could have occurred. Or we may have a potential explanation, but one that is less than convincing. Not even the atheist thinks we have sufficient reason to regard it as the actual explanation.[29] In either case, the fact in question remains, for the moment, unexplained.

Here's an example. A person may make a sudden recovery from an illness, which leaves her doctors entirely baffled. All they can say is, "Well, sometimes this occurs. But we have no idea why." The theist may wish to attribute this recovery to divine agency. Yet everyone concerned may admit that a natural explanation is possible and that one day it might be found. Perhaps medical researchers will discover the mechanism responsible for such apparently "miraculous" recoveries. Or they may be able to show that, given the mechanisms controlling this illness, such an outcome occurs entirely by chance, in a certain percentage of cases. In those circumstances, the outcome might still be surprising, since it occurs in only a small proportion of cases. But it would not be unexplained.[30] What's important is that *at the moment* we lack a natural explanation of the event in question.

Let's take another example. For a number of years, beginning in 1981, a group of six young people in Bosnia-Herzegovina reported having visions of a supernatural being, namely the Virgin Mary. Careful studies showed that on the occasion when the alleged vision occurred, they knelt, ceased praying aloud, ceased to respond to external stimuli, turned their eyes towards precisely the same place in the room, moved their eyes in a way that corresponded to their reports of the vision, and then returned to their normal state of consciousness. All the alleged visionaries performed each of these actions at almost precisely the same moment, but without any detectable sign of collusion.[31] If the reports are correct, they indicate a puzzling phenomenon, which many Roman Catholics were quick to attribute to supernatural agency. But once again, we can at least conceive of a potential explanation—perhaps that the collusion in question was occurring subliminally, below the level of consciousness. But one might argue that until this proposed explanation is developed and corroborated, it does not deserve our support. It has not won the right to be called the *actual* explanation of the event.

4.3.2.2 Naturally Inexplicable Facts

There is, however, a second class of facts lacking natural explanations. These are facts that are naturally inexplicable *in principle*. Given what it means to offer a natural explanation, we know that we could never have a natural explanation of *this*. All the atheist could ever say is that it is a "brute fact." It just is as it is; end of story. Now the atheist may balk at the idea that there exist such facts. He may argue that those facts the theist regards as naturally inexplicable are merely unexplained. Or he might insist that if naturally inexplicable facts do exist, they are few in number. But it is at least possible that there exist facts of this kind.

What kinds of facts might fall into this category? There are two obvious candidates for the role of naturally inexplicable facts, namely the very existence of both the universe and of laws of nature.[32] Richard Swinburne argues that these facts are "too big" for scientific explanation in the sense that all scientific explanations take them for granted.[33] I have already suggested (4.1.1) that the two facts Swinburne cites may, on closer investigation, collapse into one. But let me leave that issue aside for the moment. Let me concede that there may be facts which are, in principle, naturally inexplicable. My point is that such facts often function as the *explananda* of proposed theistic explanations. How we might test such a proposed explanation is a question to which I shall return (7.1.3).

4.3.3 Facts Having Natural Explanations

So much for facts that lack—either *de facto* or *in principle*—natural explanations. But alongside facts lacking natural explanations, there is another class of *explananda* to which theistic explanations can be applied, namely facts that have natural explanations. In some cases, the natural explanations in question are undisputed. The atheist and the theist agree that these facts can be naturally explained; what the theist is offering is a *complementary* explanation. But in other cases, the theist may dispute the natural explanation. He may (or may not) concede that the alleged natural explanation is a potential explanation of the fact in question. But even if he does, he will still maintain that it is not the actual explanation. In this latter case, the theist is offering a *competing* potential explanation, arguing that it should be accepted as the actual one. This distinction gives us two further classes of *explananda*.

4.3.3.1 Facts With Accepted Natural Explanations

Let's begin with the first of these: the class of facts whose natural explanation the theist does not contest. The existence of *explananda* of this sort assumes that the theist rejects an occasionalist view of divine action. But as we have seen (4.3.1), many theists do reject occasionalism, and it is their views in which I am interested here. Examples of explanations of this kind are not hard to find. When the biblical prophets affirm that God brought about the destruction of Jerusalem in 586 BC to punish Israel, they are not affirming that no natural explanation *could* be offered of this event. Indeed, they implicitly concede that such an explanation is possible. The prophet Jeremiah, for instance, criticises the political alliances of the kings of Judea with Egypt, which brought down upon the Jewish state the wrath of the Babylonians. There is nothing supernatural, nothing miraculous (if you like) about the result that followed. It is a fact that has a natural explanation, one the biblical writers do not dispute. What they offer is a complementary explanation, one that appeals to divine action.

Are theistic explanations redundant? But if this is what the theist is doing, he must face an obvious objection: that of explanatory redundancy. If we already have a natural explanation of the fact in question, which no one is contesting, why offer a theistic one? The problem here is to be distinguished from the well-known issue of causal overdetermination. In the case of causal overdetermination we have two factors, either of which is sufficient to bring about the effect. But neither is necessary, since even if one were not present, the other would ensure that the same outcome occurred.[34] (A man is shot by two assassins and dies. Either shot is sufficient for his death to occur, but neither is necessary.) The case of a theistic explanation of a naturally explained fact is different, since the natural cause is thought to be dependent on the divine cause. *Ex hypothesi*, if God had not willed the destruction of Jerusalem, the Babylonians would not have destroyed it. God's willing of the event *is* a necessary condition of its occurrence, for it is a necessary condition of the occurrence of the event that was the secondary cause. But of course God's willing of the event is also a sufficient condition of is occurrence, for as we have seen (3.4.2), the divine will is unfailingly efficacious.

At this point, we seem to have a new kind of explanatory redundancy, except that it is now the natural explanation that appears to be redundant (3.4.4). (Once again, we can see why some theists adopt the occasionalist view.) On the theistic hypothesis, what role do natural causes play in a case such as this? Apparently, natural causes are thought to be the *means* by which God achieves his goals. (In the case of the biblical example, the natural cause of the disaster was the means by which he punished Israel.) But why should God choose any means, if he could bring about this result directly, as a basic action? If God wanted to punish sinners on Boxing Day 2004, why use a tsunami? Not only is this—from God's point of view—an unnecessary means; it is also an indiscriminate one, and so hardly the best means (5.3). Why could God not simply will that sinners experience suffering, and that non-sinners do not? Presumably we would soon make the connection, and learn our lesson. This is, of course, an excellent question. If a proposed theistic explanation is to be even a potential explanation, it must offer an answer. It must tell us why God would choose *any* created cause, let alone this one, as the means of achieving his goals.

Let me set these issues aside for the moment. If theistic explanations are intentional explanations, the charge of explanatory redundancy is perhaps not as serious as it might appear. For in the case of intentional explanations, there does seem to be a sense in which one can offer two explanations of the same fact. An intentional explanation tells us of what the agent was trying to achieve in performing this action. A natural-scientific explanation describes the mechanism that brought about the action. Neither explanation would be complete,[35] in the sense that each approach "leaves some explanation-seeking questions unanswered."[36] But as I have argued above (1.3.3), an incomplete explanation is still an explanation.[37] This is, in fact, the solution adopted by Richard Swinburne. As Swinburne writes, "the motion of my hand may be . . . explained by goings-on in the nerves and muscles of my arm, and physiological laws. It may also be . . . explained by me bringing it about, having the intention and power to do so."[38] Assuming that the motion in question was an intentional act, this seems correct. Each explanation is telling us something different about the event.

Explaining under a description. But to show that intentional and non-intentional explanations *can* be complementary is not yet to escape the charge of explanatory redundancy. The events I am discussing here are those that have an accepted natural explanation. The question the atheist can pose to the theist is this: If you accept the natural (perhaps non-intentional) explanation, why do you want to offer an intentional explanation as well? What we need to remember here is that any fact is explained only under a particular description (3.2.2). What the physiological explanation explains is *why my hand moved*; it does not purport to explain *why I moved my hand*.[39] So to say that a fact already has a successful natural explanation is to say that there exists some description of that fact under which it can be explained in non-intentional terms. So if the theist wishes to argue that the same event requires a complementary, intentional explanation, she must show that there exists another true description of the event that requires this new kind of explanation.

If this is correct, it does have a surprising implication. When setting out to prove the existence of God, theists generally begin with facts whose natural explanation they reject. They may be naturally inexplicable (4.3.2.2) or merely naturally unexplained facts (4.3.2.1), or they may be facts whose natural explanation the theist contests (4.3.3.2). But on my account, they are under no obligation to do so. A theist could, in principle, begin with a fact that has a natural explanation, one he does not contest. He could admit that there exists a true description of this fact—analogous to "why my hand moved"—under which it can be explained without (immediate) reference to God. But he could seek to show that there exists another true description of this fact—analogous to "why I moved my hand"—that demands an intentional, theistic explanation.

70 *Theism and Explanation*

In principle, a theist could argue in this way. But it is difficult to see how he could convince a non-believer. For any intentional description of the fact will seem question-begging to the atheist. The difficulty here is related to the one I mentioned earlier (3.2.2)—the fact that a theistic explanation posits the very existence of the agent to whom some intentions are being attributed. In everyday life, we already have good reason to believe that the agent in question exists and that at least some of his behaviour is intentional. We are all agreed that at least some of his behaviour has a true intentional description, even if we do not know just what that description is. But in the case of a proposed theistic explanation, what is in dispute is the very existence of the alleged agent. In other words, the atheist will see no reason to agree that any of these facts *has* a true intentional description. So it is understandable that in practice theists should begin with facts which (in their view) can be explained in no other way.

4.3.3.2 Facts With Contested Natural Explanations

Our final class of *explananda* consists of facts which have what the atheist regards as a successful natural explanation, although it is one that the theist contests. The clearest contemporary example of such an attitude is to be found among creationists, who reject Darwin's account of the development of biological species. On what basis do theists reject proposed natural explanations? Well, a theistic argument against a proposed natural explanation could take one of two forms, which mirror the atheist's arguments against proposed theistic explanations of which I wrote earlier (1.3). They could be *de facto* or *in principle* arguments.

In the first case, that of a *de facto* argument, the theist would argue that, yes, there does exist a potential natural explanation of the facts in question, one that makes no reference to God. But the theistic explanation is simply a better one. It is more consistent with the rest of our knowledge, has greater empirical content, and is simpler, more economical, and more informative. It is worth noting that while theists could argue in this way, in practice they rarely do, for reasons that will become clear in Chapter 7. (Proposed theistic explanations, I shall argue, necessarily lack many of these qualities.) The more common argument against natural explanations is an *in principle* one: it denies that the natural explanation in question is even a potential explanation. This is the case among creationists, who generally argue that Darwin's theory simply cannot explain the diversity of biological species. Here, of course, the atheist may simply reply that they are wrong.

One exception to this rule is Richard Swinburne, in his discussion of the so-called "fine-tuning" argument.[40] The fine-tuning argument takes as its starting point the idea that only a narrow range of initial conditions would make possible the emergence of beings such as ourselves. And it is highly unlikely that they should have the particular values they have by chance. It follows that the universe in which we live appears "fine-tuned"

What Would They Explain? 71

to produce beings like us. How can we explain this fact? One could argue that it is merely an observational selection effect—that given our existence, the universe had to be as it was. (If the laws of nature and initial conditions had been other than they were, we would not be here to ask the question.) As it happens, Swinburne rejects this deflationary response. The reasons he offers may be less than convincing,[41] but let me leave that aside for the moment. All I am trying to do here is to analyse the structure of his argument. What Swinburne argues is that this apparent fine-tuning would be just what we would expect, given that there existed a God who intended there to be creatures such as ourselves.

But Swinburne does not consider the theistic story to be the only potential explanation of the apparent "fine-tuning." There exists a non-theistic alternative, namely the "multiverse" hypothesis. According to this view, there may exist, either simultaneously or consecutively, a number of universes. If there were a sufficient number of such universes,[42] it would not be surprising if, by chance, one of them were conducive to the emergence of carbon-based life-forms. Swinburne responds to this alternative explanation in various ways. But one of his responses is that, unless there is independent evidence of the existence of multiple universes, the multiverse hypothesis would be both *ad hoc* and an offence against the virtue of simplicity.[43] There is something to be said for this argument, although I shall argue later for a different conception of simplicity than that favoured by Swinburne (7.4). I shall also introduce another explanatory virtue, that of ontological economy (7.5), which might seem to favour the multiverse scenario.[44] But once again let me leave that aside and focus on the pattern of Swinburne's argument. Swinburne admits that there is a rival, natural hypothesis, while arguing that the theistic hypothesis is to be preferred. And that is one of the options open to a theist when contesting a natural explanation.

4.4 THE PROBLEM OF MIRACLES

Let me end this chapter by addressing another *in principle* objection to theistic explanations, which relates to miracles. In offering theistic explanations, theists posit the existence of an agent who is capable of working miracles. Indeed they sometimes claim that he has brought about the fact-to-be-explained by means of a miracle. Does this appeal to a miracle-working agent undermine the force of proposed religious explanations? Does it constitute an argument against their explanatory force?

4.4.1 Positing Miracles

When the theist offers an explanation of an event which lacks a natural explanation—a fact which is naturally unexplained (4.3.2.1), naturally inexplicable (4.3.2.2), or whose natural explanation he contests (4.3.3.2)—is he thereby positing a miracle? Well, the answer will depend on what the *explanandum* is and what definition of a miracle you adopt. Hume's classic definition, that a miracle is "*a violation of a law of nature,*"[45] assumes that there exists a regular succession of events which the miracle interrupts. This would certainly apply to many proposed theistic explanations. Christian theists, for instance, attempt to explain Jesus' empty tomb by saying that God raised him from the dead. If this were true, it would certainly represent a miracle in a Humean sense. But what of the "big bang," on the assumption that this was the beginning of the universe?[46] Would a theistic explanation of this event involve a miracle? It would not, if we understand a miracle as a violation of a law of nature.[47] We could, of course, adopt another definition of a miracle, perhaps William Lane Craig's "event which lies outside the productive capacity of nature."[48] Is this applicable to a theistic explanation of the big bang? One could argue that it is, at least on the assumption that it is beyond the productive capacity of anything, nature included, to give rise to itself.[49] In any case, even if not all proposed theistic explanations involve miracles, at least some of them do. And all proposed theistic explanations posit an agent who is capable of working miracles. Even if God does not in fact interrupt the regular workings of the natural world, he could at any moment choose to do so. What implications, if any, does this have for the explanatory force of the theistic hypothesis?

4.4.2 The Objection to Miracles

Some authors have argued that an "explanation" that posits an agent capable of miracles is no explanation at all. We find a clear expression of this view in the work of the historian of religions, Morton Smith, in a passage worth citing at length.

> A basic supposition of sound historical method . . . is, in classical terms, "atheism." I say "in classical terms" because the adjective "atheist" was regularly used in classical times to describe, for instance, the Epicureans, who insisted that there were gods, but denied that they ever descended to any special intervention in the world's affairs. It is precisely this denial which is fundamental to any sound historical method. [The historian requires] a world in which . . . normal phenomena are not interfered with by arbitrary and *ad hoc* divine interventions to produce abnormal historical events with special historical consequences. . . . The historian's task . . . is to calculate the most probable explanation of the preserved evidence. Now the minds of the gods are inscrutable and their actions, consequently, incalculable. Therefore, unless the possibility of their special intervention can be ruled out, there can be no calculation of most probable causes—there would always be an unknown probability that a deity might have intervened.[50]

What Would They Explain? 73

There is an element of truth in this claim. If the actions of the gods—or in this case, the actions of God—were entirely "incalculable," being "arbitrary," then invoking the gods would fail to explain. We could not say what would follow if a theistic hypothesis were true; such a hypothesis would not count as even a potential explanation (5.1). But is it the case that the actions of an agent capable of miracles are incalculable?

Before answering this question, let me look at another expression of the same objection. In his discussion of modern creationism, Robert Pennock argues that

> empirical testing relies fundamentally upon the lawful regularities of nature which science has been able to discover and sometimes codify in natural laws. For example, telescopic observations implicitly depend on the laws governing optical phenomena. If we could not rely upon these laws—if, for example, even when under the same conditions, telescopes occasionally magnified properly, and at other occasions produced various distortions dependent, say, upon the whims of some supernatural entity—we could not trust telescopic observations as evidence. . . . Lawful regularity is at the heart of the naturalistic world view and to say that some power is supernatural is, by definition, to say that it can violate natural laws. . . . But without the constraint of lawful regularity, inductive evidential inference cannot get off the ground.[51]

Again, there is surely some truth in these remarks. If the theist is to have any trust in our knowledge of the world, he is bound to assume that his God will not work *too many* miracles. And of course there is something odd about the idea of a God who establishes the laws of nature only to violate them, a fact that has led some theologians to reject belief in miracles on religious grounds.[52] But Pennock's objection is a stronger one. It suggests that positing an agent who can work miracles is fatal to the task of explanation.

4.4.3 A Rational Agent

In order to assess the force of this objection, let me return to my initial comments regarding abductive reasoning and explanation (2.1.2). I argued in Chapter 2 that a potential explanation of some *explanandum* (E) is one that satisfies the second premise of Peirce's abductive schema. It will show that, given the truth of H, E is what we would expect. In the case of an intentional explanation, it will do this by positing certain beliefs and desires and then offering a practical syllogism that has the *explanandum* as its conclusion. The practical syllogism, I shall argue later (Appendix 2.1), will include the following elements.

74 *Theism and Explanation*

(1) There exists a rational agent A with intended goal G.
(2) A has beliefs $B_1, B_2, \ldots B_n$ relating to the attainment of G.
(3) If $B_1, B_2, \ldots B_n$ were true, E would be the best way of achieving G.
(4) Rational agents always choose the best way of achieving their goals.
(5) Therefore A will do E.

The key premises to note are (3) and (4). The objection levelled by Smith and Pennock assumes that our explanation is nomological, that it cites laws connecting the agent's observed behaviour with some a particular set of beliefs and desires. But whether or not such laws exist (Appendix 3.3.1), an explanation of this form does not rely on them. What it relies on is a rationality principle (5.2 and Appendix 1.3). It predicts an agent's behaviour by assuming that she will act in a way that is consistent with her beliefs and desires in order to achieve her goal (5.2–5.3).

In other words, the objection put forward by both Smith and Pennock assumes a false dichotomy. It assumes that the world is either governed by natural laws or it is the product of a mere "whim" on the part of a supernatural agent. But these are not the only options. The world could, conceivably, be the work of a supernatural agent acting rationally in order to achieve his goals. If we posit a particular goal, we might be able to predict his behaviour. The fact that this agent is capable of working miracles is neither here nor there. The key question is: What would be the most rational way for such an agent to act in order to achieve this goal? The answer may or may not include miracles.[53]

4.4.4 Hume's Argument

What if we did decide that the most rational way for God to act, in these circumstances, was by way of a miracle? Then a miracle is what we would expect to observe, given the theistic hypothesis. But the atheist might simply refuse to recognise any alleged miracle as a miracle. He might, in support of this refusal, appeal to David Hume's argument, that it is always more probable that a miracle report should be false than that a miracle has occurred. If Hume is right, then we would never be in a position to verify this particular theistic prediction. We would never be justified in regarding any observed fact *as* a miracle.[54] If this is correct, then at least one group of proposed theistic explanations—those which posit miracles—seems doomed to failure.

But was Hume right? Hume's apparently simple argument, which he hoped would settle the question once and for all,[55] is still being debated. I cannot hope to end the debate here. Let me just point out a weakness in Hume's argument, which highlights the need for a fuller discussion. The argument rests on the idea that we can estimate the prior probability of a miracle occurring, and that this prior probability is exceedingly low. But how might we estimate its prior probability? Hume's discussion suggests that we ask how often the alleged miracle has occurred in the past. But in the case of most alleged miracles, the answer will be "never." An event of this kind will not have occurred before. If we make this the basis of our reasoning, the result will be a prior probability of zero. The alleged miracle in question is simply impossible.

At times, Hume writes as if this were true, as if miracles were indeed impossible. In one passage, for instance, he writes that

> there must . . . be a uniform experience against every miraculous event, otherwise the event would not merit that appellation. And as uniform experience amounts to a proof, there is here a direct and full *proof*, from the nature of the fact, against the existence of any miracle.[56]

The problem is that he immediately speaks of that proof being "destroyed" and the miracle "rendered credible" by an opposite, more powerful proof. And he argues that the testimony to a miracle can never provide such proof. But this last argument seems redundant. If the prior probability of the miracle is zero, no amount of testimony could outweigh it.

Hume's mistake lies in the way he assesses prior probability. To do so by counting the number of previous instances seems wrong-headed. It certainly flies in the face of scientific practice. As John Earman writes,

> scientists not uncommonly spend many hours and many dollars searching for events of a type that past experience tells us have never occurred (e.g. proton decay). Such practice is hard to understand if the probability of such an event is flatly zero, and the probability of the putative law asserting the non-occurrence of this type of event is unity.[557]

Yet Earman's criticism also indicates a way forward. On what basis do scientists search for previously unobserved events? Presumably because they have a promising theory which predicts that this event will sometime occur, in these circumstances. (As I write, scientists have just switched on the Large Hadron Collider near Geneva, in the hope of [*inter alia*] discovering the Higgs boson, a hitherto undiscovered particle whose existence is predicted by the standard model of particle physics.) The likelihood of the event occurring is dependent on the strength of the theory that predicts it. Applied to reports of miracles, and adopting the probabilistic framework of Hume's argument, this suggests that the prior probability of a miracle is dependent on the prior probability of the theistic hypothesis. To put this another way, it would be reasonable to accept a hypothesis that involved a miracle only if we already had reason to believe that there existed a being capable of working miracles. What reasons might we have for believing this? I shall be addressing that question in the chapters that follow.

5 Potential Theistic Explanations

> What a book a devil's chaplain might write on the clumsy, wasteful, blundering, low, and horribly cruel works of nature.
>
> Charles Darwin

In my opening chapter (1.3), I distinguished between potential and actual (or successful) explanations. I suggested that I needed this distinction—or something like it—in order to distinguish between *de facto* and *in principle* objections to proposed theistic explanations. A *de facto* objection accepts that some accounts of divine action are potential explanations. If they were true, then the explanandum is what we would expect. But it argues that such proposed explanations have been superseded by secular alternatives, which we have more reason to accept. An *in principle* objection goes further. It argues that no account of divine action could have any explanatory force. Even if such an account were true, there is no conceivable state of affairs which it could be said to explain.

In this chapter, I shall argue that this *in principle* objection is wrong. One can at least conceive of situations in which talk of divine action would be explanatory. In this sense, the atheist has no "silver bullet," which will "put a merciful end to all the nonsense."[1] He cannot assume, without further investigation, that a proposed theistic explanation is worthless. But he can ask if *this particular* story of divine action constitutes a potential explanation of *this particular* state of affairs. And the key question here is that posed by David Hume: Is this state of affairs what we would expect of "a very powerful, wise, and benevolent Deity?"[2] If it is not, then no talk of divine action could explain it.

But I'm leaping ahead. Let me pause for a moment to summarise the conclusions I have reached. What is required of an account of divine action if it is to be considered a potential explanation of some state of affairs? In Chapter 3, I described the first condition that such a proposed explanation must meet. It must do more than posit the mere *existence* of a creator God (3.2.3). Such a posit fails to single out the fact to be explained, since on the theistic hypothesis whatever occurred would happen because God willed it. If a proposed theistic explanation is to have any significant degree of empirical content, it must view the *explanandum* as a means towards a divinely-willed end. It must posit the existence of a particular divine intention. A second condition has to do with the coherence of theism (3.3). We need to have some confidence that the theistic hypothesis does not embody hidden

78 *Theism and Explanation*

contradictions. For if it does, then given the *ex contradictione quodlibet* principle of classical logic it could apparently explain any fact you should care to name. (I did, however, concede that apparent incoherence is not a fatal objection: we might have reason to keep working on an apparently incoherent hypothesis, in the hope of arriving at a coherent one.) A third condition has to do with the very idea of a theistic explanation, viewed as a causal explanation (3.4). The theist needs to be able to show that there is some sense of the word "cause" that is applicable to God.

The present chapter will build on these conclusions, offering a further condition that a proposed theistic explanation would have to meet. This condition is a necessary one. If a proposed theistic explanation cannot meet the standard I am about to propose, it is not even a potential explanation. It has no explanatory force at all. And if no proposed theistic explanation could satisfy this condition, there would exist a decisive *in principle* objection to proposed explanations of this kind.

5.1 THEOLOGICAL SCEPTICISM

A theistic explanation, I have argued, is an intentional explanation (3.2). An intentional explanation works, if it works at all, by positing that the agent in question has a particular set of beliefs and desires giving rise to a particular intention (Appendix 1.2). To explain a particular event as the work of this agent, it needs to be *what we would expect her to do*, given that intention. So far, so good. But what about a divine agent? Do we know how we would expect him to act, given a particular intention? Are we in a position to make such judgements?

It is tempting here to take the side of the sceptic. Even a very moderate sceptic might argue that talk of divine action takes us

> quite beyond the reach of our faculties. . . . We are got into fairy land, long ere we have reached the last steps of our theory; and *there* we have no reason to trust our common methods of argument, or to think that our usual analogies and probabilities have any authority. Our line is too short to fathom such immense abysses.[3]

There are two ways in which this sceptical objection might be developed. The first is by looking at the nature of God. The sceptic might argue that here is an agent so different from any other agent with which we are familiar that we cannot make any predictions about his behaviour. We have no basis on which to do so. I shall examine this objection in a moment, under the heading of "theological scepticism." A second form of scepticism focuses on our ability to make modal judgements. It suggests that we cannot judge how God would act, not so much because of our ignorance of the nature of God (theological scepticism), but because of our ignorance of the options available to him. We simply do not know what courses of action are open to a divine agent. Since I have yet to discuss the role of modal judgements in proposed theistic explanations, I shall examine this form of the sceptical objection later, under the heading of "modal scepticism" (5.4.3). But the outcome of each of these two forms of scepticism—theological and modal—is the same. If we cannot make such judgements, then the *in principle* objection is correct: an account of divine action cannot be even a potential explanation, of any state of affairs. End of story.

5.1.1 Design Arguments

A contemporary expression of *theological* scepticism can be found in the work of Elliot Sober. Sober employs his theological scepticism in order to argue against intelligent design theory. But his sceptical objections are applicable to any kind of proposed theistic explanation. So his arguments against intelligent design will make a useful starting point for my discussion.

Like Robin Collins and Richard Swinburne (2.1.3.1), Sober makes use of confirmation theory in order to analyse the theist's arguments. He argues that the design argument is most plausibly understood to rely on the "likelihood principle." This principle reads:

> Observation O supports hypothesis H_1 more than it supports hypothesis H_2 if and only if $Pr(O|H_1) > Pr(O|H_2)$.[4]

In most forms of design argument, hypothesis one (H_1) is assumed to be design and hypothesis two (H_2) is thought to be chance. One might, of course, argue that chance is not the only alternative to design. Since 1859 we have had an alternative, at least in the case of biological systems, namely natural selection. But the advocates of intelligent design (against whom Sober is writing) argue that the Darwinian hypothesis cannot do the job, that it is not even a potential explanation of the complexity and diversity of living organisms. This, they believe, justifies their view that the only alternative is chance.[5] So if O represents the observed fact, C represents the chance hypothesis, and D represents design, their argument rests on the following claim:

$Pr(O|D) > Pr(O|C)$.

In other words, they argue that the observed facts are more likely given the hypothesis of design than given what they regard as the only alternative, namely chance.

5.1.2 No Victory by Default

Sober's response to this claim makes two points. First of all, he argues that the design hypothesis (if it is a hypothesis) does not win by default. To claim victory for a design hypothesis, it is not enough to show that $Pr(O|C)$ is very low—that the facts we observe are extremely unlikely to have occurred by chance. We also need to show that the likelihood that we should observe the same facts is higher, given design. And to do this, we need to be able to predict what would follow if the hypothesis were true.

I shall look at Sober's claim that proposed explanations cannot win by default later (7.1.3). I think it is true (6.2.2), although I am not convinced by the particular arguments he offers. But his underlying point seems uncontroversial. If we are to take a proposed explanation seriously, we must be able to predict what would follow if it were true. Sober's argument is that in the case of a proposed theistic explanation this condition cannot be fulfilled. He formulates his objection in terms of testability: if one cannot say what would (and would not) follow if a hypothesis were true, then that hypothesis is untestable. But there is a prior and more important question. If Sober is correct, the problem is not merely that the proposed theistic explanation is not testable; we cannot know that it is even a *potential* explanation of the fact in question. A potential explanation, I have argued (2.1.2), is one that satisfies the second premise of Peirce's abductive schema.

(1) The surprising fact, E, is observed.
(2) But if H were true, E would be a matter of course.
(3) Hence, there is reason to suspect that H is true.

If we cannot know what would follow, given the truth of a theistic hypothesis, then we cannot say whether it meets this condition. We do not know if the *explanandum* is what we would expect, given the truth of the *explanans*. If this were true, it would constitute a strong *in principle* objection to all proposed explanations of this kind.

So on what grounds does Sober argue in support of what I am calling "theological scepticism"? He argues that theists simply *cannot* specify how their posited designer would be expected to act, in order to achieve his goals. Why? Because to do so, writes Sober, would require

> further assumptions about what the designer's goals and abilities would be, if he existed. Perhaps the designer would never build the vertebrate eye [for example] with features $F_1 \ldots F_n$ either because he would lack the goals or would lack the ability. If so, the likelihood of the design hypothesis is zero. On the other hand, perhaps the designer would want to build the eye with features $F_1 \ldots F_n$ and would be entirely competent to bring this plan to fruition. If so, the likelihood of the design hypothesis is unity. There are as many likelihoods as there are suppositions concerning the goals and abilities of the putative designer. Which of these, or which class of these, should we take seriously?[6]

It is true, Sober concedes, that we can identify the products of human design. But we can do so only because we know something of the goals and

Potential Theistic Explanations 81

abilities of human designers.[7] Perhaps we could identify the designed products even of extraterrestrial intelligent beings, on the assumption that they are the products of an evolutionary process similar to that which produced us. The problem is that the less similarity there is between a purported designer and ourselves, the less confident we can be in specifying how he might be expected to act. When it comes to God, who of all designers surely resembles us the least, we are entirely in the dark. This inability to specify how a putative designer might be expected to act is, Sober argues, "the Achilles' heel of the design argument."[8] Is there a way of avoiding this sceptical conclusion? Well, Sober notes, the theist may be tempted to argue that we *do* know what God intended. We can discover his intention by inspecting the products of his design, namely what we see around us.[9] But of course this merely begs the question, which is whether what we see around us *is* the product of divine design. Or theists might argue that

> if the *existence* of the vertebrate eye is what one wishes to explain, their hypothesis is that the intelligent designer constructed the vertebrate eye. If it is the *characteristics* of the vertebrate eye (the fact that it has features $F_1, F_2, \ldots F_n$), rather than its mere existence, that one wants to explain their hypothesis is that an intelligent designer constructed the vertebrate eye with the intention that it have features $F_1, F_2, \ldots F_n$ and that this designer had the ability to bring his plans to fruition.[10]

But this reasoning is empty, since it would enable the proposition *God created it* to "explain" anything at all. More precisely, such reasoning merely builds into the theistic hypothesis "the observations we seek to explain."[11] For this reason, I would add, it would be another case of what Philip Kitcher calls "spurious unification" (3.2.3.1).[12]

Sober's view seems to be that this is a kind of *in principle* objection. However, I have already described it as a *de facto* one (2.2.1). The following argument does constitute a potential explanation of E.

(1) God wills E.
(2) Whatever God wills comes to pass.
(3) Therefore E.

For it does correspond to the second premise of Peirce's schema (2.1.2). The problem is that it does so in an almost trivial fashion, which is little more than a restatement of E. And it is a potential explanation we have good reason not to accept, since it would be untestable (7.1). Sober does concede that the theist could keep postulating divine goal-ability pairs until she finds one which *does* explain the world as we see it. But, he argues, one cannot simply invent such auxiliary hypotheses at will. They need to be independently testable and, ideally, to have passed independent tests.[13]

5.1.3 Is Sober Correct?

What are we to make of Elliot Sober's criticisms? Unlike Sober, I am not using confirmation theory to analyse theistic explanations, for reasons I have already given (2.1.3.2). Nonetheless, there is much here with which I would agree. If we are to judge a theistic explanation to be a potential explanation, we must be able to specify what would follow if it were true. And we must be able to specify this in a way that is *independent* of the fact that we know the *explanandum* to be true. Given a deductivist account of intentional explanations (2.1.4), we must be able to produce an argument that has the *explanans* among its premises and a description of the *explanandum* as its conclusion. I shall refer to this as the *criterion of independent specification*.[14] Its significance was already recognised by David Hume. As I noted earlier, Hume posed the question that I shall argue is central to the success of any theistic explanation. "Is the world considered in general, and as it appears to us in this life, different from what a man or such a limited being would, *beforehand*, expect from a very powerful, wise, and benevolent Deity?"[15] If some fact about the world is not what we would expect of such a being, then appeal to the actions of God cannot be said to explain it.

5.2 The Rationality Principle

But is Sober's scepticism warranted? Do we need to be theological sceptics? Let's approach this question afresh. Sober's objection to the design argument is that it places no constraint on how a putative divine designer might be expected to act. The supposed omnipotence of God—the idea that he could do anything that is logically possible—merely makes this problem worse. As he writes, "an engineer who is more limited would be more predictable."[16] But is this correct? Do proposed theistic explanations place no constraints on how God might be expected to work?

5.2.1 An Explanatory Constraint

I have argued that a proposed theistic explanation is one that views the *explanandum* as the means of achieving a divinely willed goal. More precisely, it attributes to God the desire to achieve a particular end, and invites us to see the *explanandum* as a means towards this end. It is true that some proposed theistic explanations may not do this. They may deserve condemnation, since—as Sober suggests—they merely build into the hypothesis "the observations we seek to explain."[17] But all this means is that *some* proposed theistic explanations are flawed. It does not mean that *all* proposed theistic explanations are flawed or that *no* account of divine action could have any explanatory force. If the theist proposes a divinely-willed goal and suggests that the *explanandum* is the means by which God achieves this goal, then her proposed explanation does face a constraint. It may not be constrained by laws. And, as Sober suggests, appeal to analogies will not take us very far, since the divine agent is so unlike any other agent with which we are familiar. But a proposed theistic explanation is constrained by the presumption of rationality upon which all intentional explanations rely (3.2.1; Appendix 1.3). It assumes that God will act in a way that is consistent with his beliefs and desires and that he will act in a way that would bring about his goal. Just what this means, in the case of a divine agent, is a question to which I shall return in a moment (5.3).

5.2.2 The Panda's Thumb

Sober's neglect of this rationality principle is evident in his criticism of Stephen Jay Gould's essay on "the panda's thumb." In that essay, Gould describes his childhood encounter with a panda at Washington Zoo. He was struck by the panda's ability to strip the leaves off shoots of bamboo, apparently with the aid of a flexible thumb. "This puzzled me," he writes, "I had learned that a dexterous, opposable thumb stood among the hallmarks of human success. We had maintained, even exaggerated, this important flexibility of our primate forebears, while most mammals had sacrificed it in specializing their digits."[18] Then, to his further amazement, he observed that the panda has five *remaining* digits. Had the panda evolved a sixth finger? In due course, he discovered that it had not. The panda's "thumb" is, in fact, a cobbled together contraption, fashioned by variation and natural selection from bones and muscles that already existed in the wrist. It is, as Gould writes, "a somewhat clumsy, but quite workable" response to a need.

Gould's point is that arrangements such as this—there are plenty of them in the natural world—are strong evidence in support of Darwin's theory of evolution. As Gould writes,

> our textbooks like to illustrate evolution with examples of optimal design—nearly perfect mimicry of a dead leaf by a butterfly or of a poisonous species by a palatable relative. But ideal design is a lousy argument for evolution, for it mimics the postulated action of an omnipotent creator. Odd arrangements and funny solutions are the proof of evolution—paths that a sensible God would never tread but that a natural process, constrained by history, follows perforce. No one understood this better than Darwin himself.[19]

I shall refer to this shortly as a "suboptimality argument" against proposed theistic explanations. What is of interest here is that Elliot Sober disagrees with this argument.

> Gould thinks he knows what God would do if He built pandas, just as Paley thought he knew what God would do if He built the vertebrate

eye. But neither of them knows this. Both help themselves to *assumptions* about God's goals and abilities. However, it is not enough to make assumptions about these matters; one needs independent evidence that these auxiliary assumptions are true.[20]

Let me begin with what is correct about this response. It is surely right to ask for independent evidence of the truth of the assumptions that are being employed. I have insisted on this from the beginning. But as I argued in Chapter 3 we are perfectly at liberty to make such assumptions and then see what follows from them. This is precisely what it means to offer a theoretical explanation, supported by abductive reasoning. So we are entitled to posit the existence of a God having the requisite "goals and abilities" (to use Sober's terms) and then ask what we would expect to observe as a result. If the *explanandum* is among the things we would expect to observe, given this hypothesis, then we would have satisfied the second premise of Peirce's abductive schema (2.1.2). Of course, the conclusion of Peirce's schema is a modest one. At best, such reasoning only gives us *reason to suspect* that the hypothesis is true; some kind of corroboration is required (7.1). And it is here that Sober's requirement (and my *desideratum*) of testability comes into play (7.1).

But Sober thinks we cannot go even this far, that we cannot say what would follow if the theistic hypothesis were true. And at this point I must side with Gould against Sober. For Gould's argument employs the rationality principle that I have suggested lies at the heart of all intentional explanations. It assumes that a divine agent will act rationally, in order to achieve his goals. Gould rightly senses that this places some constraints, not perhaps on the divine agent himself (5.4.1), but on what we may plausibly attribute to him. So far as I am aware, no theist has specified the divine purpose that was allegedly served by the creation of the panda's "thumb." But let's posit one. Let's assume, for instance, that God's plan of creation required an animal that could strip bamboo. Gould's point is that the panda's "thumb" is not the kind of mechanism we would expect God to create, in order to achieve his purpose. Gould's argument may be incomplete, as I shall argue in a moment, or it may be faulty in some other way. But he is surely asking the right kind of question. His argument rests on the assumption that the posited divine agent will act rationally. And this rationality principle places constraints on how God might be expected to act.

5.3 THE OPTIMALITY CONDITION

But of course God is no ordinary agent. So we can also ask what the rationality principle entails, when applied to God. A key consideration here is precisely the one to which Sober draws attention—the fact that the agent posited by a theistic explanation is unique. He has characteristics possessed by no other agent. First of all, he is assumed to be omniscient. This means that his beliefs simply mirror the way the world is: for any proposition p, "if p, God knows that p."[21] Secondly, he is assumed to be omnipotent. This means that there are no constraints on how he might realise his intentions, other than those of logical possibility. If a consistent description can be given of an action, then God can perform it. Thirdly, he is thought to be morally perfect. At the very least, I shall argue, this means that God will seek to minimise suffering. So the key question is: What would be the most rational way in which an omnipotent, omniscient, and morally perfect agent could bring about his intended goal?

5.3.1 The Divine Agent

Given the nature of the posited divine agent, there are a number of factors that shape human action which we can exclude from the outset. Firstly, it cannot be the case that God acts on the basis of *false* beliefs or on the basis of *unconscious* or only *partly recognised* desires. As an omniscient agent, God has no false beliefs or unrecognised desires. Secondly, it cannot be the case that God is *constrained* in his choice of means towards an end. As an omnipotent agent, God acts under no constraints, other than that of the logically possible, which is really no constraint at all. Thirdly, God cannot suffer from *weakness of will* (*akrasia*). It is inconceivable that he should will an action, but because of his own weakness fail to bring it about. As we have seen (3.4.2), the divine will is unfailingly efficacious. Fourthly, God cannot be under any compulsion to adopt any *means* towards an end. He could bring about whatever he wills merely by willing it: if he chose, all of his actions could be basic actions (3.4.2). God could create a world as directly as I move my arm.[22] But if God is morally perfect, has no false beliefs, and suffers no constraints on his action, what follows? On the assumption that he is rational agent we can assume whatever he wills, he would choose the best possible means of achieving it. I shall refer to this as the *optimality condition* and shall argue that it is the most important constraint on a proposed theistic explanation.

5.3.2 Suboptimality Arguments

What the optimality condition offers is something very important: a test of whether a proposed theistic explanation is even a *potential* explanation of the fact to be explained. The key question is: Given the posited divine goal, is the *explanandum* the best way in which this goal could be realised? If not, then we cannot plausibly attribute it to God. It is true that I still need to show that we can answer the question. Perhaps there is no "best means" of achieving some goal, or perhaps we cannot know what it is. I shall come to these objections in a moment (5.4). But before I do so, let me spell out my argument a little more clearly.

If we accept that proposed theistic explanations must meet an optimality condition, it offers us a way of assessing their explanatory force. Strictly speaking, it is not the *explanans* but the *explanandum* that must meet this condition. Given a posited divine intention, the *explanandum* must be the best way in which this intention could have been achieved. If it is not, then positing this intention simply fails to explain, for the *explanandum* is not what a theistic hypothesis would predict. In these circumstances, the proposed theistic explanation is not even a potential explanation of the fact in question, since it fails to satisfy the second premise of Peirce's abductive schema (2.1.2).

(1) The surprising fact, E, is observed.
(2) But if H were true, E would be a matter of course.
(3) Hence, there is reason to suspect that H is true.

So how might an atheist discredit a proposed theistic explanation? He could do so by arguing that there exists a better way in which God could have achieved his goal. It would follow that the *explanandum* is a less than optimal means to the posited end, and cannot plausibly be attributed to God.

Such suboptimality arguments against proposed theistic explanations are not new. Even in the eighteenth century, David Hume countered the theistic hypothesis by referring to "the inaccurate workmanship of all the springs and principles of the great machinery of nature."[23] And Charles Darwin supported his theory of evolution by natural selection by reference to the phenomenon of "rudimentary, atrophied, or aborted organs."

> I have now given the leading facts with respect to rudimentary organs. In reflecting on them, every one must be struck with astonishment: for the same reasoning power which tells us plainly that most parts and organs are exquisitely adapted for certain purposes, tells us with equal plainness that these rudimentary or atrophied organs are imperfect and useless.[24]

Given the theory of creation, Darwin argues, the existence of such organs represents a "strange difficulty," but on his theory it can be accounted for; indeed it "might even have been anticipated."[25] Following Darwin, such arguments have been common among defenders of evolution, who have argued that "the imperfection of living organisms . . . [does] away with the idea that they were created by an omnipotent and omnibenevolent creator."[26] Stephen Jay Gould's "panda's thumb" argument, which I examined a moment ago (5.2.2), is a product of this same tradition. A more recent example of a suboptimality argument is to be found in a review by A. C. Grayling of a new book on the intelligent design controversy:

> Your average engineer, tasked with building a human being, would not separate the entrances to the trachea and oesophagus with a movable

flap tagged with an instruction not to breathe while you eat, or the organs of generation not just next to but partially carrying the organs of excretion, or redundant bits of anatomy than can become infected and kill their owners, or permanent vulnerability to large numbers of invasive life-threatening organisms, or cells that constantly mutate in potentially life-threatening ways, or the origin of the optic nerve slap in the middle of the retina, or. . . . and so endlessly on. . . . Intelligent design? Look in a mirror for the horse-laugh answer to that one.[27]

As one might expect, the force of such suboptimality arguments is a much discussed issue in the intelligent design literature. But the discussion is hampered by a failure to think clearly about the structure of theistic explanations. Proponents of suboptimality arguments write as though theistic explanations were simple causal attributions, merely attributing some feature of the world to God. Their suboptimality argument runs as follows.

(1) If God is responsible for this apparent design, we would expect it to be perfect.
(2) It is not perfect.
(3) Therefore God is not responsible.

This implies that a theistic explanation merely attributes some fact to divine action, and I have argued that an explanation of this form would lack empirical content (3.2.3). And couched in this form, a suboptimality argument is too easy to defeat, for it is far from clear what "perfection" in this context might mean.

Even Gould's "panda's thumb" argument suffers from this weakness. Gould argues that the design of the "thumb" could have been more efficient than it was. You would expect better of an omnipotent, omniscient, and morally perfect creator. I have already argued that this is the correct *kind* of question to ask. But it needs further specification. For efficiency must be measured against some goal, and Gould never specifies what that goal might be. After all, the "thumb" in question is quite workable. So what does he object to? That it is apparently cobbled together? Well, that might provide evidence of its evolutionary history, but this is a different argument. It's no longer a suboptimality claim. And if the "thumb" is somehow imperfect, is Gould implying that God should have created a perfect panda? But then what would a perfect panda look like? As Paul Nelson writes,

> given the conventional concept of the creator, there seem to be *no* limits on what is possible, nor any reason (short perhaps of logical contradiction) why one hypothetically possible panda should be preferred, as a counterfactual ideal, to another. If "perfection" is limited only by the extent of one's imagination, then specifying an ideal phenotype, for the panda or any other organism, quickly becomes a fanciful exercise. Why couldn't the creator have given pandas the ability to fly?[28]

88 Theism and Explanation

Why not, indeed?

Now there may be an answer to this last objection. Perhaps there is an essence of what it is to be a panda which would be violated by giving pandas wings, but not violated by giving them a more efficient "thumb." Perhaps a panda with wings would no longer be a panda. But I don't want to pursue that line of argument here. My point is that Nelson's criticism of Gould's argument is misplaced. It is true that Gould's suboptimality argument is not, as it stands, a strong one. But this is because he has not thought clearly about the structure of proposed theistic explanations. And the theist has, in any case, given him no explanation which he could counter. So what Gould offers is merely a sketch of a suboptimality argument.

Let me explain. I have argued that to have any significant degree of content, a proposed theistic explanation must posit, not merely that the *explanandum* was produced by God, but that it was produced by God in pursuit of some goal (3.2.3). It cannot be a simple causal attribution. (It is against such vague references to a "divine plan" that Darwin seems to have rebelled [1.3.2], arguing, quite correctly, that they lacked empirical content.[29]) It follows that the optimality condition is a condition imposed *on a theistic explanation*, that is to say, one that specifies such an intention. It is up to theists to specify just what God had in mind when he created pandas. And it will not do merely to add "God willed it" to our existing description of a panda. That would be a spurious "explanation," of the kind that Sober criticises (5.2.2). The theist must explain what divine purpose God had in mind in creating such beings. *Only then* can we ask if a better implementation of that intention is conceivable.

It follows that what the optimality condition specifies is not some kind of overall optimality—a "perfect panda," whatever that would be. It is optimality *in relation to a specified divine purpose*. It is up to the theist to nominate just what that purpose is. Unfortunately, theists do not offer us much guidance when it comes to pandas. (It is striking how few facts theists actually try to explain, despite their grandiose claim that theism is a hypothesis of universal scope [7.2.2].) So let me follow up on my earlier suggestion (5.2.2). Let's posit that God created pandas because he wanted to create an animal that would strip bamboo. Then Gould's suboptimality argument would come into play. He could argue that this "thumb" is an inefficient way of stripping bamboo. It is not the kind of design we would expect of an omnipotent, omniscient, and morally perfect creator. Once again, one could take issue with his conclusion—the idea that God must aim at "efficiency" is particularly questionable (5.4.1)—but the optimality condition on which Gould's argument rests is surely correct.

5.3.3 Optimal Divine Action

At what conclusion have I arrived? It is that a proposed theistic explanation of any fact must be regarded as a pseudo-explanation if the *explanandum*

Potential Theistic Explanations 89

is not the optimal way of achieving the posited divine goal. But what does "optimal" mean in this context? It means the most rational way of achieving the posited goal, given perfect knowledge and power as well as moral perfection. But this merely shifts the question, which now becomes: What does it mean for an action to be the most rational action in pursuit of a goal? What we need here are criteria of rational action. I shall offer three such criteria (Appendix 1.3), although my list does not pretend to be exhaustive. In general, an agent is acting rationally in pursuing a particular goal if she acts consistently with her beliefs and desires, in a way which is likely to attain the goal, and which requires the least expenditure of time and effort. This gives us three criteria of rational action: consistency, efficacy, and efficiency.

At least one of these seems inapplicable to a divine agent, namely the criterion of efficiency. A divine agent has no need to conserve his time and energy.[30] Nor does he need to create creatures that would achieve their goals efficiently, unless that efficiency had some desirable consequence (such as the minimising suffering). This may enable the theist to respond to an earlier objection—the idea that God has no need to choose means to an end, since he could achieve his ends directly, by way of basic actions (4.3.3.1). The theist could respond that while this course of action might appear to be more efficient, God has no need to act efficiently.

However, the theist still needs to specify why God has chosen *this particular* means, to achieve the posited goal. And here another criterion of rational action comes into play. We expect a rational agent to act in a way that is consistent with his other beliefs and desires, or (if you prefer) consistent with his character.[31] From God's point of view, it may not matter that evolution by natural selection (for example) takes a long time. He has plenty of time to waste. But on the assumption that God is morally perfect, it does matter if natural selection necessitates considerable suffering. Would it be rational for an omnipotent, omniscient, and benevolent being to choose *this* particular way of bringing living creatures into existence? We can now see that at least some forms of the atheist's argument from evil are, in fact, suboptimality arguments.[32] They try to render the theistic hypothesis of divine creation implausible by suggesting that God could have created a world containing less suffering.[33]

At this point, we can also understand the appeal of an uncompromising, young-earth creationism, one that takes the opening chapters of Genesis at face value. Remember the criterion of independent specification? Let's apply it to the creation of the world. If we were to specify how an omniscient, omnipotent, and morally perfect God would create a world, *independently of what we now know of the world's origins*, what would we come up with? One could argue that we would produce an account that at least resembles Genesis 1. After all, such a deity would not need to engage in a lengthy process of creation. He would not need to "use" evolution, for instance, in order to produce beings like us. He could achieve his ends directly, simply by willing them or (as the book of Genesis has it) by speaking his creative word. In one such act, or in a series of such acts (perhaps over six days—why not?),[34] he could have created every aspect of the world as we now find it. And if God were a rational agent, would he not have chosen this, the most painless way of bringing creatures into existence?

My discussion has assumed that a hypothesis has what we might call "explanatory force" if it is at least a *potential* explanation of the fact in question. What I am suggesting here is that if we were to choose between two theistic hypotheses, the one being the Genesis account and the other being some form of theistic evolution, we would have more confidence in the explanatory force of the first than the second. Now it may be that we can have little confidence that *any* theistic hypothesis has explanatory force (5.5)—that it really is a potential explanation of any state of affairs. But insofar as we can make such judgements—and I think we can, albeit cautiously—then the Genesis account of creation has greater explanatory force than any story about a divinely-guided process of evolution. Natural selection is not what we would expect, given the posited character and capacities of God.

I should, perhaps, add that this is not an argument in favour of a literal reading of Genesis 1–3. The reader will not be surprised to learn that I am no supporter of young-earth creationism. But one can regard a hypothesis as a potential explanation of some state of affairs—one can agree that it has explanatory force—while believing that there are excellent reasons why we should not accept it. What those reasons might be is a question to which I shall return.

5.4 ARGUMENTS AGAINST OPTIMALITY

There are a number of objections that could be raised to my optimality condition. I shall consider four. The first is that God is not obliged to act optimally; the second is that there *is* no optimal divine action; the third is that we cannot make such judgements; the fourth is that talk of intelligent design does not entail that the design in question *is* optimal. Let me address each objection in turn.

5.4.1 God is Not Obliged to Act Optimally

The first objection is that the optimality condition is simply inapplicable to a divine agent. Such an agent, it might be argued, is supremely free. He can act in any way he chooses, and is not obliged to choose the optimal course of action (assuming there is one). As Laura Garcia argues, "God has no need to minimize the amount of time or effort or expense and he is not subject to time constraints, natural laws, etc. It may be that a given means is optimal with respect to its cost to other goals or purposes of his, but even here it is not clear that God is required to realise that means."[35] So Garcia admits that there may be an optimal divine action, but denies that God is obliged to follow it. Now if we remember that the optimality condition is an expression of the rationality principle, this argument seems an odd one. For it suggests that God is not obliged to act rationally. And I'm not sure what to make of that idea. Would any theist wish to affirm that God has acted irrationally?

In any case, in the present context the objection is misplaced. The optimality condition is not intended to be a constraint on God; it is intended to be a constraint on us. More precisely, it is a constraint on the offering of theistic explanations. The point is not that God is obliged to do this or that, but that we are obliged, by the nature of intentional explanations, to regard the divine agent as a rational agent. My argument in favour of the optimality condition is epistemological, not metaphysical (or theological). One might want to take it further, to argue that God is obliged to act optimally. But this would be a different argument. The optimality condition I am advocating stems from the nature of intentional explanations, not from any theological claim.

5.4.2 There Is No Optimal Divine Action

A second objection relates to the optimality condition itself. Let's accept that we must regard God as a rational being, who chooses the best possible way of realizing his intentions. We still have to make sense of the idea of the *optimal realization* of a divine intention. This idea resembles that of a *best possible world*, to which it is closely related. For the optimality condition entails that if this world is created by God, then it is the best possible realization of whatever intentions God had in creating. It follows that it *is* the best possible world, although (as we shall see) in a more clearly specified sense. But the difficulties surrounding the idea of a best possible world are now widely recognised. Could the same objections not be levelled at my idea of an optimal realization of a divine plan?

5.4.2.1 No Best Possible World

There are two major objections to the idea of a best possible world. The first is that there may be no "single scale of value" against which different possible worlds could be ranked.[36] After all, there are many different sorts of values. How are they to be compared? "Some world A might be better than rival world B in some respects, but with B surpassing A in others, and the relevant values not such that they could be summed over and compared overall."[37] The second is that such values may have no upper limit. If we are speaking of mere "additive value," in the sense that a world with $n + 1$ creatures is better than a world with n creatures, then there is clearly no limit to how good a world could be.[38] The same may be said of the value of diversity, in the sense of the range of natural kinds which a world could contain. For any world, there could be another displaying a greater diversity. What if we were to say that the best world is one which contains the best kinds of beings, those which exhibited the highest level of perfection? Here, too, it seems there is no upper limit. "For each level of finite goodness or knowledge" such beings might have, "there is always a higher level."[39] So it may be that the very idea of a best possible world is incoherent. Can the same not be said of the idea of the optimal realization of a divine plan?

5.4.2.2 Four Responses

This is a serious objection. What responses might I offer, in defence of my optimality condition? Can that condition be defended? Does it rest on an idea that turns out to be incoherent: the idea of a best possible world?

The incoherence of theism. A first response would be to come out of the corner fighting, for it may be that this objection can be turned against the theist. After all, my optimality condition seems a plausible one. Surely we would expect an omnipotent, omniscient, and morally perfect creator to create the best possible world? And if he has a plan for the world, we would expect him to implement that plan in the best possible way. If the idea of a best possible world, or the best possible implementation of a divine plan, is an incoherent one, so much the worse for the theist. If there is nothing wrong with the logic of this argument, then the incoherence of the *conclusion* reflects an incoherence in its *premises*. What is at fault, it could be argued, is the very idea of God. What the argument shows is that there cannot be a being who is omniscient, omnipotent, and morally perfect. Even to speak of God as "perfectly good" would be to fall into confusion; it is as if we were to speak of something as "perfectly long."[40] I spoke earlier (3.3) about the idea that theism may be disqualified as a hypothesis because it is incoherent. This is one way in which that argument could be pursued.

There is no parallel. However, I shall not pursue that first response here. Instead, I shall offer a second response. I shall argue that the idea of an optimal realization of a divine plan is not faced with the same objections that can be brought against the idea of a best possible world. As we have seen, the idea of a best possible world is problematic because of the diversity of the values that must be compared and the fact that those values have no upper limit. But the idea of an optimal realization of a divine plan faces neither of these difficulties. The optimality in question is more clearly defined: it is "best relative to the ends and purposes one has in mind."[41] And while the optimality condition may *entail* that a world created by God would be the best possible world—although once again in a more clearly defined sense—the two ideas are not identical. The optimality condition is not something one applies to the world as a whole. Indeed it is not clear, at least to me, how one might go about offering an explanation of "the world as a whole." What we are interested in are explanations of *particular facts* about the world, however broad their scope. (The existence of the world is also a particular fact.) It may not make sense to speak of a best possible world, but it does make sense to speak of the best possible realization of particular divine intention.

A comparative judgement will suffice. But perhaps this reply does not yet dispose of the objection. So let's grant the objector his point and look at the worst-case scenario. Let's assume that the idea of a best possible realization of a particular divine plan is incoherent. Or let's assume that it is coherent, but unworkable, of no practical use, since we are not in a position to say what it would entail (5.4.3). Would my argument lose all force if I were to abandon this idea? No, it would not. It does not matter if there *is* no optimal realization of a divine plan. Nor does it matter if there is such a thing, but we could never know what it entails. What matters is that we can conceive of a state of affairs which, from the point of view of a rational creator, would be *better* than that which actually obtains.

Let me expand on this response indirectly, by examining a parallel response which William Rowe makes to his critics. Rowe defends the principle (let's call it the "better world" principle), which states that

> if an omniscient being creates a world when there is a better world it could create, then it would be possible for there to be a being morally better than it.[42]

On the assumption that there *is* a best of all possible worlds (that the idea makes sense), what follows from this principle? There are two possibilities. It may be that this world *is* the best possible world, in which case God, understood as the morally unsurpassable creator of this world, may exist. Or it may be that this world *is not* the best possible world, in which case it cannot be that God, understood as the morally unsurpassable creator of this world, exists. It follows, Rowe argues, that the theist is faced with an unpalatable choice. He must either claim that this world is the best of all possible worlds (and face the ridicule of those who, like Voltaire, regard this suggestion as morally offensive, if not absurd) or he must abandon his faith.

But there is apparently a way out, which is comparable to the objection I have been considering. The theist can argue that the idea of a best possible world is a nonsense. To create such a world is logically impossible, and you cannot fault God for failing to do what is logically impossible. So God would not be a morally imperfect being by creating a world which is less than the best possible. Rowe's response to this argument is a simple one. It is to point out that *even if* there is no best possible world—in fact *precisely if* there is no best possible world—there is always a world better than any which God might choose to create. So if one accepts the "better world" principle, there can never be a morally unsurpassable (morally perfect) being.[43] This, of course, resembles my first, *incoherence of theism*, response.

In Rowe's case, this response works only if possible worlds can be compared in terms of overall value. If they cannot, not only is there no *best* possible world, but there is no *better* possible world. But as we have seen, this objection is not one I have to face. On the assumption that we *can* compare different possible realizations of a divine plan (some, for instance, causing more suffering than others) there exists parallel response in defence of my own position. It may be that there is no *best* possible realization of a divine plan—in this context, perhaps, "optimal" makes no sense—but that does not mean that there are not *better* and *worse* realizations of a divine plan. The fact that there may be no upper limit to how well God might have acted is no fatal objection. If we examine the *explanandum* and can envisage a better way in which the posited divine intention could have been implemented, then the theistic explanation is no explanation at all.

What follows from this discussion? I have argued that it does make sense to speak of the best way in which a divine intention could be implemented. If so, then we are right to invoke the optimality condition. We cannot plausibly attribute to God a suboptimal solution. But if I am wrong—if there is no best way in which a divine intention could be implemented, since there could always be a better—then the very idea of a divine agent seems questionable. Either way, it seems that the theist will have some questions to answer.

5.4.3 We Cannot Make Such Judgements

So far I have argued against the objection that God is not obliged to act morally and against the idea that there exists no optimal realisation of a divine intention. As a coda to that argument, I have suggested that even if it were true that there is something incoherent in my appeal to optimality, it would suggest there is something wrong with the very idea of a theistic explanation. Let me turn now to a third objection. It is another form of scepticism, similar to that expressed by Elliot Sober. But it is a *modal* rather than a (directly) *theological* scepticism. The objection runs as follows.

To ask if it would have been rational for God to realise *this* intention in *this* way assumes that he had other ways available to him. But how do we know this? How do we know that the *explanandum* was not in fact the *only* means available to him? We may *think* that we can envisage a better way in which the posited divine intention could have been achieved. We can produce what appears to us a consistent description of a better state of affairs and argue that since God is omnipotent, he could have brought this about. But how do we know that this state of affairs *is* logically possible? After all, there are many ideas that appear at first sight to be free from contradiction. The idea that there should exist a barber who shaves every man who does not shave himself seems perfectly reasonable, at first sight. Contradictions emerge only after closer examination. We may, for instance, *think* that there could exist free beings who always choose the good. But that may be only because there is a contradiction here which we have not yet discovered.

Here's one response to this objection. In claiming to possess modal knowledge, we are not claiming to possess *incorrigible* modal knowledge. Our judgements in this respect are fallible, like all other judgements regarding matters of fact. But they are judgements, however provisional, which we are required to make if we are to evaluate proposed theistic explanations (5.2–5.3). Indeed they are judgements we are required to make if we are to *offer* theistic explanations (5.4.3.2). This initial response is surely correct, but it fails fully to come to terms with the question. For what is being suggested here is that we cannot have even corrigible knowledge, or make provisional judgements, in this area. It is this stronger objection that I am describing as "modal scepticism."

5.4.3.1 Modal and Theological Scepticism

The term "modal scepticism" seems to have been coined by Peter van Inwagen, who deploys it principally in response to the atheist's argument from evil. Van Inwagen denies that we can make reliable, intuitive judgements about what is possible in "circumstances remote from the practical business of everyday life."[44] A good case can be made for the reliability of certain *everyday* modal judgements. We know, for instance, that the table placed under the window could have been placed a metre to the left. Experience shows that we are often successful in making such judgements. But why should we assume that our capacity for modal judgements goes beyond these everyday matters? Our supposed ability to make such judgements may be no more reliable than a supposed ability to judge by eye the distance of the moon from the earth.[45] We simply cannot do it, and if we think we can, we are fooling ourselves.

It should be clear that van Inwagen's modal scepticism entails a particular form of theological scepticism. It entails a scepticism regarding our knowledge of the possibilities available to a divine agent. After all, judgements about how God could act are, of all judgements, the most "remote from common life and experience."[46] If the modal sceptic is correct, we are in no position to know what kind of a world an omnipotent, omniscient, and morally perfect God would create. I have been assuming that we can identify various ways in which God might have acted, and that we can judge some to be better than others. But if the modal sceptic is correct, we simply cannot do this, for we do not know the possible courses of action that were open to God. So we cannot say what an optimal (or even a better) means of achieving a divine goal would look like.

5.4.3.2 The Implications of Modal Scepticism

There is much to be said for a moderate dose of modal scepticism. It is surely true that our ability to make such judgements is limited. (I have already cited David Hume's suggestion that "our line is too short to fathom such immense abysses"[47] [5.1].) But from the fact that our ability to make such judgements is limited, it does not follow that we have no ability at all. One could accept van Inwagen's arguments, but argue that they support nothing more than a moderate modal scepticism. However, for the sake of the argument let me concede the modal sceptic his point. Let's say that we cannot claim modal knowledge in matters "remote from the practical business of everyday life." (There is presumably some point on the remoteness scale where such judgements become unreliable. Let's assume we can specify what that is, so that—in true Socratic manner—we can know what we do not know.) What would follow? What I want to suggest is that a consistent modal scepticism has some devastating consequences.

A first result of adopting a consistent modal scepticism is that the theist could no longer appeal to the doctrine of divine omnipotence. Divine omnipotence is commonly defined as the ability to do whatever is logically possible. But what happens to this doctrine if we cannot know what is logically possible? Worse still, what happens if the very category of the logically possible is empty?[48] In this case, the doctrine of divine omnipotence is also empty. It has no content at all. So one wonders how far van Inwagen wants his modal scepticism to be taken.

A second, related consequence has to do with the issue at hand. For when modal scepticism becomes theological scepticism, it constitutes a powerful *in principle* objection to theistic explanations. I have argued that to offer a potential theistic explanation is to posit an particular divine intention and to argue that the *explanandum* is how we would expect God to act, given that intention. But of course it is precisely our ability to make such judgements that the modal sceptic denies. It follows that, given modal scepticism, a proposed theistic explanation could not be regarded as even a *potential* explanation, of any fact at all. And if (*per impossibile*) it did establish itself as a potential explanation, it would suffer from the flaw of being entirely *ad hoc*. There is no way it could be tested, for to test such an explanation is to ask *what else* would follow, if it were true. (These are precisely the arguments which Elliot Sober deploys, to which modal scepticism would give new force.) So an atheist might welcome a thoroughgoing modal scepticism. It would be nothing less than the "silver bullet" the atheist seeks.

5.4.4 Intelligent Design is Not Optimal Design

I shall conclude this discussion with an objection to suboptimality arguments that has recently been articulated by William Dembski, a leading figure in the "intelligent design" movement. Dembski repeats some of the objections to the idea of "optimal design" which I have discussed above. He then notes (somewhat disingenuously) that "taken strictly as a scientific theory, intelligent design refuses to speculate about the nature of the designing intelligence."[49] It is only when the discussion moves to theology that this issue arises, being transformed—Dembski argues—into the familiar problem of evil. The theist, he writes, must "reconcile the following three propositions: (1) God is good; (2) God is all-powerful; (3) Evil exists."[50] Dembski is confident this can be done, since (as he puts it) "philosophical theology has abundant resources for dealing with the problem of evil."[51] In any case, what was originally well designed can become corrupted: teleology can become dysteleology. "The perversion of design," Dembski argues, "is not explained by denying design, but by accepting it and meeting the problem of evil head on."[52]

But Dembski's comments understate the difficulty of the theist's task. It is not enough to *reconcile* the three propositions which Dembski lists, in the sense of showing they do not give rise to a contradiction. It is not sufficient to show that affirming the existence of God is *compatible* with recognizing the existence of evil. In the present context—that of offering explanations that posit the existence of such a God—the theist must show that the world with all its suffering is *precisely what we would expect* an omnipotent, omniscient, and morally perfect being to create. He must show that this world is what we "would, *beforehand*, expect from a very powerful, wise, and benevolent Deity."[53] In Hume's *Dialogues*, Philo makes this very point against Cleanthes.

> I will allow, that pain or misery in man is *compatible* with infinite power and goodness in the Deity, even in your sense of these attributes: What are you advanced by all these concessions? A mere possible compatibility is not sufficient. You must *prove* these pure, unmixed, and uncontrollable attributes from the present mixed and confused phenomena, and from these alone.[54]

This is why the most powerful form of the atheist's argument from evil is an evidential argument that compares two hypotheses, the theistic hypothesis and the "hypothesis of indifference." According to the theistic hypothesis, the world was created by an all-powerful and benevolent deity. According to the hypothesis of indifference, "neither the nature nor the condition of sentient beings on earth is the result of benevolent or malevolent actions performed by non-human persons."[55] Which of these, the atheist asks, would render the observable facts less surprising, if indeed it were true? That is the question which the explanation-offering theist must face.

5.5 THE CONSEQUENCES OF SCEPTICISM

Let me end this chapter by seeing if I can sharpen up my argument, expressing my claims with a little more precision. I suggested earlier

(2.1.2) that a hypothesis (H) should be regarded as a potential explanation of some fact (E) if it meets the requirement of the second premise of Peirce's abductive schema. I also argued (2.1.4) that an intentional explanation takes us from H to E—meeting the requirement of that second premise—by way of an argument. More precisely, an intentional explanation is a kind of practical syllogism (Appendix 2.1), which has a particular intention as its premise and a description of the *explanandum* as its conclusion. While a hypothesis that meets this requirement has explanatory force, our confidence about its explanatory force may vary. We will be confident about the explanatory force of an intentional hypothesis to the extent that we are confident about the truth of the premises of the practical syllogism involved.

What I have argued in this chapter, against theological and modal sceptics, is that in the case of a divine agent we can have *some* degree of confidence in the premises of such a syllogism. By using the rationality principle, we can form some idea of how a divine agent might be expected to act, given a posited divine intention. Complete scepticism in this regard is unwarranted. As we have seen, if complete scepticism were warranted, it would be an apparently decisive *in principle* objection to proposed theistic explanations, since it would render this kind of syllogism impossible. So the atheist might hope that the sceptic is right. But my argument has proceeded on the assumption, backed up by appeal to the rationality principle, that we are not required to be complete sceptics.

Nonetheless, I have also suggested that the sceptics have a point. A degree of scepticism does seem warranted. To say that the *explanandum* is, or is not, the best way in which God could have achieved a posited goal involves a difficult judgement, about matters that are "remote from common life and experience."[56] Even if we *can* fathom this particular abyss, we cannot have a high degree of confidence in the judgements we make. And this means that we cannot be confident that whatever we specify *really is* the best means of achieving a posited divine goal. Assuming, for example, that Mackie's famous argument against the free will defence is correct—that God could have created free creatures who always chose the good—then it is striking how long it took for someone to come up with it. Even now, if my students' reactions are anything to go by, it can take a while to see that this *is* a logically possible state of affairs.

To what point has this discussion led? If an account of divine action is to be even a potential explanation of some state of affairs, we must be able to specify how we would expect a divine agent to act in order to achieve his goals. Only then would the account of divine action have any explanatory force. Using the rationality principle, I have argued, we can indeed make some provisional judgements in this regard. But the flip-side of that principle, in the case of a divine agent, is what I have called an optimality condition. We are warranted in regarding a theistic hypothesis as a potential explanation of some state of affairs *only if* we cannot conceive of any better way in which the posited divine goal could have been attained. If we cannot make any of these judgements, as sceptics would argue, then there can be no theistic explanations. But even if we can, we can have only a modest degree of confidence in the outcome. We can never be confident that any particular theistic hypothesis has explanatory force. It follows that even a moderate degree of scepticism—such as that urged by many theists themselves—will undermine our confidence in a proposed theistic explanation.

6 Inference to the Best Explanation

> "Tracks," said Piglet. "Paw-marks." He gave a little squeak of excitement. "Oh, Pooh! Do you think it's a—a—a Woozle?"
> "It may be," said Pooh. "Sometimes it is, and sometimes it isn't. You never can tell with Woozles."
>
> A. A. Milne

Let me begin this, the penultimate chapter of my enquiry, by summarising the conclusions I have reached. I began by identifying a number of objections to proposed religious explanations. The first is that theistic explanations exclude no possible state of affairs; the second is that the actions of an agent who can work miracles would be unpredictable; the third maintains that the very concept of God is incoherent; the fourth suggests that the will of God cannot be a cause and hence cannot be invoked in an explanation. I did, in a footnote, allude to a fifth objection.[1] It is the idea, based on Hume's principle of proportioning cause to effect,[2] that we would never be warranted in positing a being of infinite power in order to explain a finite effect.[3] I have not dwelt on this objection since at least some of its force is captured by my optimality condition (5.3.3). As the reader will recall, this suggests that if you posit a being of infinite power and goodness, the *explanandum* may not correspond to how we would expect him to act.

After examining each of these objections, I decided that none constitutes a "silver bullet," a decisive objection which would warrant a summary dismissal of a theistic hypothesis. With regard to the first objection, I suggested ways in which proposed theistic explanations could be formulated so as to have empirical content. With regard to the second objection, I argued that if we assume that the divine agent is a rational agent—an assumption that underlies all intentional explanations—then his behaviour is not entirely unpredictable. With regard to the fifth objection, I suggested that we cannot, *a priori*, exclude the bare possibility that a proposed theistic explanation might satisfy the optimality condition. It does, however, constitute a significant hurdle for the theist.

What about the objections three and four, both of which argue that there is something incoherent about the very idea of a theistic explanation? There is certainly a *prima facie* case here for the theist to answer. One could argue that he is obliged to show that his hypothesis does not embody contradictory claims. Can this be done? I don't know. Richard Swinburne admits that the theist can avoid the charge of incoherence only by appealing to the fact his language about God is being used analogically (3.3.3).[4] But if we cannot attribute any literal meaning to this analogical language—if our talk of a divine agent must remain shrouded in a cloud of unknowing—it is hard to see how we could demonstrate its internal coherence. How could we ever be confident that it does not embody hidden contradictions?

Does this constitute a decisive objection to any proposed theistic explanation? Probably not. I shall argue later (7.6) that an inability to offer a literal description of divine action *counts against* proposed theistic explanations. It gives us reason to prefer explanations that are more informative. But it is not clear, at least to me, that it immediately disqualifies them. And I have argued that there are occasions in which we would be acting rationally in accepting an apparently inconsistent hypothesis, at least in the sense of continuing to work on it (3.3.4). If this is true, then even if you could show that a theistic hypothesis was internally incoherent, this would not *necessarily* warrant its *immediate* dismissal, if that hypothesis had other features in its favour. What those features might be, and whether a proposed theistic explanation might ever possess them, are questions I shall be addressing in these final chapters.

If the atheist concedes this much, then she lacks a silver bullet. Even if she believes that there exists a strong presumption against proposed theistic explanations—a position I shall defend myself—she must argue against them on a case-by-case basis. But her argument can take one of two forms. She can argue that such a proposed explanation is not even a *potential* explanation of the fact in question. According to this view, even if the theist's account of divine action were true, it would not explain the *explanandum*. In Chapter 5, I outlined one way in which this might be done, namely, by invoking the optimality condition (5.3.3). The atheist could undermine the force of a proposed theistic explanation by arguing that there exists a better way in which God could have achieved his posited goal. And the obvious candidate for a "better" way would be one involving less suffering.

But the atheist can also adopt a second line of criticism, one that focuses on the reasons we might have to accept a proposed theistic explanation, one that has been shown to have some explanatory force. This is a *de facto* rather than an *in principle* argument. It suggests that even if the theist has a *potential* explanation of the fact in question, we have insufficient reason to regard it as the *actual* explanation. It lacks the qualities that would warrant its acceptance. The question this raises is: What are those qualities? What would constitute a sufficient reason for accepting a theistic hypothesis, given that it has been shown to be a potential explanation of the fact in question? It is to this question that my final chapters will be devoted.

6.1 INDUCTION AND ABDUCTION

I shall approach the answer indirectly, by examining Richard Swinburne's arguments for the existence of God. In a number of publications, Swinburne

Inference to the Best Explanation   103

claims that positing the existence of God offers us a successful explanation of various facts about the world. Some of these facts are very general—such as the very existence of a universe, operating in regular and predictable ways—while others are more particular. The particular facts to which Swinburne appeals have to do with the existence and nature of human beings, as well as reports of events in human history, some of which he sees as miracles. Once again, I shall not be examining the *soundness* of Swinburne's arguments. If my argument to this point is correct, that would require a careful case-by-case study. I am happy to leave that task to others. All I want to do is to examine the *structure* of his arguments, to see if that sheds any light on the questions I am addressing.

6.1.1 Inductive Reasoning

Swinburne consistently claims to be offering *inductive* arguments for the existence of God. In particular, he claims to be offering sound C-inductive arguments, which he describes as arguments that make the theistic hypothesis more probable than it would be otherwise.[5] His example of a C-inductive argument is the following.

> (1) All of 100 ravens observed in different parts of the world are black.
> (2) [Therefore] all ravens are black.[6]

This is certainly an inductive argument, indeed one made famous by Carl Hempel's discussion of inductive reasoning (7.1.2).[7] But do Swinburne's arguments take this particular form?

They do not. It is true that Swinburne's arguments are not *deductive* arguments; they do not take the form of a syllogism such as the following:

> (1) No material body travels faster than light.
> (2) My car is a material body.
> (3) [Therefore] my car does not travel faster than light.[8]

If you define an "inductive argument" as any argument that is not deductive and can support only a probable conclusion, then Swinburne's arguments can be described as inductive. But they are not inductive in the sense in which such arguments were understood by John Stuart Mill and his successors.[9] In discussions of scientific reasoning, an inductive argument is one that proceeds from the observation of particulars to the formation of a general hypothesis.[10] The principle underlying such reasoning may be summarised as follows.

> If a large number of *A*s have been observed under a wide variety of conditions, and if all those observed *A*s without exception have possessed the property *b*, then all *A*s possess the property *b*.[11]

104 *Theism and Explanation*

Since David Hume's day, there has been a philosophical debate about why we take such arguments as seriously as we do. But that this is the form of an inductive argument is not in dispute.

Now one could base an argument for the existence of God on inductive reasoning, as Mill himself recognised when discussing the argument from design.[12] A recent example is to be found in the work of William Dembski, the "intelligent design" advocate. Dembski identifies a feature of living organisms which he calls "specified complexity" and argues that this is a reliable indicator of design. His reason for doing so, he writes, is

> a straightforward inductive argument: In every instance where the complexity-specification criterion attributes design and where the underlying causal story is known (i.e., where we are not just dealing with circumstantial evidence, but where, as it were, the video camera is running and any putative designer would be caught red-handed), it turns out design actually is present.[13]

So Dembski's inductive argument has the following form:

(1) Every *observed instance* of specified complexity is explained by the acts of some intelligent agent who brought it about.
(2) Therefore, every *instance* of specified complexity is explained by the acts of some intelligent agent who brought it about.[14]

Admittedly, this is only the first step in Dembski's process of argumentation. To support his conclusion that there exists a non-natural intelligent agent, further premises are required, such as:

(3) The natural world exhibits specified complexity.
(4) That specified complexity could not have been produced by a natural agent.

But the first two steps do constitute an inductive argument. It may or may not be a sound argument[15]—it seems all but identical, interestingly enough, to that discussed by Mill—but it certainly moves from the observation of particulars to a general statement.

6.1.2 Swinburne's Arguments

What is important in this context is that this is not how Swinburne reasons. He does not, for instance, argue:

(1) Every instance of a universe we have observed has a creator.
(2) Therefore all universes (including our own) probably have creators.[16]

Inference to the Best Explanation 105

He argues instead that the existence of a universe would be less surprising, given the theistic hypothesis, than it would be otherwise.[17] It follows, he argues, that the existence of the universe confirms the theistic hypothesis. And the same pattern of argument is deployed throughout Swinburne's work. All the phenomena to which he draws our attention are, he argues, "such as we have reason to expect if there is a God, and less reason to expect otherwise."[18] For if there is a God, he would have both the power to produce such a world and reason to do so.[19]

6.1.2.1 The Likelihood of the Evidence

Let's try to set out Swinburne's pattern of reasoning in more detail. If we take E to be the evidence and H to be the theistic hypothesis, his argumentation in support of that hypothesis involves two steps. In the first, he argues that the truth of H would render E more likely than it would be otherwise. This first step can be expressed more formally as follows:

$Pr(E|H) > Pr(E|\overline{H})$.

This resembles my own account of what constitutes a *potential explanation* (2.1.2). I have argued that the underlying argument is deductive in form, while Swinburne thinks of it as somehow probabilistic. As it happens, he does not specify just what form this probabilistic argument takes. But once again Swinburne does *not* seem to be arguing inductively, in the sense of arguing from particular instances to a general conclusion. However, let's grant Swinburne his probabilistic framework, for the sake of the argument, and agree that if H renders E more probable than it would be otherwise, then H is a potential explanation of E.

Yet Swinburne is not content with so modest a conclusion. He argues that if H renders E more probable than it would be otherwise, then H is *confirmed* by E.[20] There is a sense in which this is true. To say that H renders E more likely than it would be otherwise is to say that E lends some support to H. But this is a weak sense of "confirmation"—it is a case of what we might call "incremental" rather than "absolute" confirmation[21]—for E may lend some support to H even when H is clearly false. Let me illustrate this point with an example given by Elliot Sober (who uses O for "observation" rather than E for "evidence").

> To say that H has a high likelihood, given observation O, is to comment on the value of Pr (O|H), not on the value of Pr (H|O); the latter is H's *posterior probability*. It is perfectly possible for a hypothesis to have a high likelihood and a low posterior probability. When you hear noises in your attic, this confers a high likelihood on the hypothesis that there are gremlins up there bowling, but few of us would conclude that this hypothesis is probably true.[22]

In terms of confirmation theory, the gremlin hypothesis has a low *posterior* probability because it has a low *prior* probability. What is it about the gremlin hypothesis that gives it a low prior probability? Well, one reason is that it enjoys little support from our background knowledge: it bears little relationship to those other things which we know to be true. So, as Swinburne is well aware, a key issue is the prior probability of the theistic hypothesis, and a key issue in determining this is the role of background knowledge. I shall come back to these questions shortly (7.2).

We can approach the same question more formally, by way of the Bayesian reasoning that forms so important a part of Swinburne's argumentation. As we have seen (2.1.3.1), the relationship I have been discussing—that between likelihood and posterior probability—is formalised by Bayes's theorem:

$$\Pr(H|E) = \frac{\Pr(E|H) \times \Pr(H)}{\Pr(E)}.$$

If, with Swinburne, we assume that a hypothesis is confirmed to the degree that it is rendered probable—and I have already hinted at an alternative account (2.1.3.2)—then Bayes's theorem also gives us the degree to which a hypothesis is confirmed. Let's see how this works by assigning some figures, more or less at random. Let's say that the prior probability of *E* is 0.2. (It is a *surprising* fact that we're trying to explain.) And let's say the likelihood of *E*, given *H*, is 0.9. (*H* has a high degree of explanatory force.) Can we say that *E* confirms *H*? Yes, in the weak sense of "confirm" we can. It renders it more likely than it would be otherwise. But by how much? Well, it depends on the prior probability of *H*. If the prior probability of *H* is low, let's say 0.1, then its probability is raised to 0.45. This is impressive, but it falls short of demonstrating that *H* is probably true (if that is what you are interested in doing).[23]

6.1.2.2 The Probability of Theism

So the second step in Swinburne's reasoning is to turn these various C-inductive arguments, as he calls them, into a P-inductive argument.[24] A P-inductive argument is one that makes the conclusion more probable than not. Swinburne argues that the prior (or "intrinsic") probability of theism is high, at least "relative to other hypotheses about what there is."[25] For prior probability, he claims, will be directly proportional to the simplicity of a hypothesis, its narrowness of scope, and its conformity to background knowledge.[26] Swinburne argues that background knowledge need not be taken into account when assessing the theistic hypothesis, since theism "purports to explain everything logically contingent (apart from itself)."[27] But this means that the theistic hypothesis leaves nothing in the background: the relevant evidence is everything (except God himself). I think this argument is flawed, for reasons to which I shall return (7.2.2). In any case, having dismissed background knowledge, Swinburne is left with simplicity and scope. He argues that of these two the criterion of simplicity is the more important, and that on this criterion theism ranks very highly.

Given this conclusion regarding prior probability, there remains the task of assessing the degree to which the evidence supports theism. Swinburne does this by performing the requisite Bayesian calculations. He admits that his probability estimates are "arbitrary," but claims that they do "capture, within the roughest of ranges, the kinds of probabilities involved."[28] At first, Swinburne leaves aside the evidence of religious experience, the force of which depends upon whether a person has herself had a religious experience,[29] and the evidence of history, which he considers at more length elsewhere. Leaving these aside, Swinburne concludes that "it is something like as probable as not that theism is true."[30] In other words, the posterior probability of theism is roughly 0.5. But he argues that if we add the evidence of religious experience and of history, then we can conclude that "theism is more probable than not."[31]

6.1.3 Abductive Reasoning

Even if one grants the force of these calculations—and each step along the path is contestable—one might argue that they do not take us very far. The Christian theist will still want to demonstrate that his particular variety of theism, with all its additional claims, is probably true. And this is no easy task. Alvin Plantinga, for instance, argues that even if we assign a probability of 0.9 to theism, we will not be able to demonstrate the probable truth of the Christian faith. Making generous estimates along the way, Plantinga calculates that the probability that Christianity is true could not exceed 0.35.[32] But let me leave such considerations aside, for my primary interest here is in the structure of Swinburne's arguments and the criteria he is using. What can we say about the structure of these arguments?

My proposal is that Swinburne's overall argument is best thought of as a type of abductive reasoning, although he himself does not employ this term. In arguing that what we observe around us is "such as we have reason to expect if there is a God, and less reason to expect otherwise,"[33] Swinburne is in fact arguing not inductively but abductively.

It is true that abductive reasoning could be *supported* by an inductive argument. One could set out an inductive argument—one that argues from past instances—in support of the second premise of Peirce's abductive schema (2.1.2). If all observed events of type E were produced in the manner indicated by hypothesis H, this would give us some reason to think that H was the explanation of E. Intelligent design advocate Stephen Meyer, for instance, to whose work I referred earlier (2.1.1), offers an argument of precisely this form. In what has become a controversial article,[34] Meyer offers a "best explanation" account of what he calls "biological information." In the course of doing so, he argues inductively, from our previous experience of intelligent designers. But as I have already suggested (6.1.2), there is no evidence that Swinburne is offering an argument of this kind, one that refers to previous observed instances of the fact in question. Swinburne does claim that the explanation he is offering is a species of personal, or (as I have described it) intentional explanation.[35] So it is presumably an intentional explanation that meets the requirement of Peirce's second premise by taking us from H to E. But other than assuming that it is probabilistic in form, Swinburne never spells out just what kind of argument this involves. My own view will by now be familiar. It is that an intentional explanation is best regarded as a species of deductive argument.

6.2 THE BEST EXPLANATION

It seems, then, that Swinburne's arguments for the existence of God follow, more or less, the pattern of Peirce's abductive schema. They are, therefore, best analysed as abductive arguments, of the form I discussed at the starting point of my enquiry (2.1.2). I shall argue in a moment (6.2.1) that abductive reasoning can be defended as a form of inference to the best explanation (IBE). And, as a number of authors have argued,[36] IBE is particularly well-adapted for a defence of theism. Firstly, it can be used to support the positing of *unobservable* (or at least unobserved) entities. To mount a directly inductive argument, of the kind offered by William Dembski (6.1.1), requires the theist to produce past instances in which this posited cause can be observed at work. But IBE allows us to posit a cause which we have never before observed at work. Secondly, and for precisely the same reason, IBE can be used to support *singular* causal claims (4.2.1). Even if we know of only one event of the type in question (such as the "big bang," commonly, but no longer universally,[37] thought to mark the beginning of our universe), we can legitimately posit a cause and argue for its existence in the manner Peirce indicates. All we need is a non-inductive way of arguing that "if H were true, E is what we would expect" (2.1.2), that is to say, one that does not need to appeal to past instances of this correlation. And in the case of intentional explanations, this is precisely what we have (Appendix 1.3), in the form of the rationality principle (5.2).

6.2.1 The Problem of Abduction

But I'm now jumping ahead of myself. Let me return to the question of abduction, for at first sight this might seem a poor kind of argument. To Peirce's credit, he is very careful in the wording of his schema. Its conclusion is not "H is true," but "there is reason to suspect H is true." But let's be less cautious for a moment, and formulate an abductive argument without such qualifications.

(1) The surprising fact, E, is observed.
(2) But if H were true, E would be a matter of course.
(3) Therefore H is true.

Such an argument would embody a well-known logical fallacy, namely that of affirming the consequent.[38] It is a fallacy of the *The streets are wet; if it has been raining, the streets would be wet; therefore it has been raining* variety. In symbols, the argument involved would have the following, invalid form.

P ⊃ Q

Q
―――
∴ P

If this is how we justify our belief in unobservables, then A. J. Ayer was surely right: the inference involved is illegitimate.[39]

Let me illustrate the difficulty. I suggested earlier (3.1) that the discovery of electrons was a scientific discovery backed up by abductive reasoning. One of the factors that led to the discovery of electrons was the attempt to explain the behaviour of cathode rays. In particular, J. J. Thomson suggested that the behaviour of cathode rays could be understood if we assume that they "mark the paths of particles of matter charged with negative electricity."[40] But the danger with such reasoning is that there are other ways in which cathode rays could be explained. In fact, in Thomson's day there was a competing hypothesis, namely that of "some process in the aether."[41] I shall reflect later on how Thomson chose between these competing hypotheses, in order to argue that the electron hypothesis was the better explanation (7.1). For the moment, I want to note merely that the electron hypothesis was not the only potential explanation of the data. And even if it were, Thomson could not have excluded the possibility that another, preferable explanation existed.

The general principle should be clear. The mere fact that some hypothesis would explain the data, if it were true, does not entail that it is true. As Alan Musgrave writes, "any sane philosopher can think of countless cases where an explanation of some surprising fact is false. It is a surprising fact that fossils are found on mountain tops. One explanation is that Martians came and put them there to surprise us. But this explanation is not true."[42] What makes us think the Martian hypothesis is not true? It is the fact that we have a better explanation. So perhaps we can reformulate Peirce's abductive schema as a form of inference to the best explanation (IBE).

(1) The surprising fact, E, is observed.
(2) If H were true, E would be a matter of course.
(3) No available competing hypothesis would explain E as well as H does.
(4) Therefore H is true.

110 *Theism and Explanation*

Does this solve our problem? No it does not. I have already explored this line of argument when discussing scientific realism (3.1.2) and found it wanting. The problem with this schema is—as Musgrave writes—that it is merely "a souped up version of the fallacy of affirming the consequent."[43] It assumes that the best available explanation of some fact is the true one. And as van Fraassen has reminded us (3.1.1), this assumption is indefensible: the best explanation available may well be a false one. So the fact that it is the best explanation cannot warrant the conclusion that it is true.

Could it warrant a weaker conclusion, not about the truth of H, but about the rationality of accepting H? Our revised Peircean schema, which adds a premise (4), would take the following form.[44]

(1) The surprising fact, E, is observed.
(2) If H were true, E would be a matter of course.
(3) No available competing hypothesis would explain E as well as H does.
(4) It is reasonable to accept the best available potential explanation of any fact.
(5) Therefore it is reasonable to accept H.

As I suggested earlier (3.1.2), this argument *is* defensible, at least if we carefully define what we mean by "accept." Its key principle is premise (4), the claim that it is reasonable to accept the best available explanation of any fact. This is not defeated by the observation that the best available explanation may turn out to be false. For it may be reasonable to accept a falsehood, provided (of course) that one does not know it is false. Many late medieval Europeans accepted the geocentric view of the universe put forward by Ptolemy (ca. AD 100–170). Does the fact that Ptolemy's cosmology was false make this an irrational choice? No, it does not. For until the work of Nicolaus Copernicus (1473–1543), Ptolemy's cosmology *was* the best available explanation of the movements of the heavenly bodies.[45] Indeed before the arrival of the Copernican hypothesis, it may have been irrational to accept any other explanation of the movement of the heavens.

6.2.2 The Best Explanation

If we adopt my revised Peircean schema, then a key question is: By what criteria do we judge H to be the best explanation of E? It is important to note that a parallel question may be asked if H is the only explanation on offer. For even if it has no rivals, we still want H to possess those features by which we might judge it to be the best explanation, if it had competitors. In Musgrave's words, we would like H to be a "satisfactory" explanation of E.[46] This is an important point for the evaluation of proposed theistic explanations, for it means they do not win by default. If the only proposed explanation on offer is a bad one, it would be better to admit that we have no (satisfactory) explanation at all.[47]

What if the proposed theistic explanation were the only *possible* explanation of some fact? What if the fact in question were naturally inexplicable, not merely (contingently) unexplained? In these circumstances, would the proposed theistic explanation not win by default, even if it did not appear to be a very good explanation? Well, we would first have to be satisfied that the fact in question *had* an explanation, that is to say, "a sufficient reason why it is thus and not otherwise."[48] For it may turn out to be a "brute fact," one lacking an explanation (4.3.2.2) and it would be better to accept this than adopt what would be an unsatisfactory explanation. And how could we know that the proposed theistic explanation *was* the only possible (not merely the only available) explanation of the fact in question? We are rarely, if ever, in this situation. And if we cannot be certain there is no alternative, and the proposed theistic explanation was less than satisfactory, we would always be justified in seeking an alternative.

If this line of argument is correct, then I can further refine Peirce's schema, by rewording premises (2) and (4).

(1) The surprising fact, E, is observed.
(2) H would be a satisfactory explanation of E.
(3) No available competing hypothesis would E as well as H does.
(4) It is reasonable to accept the best available potential explanation of any fact, provided that explanation is a satisfactory one.
(5) Therefore it is reasonable to accept H.

But this merely brings me back to my initial question: By what criteria do we judge H to be the best explanation—or a satisfactory explanation—of E? Given that H is a potential explanation of E, what other features should it possess to make it worthy of our acceptance?

It is tempting at this point to offer a "justificationist" answer to this question (2.1.3.1), similar to that favoured by Swinburne, with his appeal to confirmation theory. If a true explanation is what we want, then surely the "best" explanation is simply that which is most probably true. So we would be justified in accepting a potential explanation H if

$$Pr(H|E \& K) > 0.5$$

and there exists no competing hypothesis whose probability given E and K is higher. If we adopt this solution, we can use Bayes's theorem to take us from the likelihood of E given H to the probability of H given E and K.

But as I argued earlier (2.1.3.2), this sets too high a standard. There are many instances of people accepting scientific theories even though their posterior probability has not yet been shown to be greater than 0.5. And

112 *Theism and Explanation*

they seemed to be acting rationally in doing so. So my preferred answer to this question is the explanationist one. According to the explanationist, we may be acting rationally in accepting a theory even if we do not have sufficient evidence to demonstrate that it is probably true. What we should require of such a theory is that it display, to a greater degree that any competitor, certain explanatory virtues. It is true that it may be impossible to quantify such judgements. (Hence the attraction of Bayesian formulas.) And there may exist no algorithm, no decision procedure that will ensure that our judgements are correct. As Alan Musgrave remarks, in choosing one theory over another "two scientists may make their choices in different ways" and yet in doing so both of them might be acting rationally.[49] But something like the explanationist view does seem to underlie our best scientific practice.

6.2.3 Explanatory Virtues

If we adopt the explanationist view, then two questions arise. The first is: What features of theories count as explanatory virtues? The second is: Why do we regard these features as virtues, or *desiderata*? Let me begin with the first of these questions. In assessing the comparative merit of scientific theories, scientists and philosophers commonly refer to qualities such as explanatory power, simplicity, economy, precision, informativeness, and elegance. The problem here is that each of these qualities is notoriously difficult to define, there exists no exhaustive list, and it is far from clear just how they are supposed to function.

Let me begin with the last point, namely, how such virtues are supposed to function. William Lycan distinguishes three roles that explanatory virtues may be thought to play. They may be thought of as purely descriptive, as an account of how scientists in particular *actually choose* theories. Or they may be thought of as normative, as accounts of how we *would* choose theories, if we were acting rationally. Or they may be regarded as *practical suggestions*, part of what Alvin Goodman calls a "doxastic decision procedure."[50] In what follows, I shall be taking them primarily as normative, as criteria which distinguish justified from unjustified explanatory claims, although insofar as they can be applied to real cases, they also form part of a decision procedure, showing how we could make such choices.

Why are these features *desiderata*? What makes them explanatory virtues? I don't think I have a satisfactory answer to this question, but then I'm not sure if anyone else does, either. I began by asking what would give us sufficient reason to accept a potential explanation as the actual one. And my reply was that we have reason to accept such a hypothesis if it is the best explanation on offer. If it has no competitors, then we have reason to accept it if it possesses, to some acceptable degree, those qualities by which we might judge it to be the best, if it had competitors. I have just argued (6.2.1) that such a policy can be defended against van Fraassen's objections (3.1.1). But I have not yet produced any positive arguments in its favour. Can our use of this policy of theory choice be justified?

William Lycan argues—rightly, it seems to me—that we cannot justify such a policy. We cannot justify it precisely because its principles are fundamental. They are the principles by which we justify, which cannot be justified in turn. Lycan repeatedly cites Jeremy Bentham's principle in this context, namely "that which is used to prove everything else . . . cannot itself be proved."[51] If we look at instances of theory-choice that we judge, intuitively, to be rational, we discover that these are the kinds of principles they employ.[52] So we have reason to think that this is what it means to act rationally. End of story. For as Lycan writes, "rationality is a primitive term used to evaluate epistemic acts; particular principles are seen to "tend toward truth," because the beliefs they produce are rational, not the other way around."[53]

But while we cannot offer an epistemic justification of these principles, we can offer an explanation of why it is that we employ them. Lycan's explanation is a broadly evolutionary one, which appeals to the usefulness of such a procedure.

> Crudely, the idea is . . . that it *is* a good thing in cost-benefit terms, that we choose theories on the basis of simplicity and the other explanatory virtues. Specifically, these methods of theory choice are the ones that a wise and benevolent Mother Nature would have given us, . . . because our having these methods rather than others has survival (and welfare) advantage.[54]

Once again, to say this is not to argue that such principles are truth-conducive because they are useful.[55] Rather, it is to explain *why* we regard such principles as truth-conducive. In this context, Lycan argues, such an explanation is the best we can do.

Does it matter if you are not convinced by Lycan's arguments? Probably not. For I could also approach this matter in an entirely pragmatic manner, by referring to the bare fact that these are the criteria we employ. As Lycan notes, these are the principles that underlie what we regard, intuitively, as our best scientific practice. As a matter of fact, we prefer theories that have a high degree of testability, and are simple, ontologically economical, and informative. There are various reasons that can be given for our having this preference, but the preference itself is not in doubt. So all I need do is to appeal to this widely-held view, which is also that adopted by at least some theistic philosophers. For while not all theists present their arguments for the existence of God as "inference to the best explanation" arguments, there are some who do. And those who do—thinkers such as

Stephen Meyer, Arthur Peacocke, and Michael Banner—appeal to explanatory virtues that closely resemble those I am employing here. Even Richard Swinburne, who does not appeal to "best explanation" principles, argues that the theistic hypothesis is a theory of great simplicity and scope, and that this represents evidence in its favour (6.1.2.2). My question is: Could such philosophers be right? What chance is there that a theistic explanation could prove to be not merely a *potential* explanation, but the *best* (or at least a *satisfactory*) explanation of some fact about the world? That's the question for my final chapter.

7 Successful Theistic Explanations

"That Accounts for a Good Deal," said Eeyore gloomily.
"It Explains Everything. No Wonder."

A. A. Milne

Once again, let me begin by summarising my argument. There exists a bare, theoretical possibility that appeal to the action of God might constitute a potential explanation of some fact. However, such an explanation cannot merely invoke the existence of a divine agent. The theist would need to posit a particular divine intention and to show that the fact in question was the best way in which that intention could have been realised. This "optimality condition," as I called it in Chapter 5, sets the bar very high. It may be that if it were consistently applied (as it rarely is), it would disqualify most if not all proposed theistic explanations. On close examination, they may turn out to be not even *potential* explanations of the facts in question.

However, this is not something I can demonstrate here, for it would require a case-by-case analysis of the proposed theistic explanations on offer. So for the sake of the argument, let's give the theist the benefit of the doubt. Let's assume that the theist has satisfied the optimality condition, and has shown her account of divine action to be a *potential* explanation of some fact. What chance is there that it could be regarded as the *actual* explanation (2.1.2)? In other words, are we likely ever to encounter a successful theistic explanation, one that would warrant our acceptance?

In Chapter 6, I set out how this question should be answered. We should ask if a theistic explanation could ever be regarded as the *best explanation* of some observable fact. And I have also suggested how we might make this judgement: by assessing the proposed explanation against some list of explanatory virtues. The virtues are best thought of as *desiderata* rather than (jointly) necessary conditions: we need not demand of an explanation that it display all of these virtues.[1] And any theory choice will have to balance these various *desiderata* against each other, for they can come into conflict. As William Lycan writes, "our preference for any one of the [explanatory] virtues always comes qualified by 'other things being equal,' and the 'other things' are the respective degrees of the other virtues."[2] Unfortunately, there does not seem to be any algorithm that would guarantee a correct balance in any particular case. (Once again, one can see why people are attracted by the apparent precision of the alternative, Bayesian approach.) But the lack of a clear decision procedure does not count against

116 *Theism and Explanation*

the insight that this is how we actually choose theories. Nor does it show that we are acting irrationally in doing so.

Since there exists no definite or exhaustive list of explanatory virtues, we are forced to choose which we shall adopt. Here is my choice. A potential explanation of some fact can be regarded as its best explanation if it possesses the following features. Our preferred theory will have a high degree of testability; indeed, it will have survived independent tests. It will posit mechanisms that are at least analogous to those with which we are already familiar, and will form part of a previously successful research tradition. It will also be simple, ontologically economical, and informative. There is nothing particularly authoritative about this list. The features it names are closely related, and it may be that with a bit of reworking the number could be reduced to three or four. And more *desiderata* could perhaps be added. The fecundity of a theory—its ability to suggest new lines of research—would be one obvious addition. But one has to stop somewhere. I have chosen this particular set of virtues for reasons of convenience, and because most lists of explanatory virtues will include *desiderata* that include or at least resemble those given here. If a proposed theistic explanation were to rate poorly, when measured against these criteria, this would be a sufficient reason to seek a natural alternative.

7.1 TESTABILITY

My first *desideratum* in a hypothesis worthy of our acceptance is that it should be testable. Indeed many philosophers and scientists have regarded testability as the distinguishing mark of the sciences (and a lack of testability as the mark of a pseudo-science). In this sense, they regard testability as a necessary condition of at least a *scientific* explanation. For Carl Hempel, for instance, the "methodological unity of the sciences" consists in precisely this: that their theories are testable.

> Notwithstanding many differences in their techniques of investigation, all branches of empirical science test and support their statements in basically the same manner, namely, by deriving from them implications that can be checked intersubjectively and by performing for those implications the appropriate experimental or observational tests.[3]

Of course, testability, by itself, does not take us very far. Many theories remain testable that are now entirely discredited; indeed they were discredited precisely because they were testable (and have failed the test). As Frank Cioffi writes, "the propensity to melancholy of those born under Saturn" or "the immunity to appendicitis of people ignorant of the vermiform appendix" are both eminently testable hypotheses.[4] But they are not for that reason alone any more worthy of our acceptance. To be worthy of our acceptance, a theory should have *survived* a process of testing. To the extent that a hypothesis has survived (independent) tests, I shall speak of it as having been *corroborated*. Nonetheless, a hypothesis cannot be corroborated unless it *is* testable, so the question of testability is still a critical one.

A hypothesis is independently testable if we can use it to make predictions about facts *other than* those it purports to explain, that is to say, about different kinds of phenomena. (Here's an example from J. J. Thomson's work. "If [cathode rays] are [as posited] negatively charged particles, then when they enter an enclosure they ought to carry into it a charge of negative electricity."[5]) And if we are dealing with competing potential explanations, we should be able to make predictions that discriminate between them, that would turn out to be true given our favoured hypothesis, but not true given the alternative.

The last point is an important one. If a hypothesis is to be testable, there needs to be some chance that the prediction it makes will turn out to be false. The hypothesis must, in other words, have some degree of empirical content (3.2.3): there needs to be at least one possible state of affairs that it excludes.[6] Ideally, there will be more than one. Indeed, the greater the degree of empirical content, the better. For it is the empirical content of a hypothesis that determines its degree of testability.

7.1.1 Are Proposed Theistic Explanations Testable?

Are theistic hypotheses testable in this sense? Well, it depends on how they are formulated. I have argued that if a proposed theistic explanation is to have any significant degree of empirical content, it is not sufficient that it attribute some event or state of affairs to a divine agent (3.2.3). For if God exists, then any actual event or state of affairs is attributable to him. God is, in this respect, analogous to the poltergeist who is responsible for whatever occurs in the room. But I have also argued that a theistic hypothesis need not suffer from this defect. It can be given empirical content by being formulated as an intentional explanation, one that specifies *just why* God is supposed to have willed the fact in question. We can then use the rationality principle that lies at the heart of all intentional explanations to make predictions about how such a being would act to achieve the posited goal.

What, then, would a theist need to do in order to show that her proposed explanation has been corroborated? Let's begin with what she should *not* do. She should not treat theism as a single hypothesis. For what we might call the theistic hypothesis—let's say "there exists a God, who created the world"—is a most inadequate explanation. It has little empirical content, insofar as it fails to single out the particular facts to be explained. What the theist needs, and what she must seek to corroborate, is a hypothesis of the form "there is a God who wills G," where G is a posited divine goal. So if the theist wishes to show that her proposed explanation is testable, she must do more than show that explanations appealing to a divine agent can cover a wide range of events. She must show that this *particular* proposed explanation can cover a wide range of events.

Let me illustrate this point with an example given earlier (4.1.2). At least one prominent theist has suggested that the Indian Ocean tsunami of 2004 occurred because God was angry about the neglect of his commandments, a neglect to which the widespread sexual immorality of our age bears witness. There are many things one might say about such a proposed explanation. But the question I wish to ask here is: Could this proposed explanation be corroborated? To answer this question in the affirmative, it would not suffice to show that other events can be explained by reference to divine action. That might indicate the scope of what I shall call the theistic research tradition (7.3), but it says nothing about the corroboration of this *particular* proposed explanation. To corroborate this particular explanation, you would have to show that other events can be explained by positing a God who is angry about sexual immorality. For this is the specific explanatory claim that is being tested here.

Could this be done? I have no idea, since I know of no theists who have sought to corroborate their proposed explanations in this way. And in my experience, it is rare for a proposed theistic explanation to be expressed in a form that *is* independently testable. I have suggested that Richard Swinburne's account of theistic explanations is, perhaps, the best available. But even Swinburne's proposed explanations lack empirical content, since they lack what I shall call *intentional specificity*. They fail to spell out just *why* God would do what he is alleged to have done. Throughout his work, Swinburne argues that God is not only able to create a world such as ours, but he has "good reason to choose to do so."[7] But he also admits that "God has reason to make many other things," so that we cannot "be certain" that God would make this world.[8] So apparently there exist a range of possible divine intentions, only some of which would have led God to create the world we live in. But this is not particularly helpful. It is akin to answering the question "Why did Sally go to the doctor?" with "Being a human being, prone to illness, she would have had reason to go to the doctor, although she would have had reason not to go to the doctor as well." Well, this may well be true, but it is not very informative. What the question is asking for is the particular reason she had.

Let me make the point another way. As I have argued throughout this study, a proposed theistic explanation (H) will be potential explanation only if it satisfies the second line of Peirce's abductive schema (2.1.2). I shall argue later that an intentional explanation will demonstrate this by way of a practical syllogism (Appendix 2.1). When the agent in question is a divine agent—one who is omnipotent, omniscient, and morally perfect—the syllogism will take the following form, where E represents the fact to be explained and G the posited divine purpose.

(1) There exists a divine agent with goal G.
(2) E is the best means of achieving G.
(3) A divine agent will always choose the best means of achieving G.
(4) Therefore the divine agent will do E.

Swinburne does want to argue that if the theistic hypothesis H were true, E would be what we would expect to observe. More formally, he wishes to argue that

Pr(E|H) > Pr(E|H).

But his argument in support of this conclusion amounts to little more than the following.

(1) There exists a divine agent with expected goals $G_1 \ldots G_5$.
(2) One of $G_1 \ldots G_5$ would lead God to produce E.
(3) Therefore E.

This may be true, but this doesn't tell us very much. And it is not independently testable.

Why not? Well, there are two elements missing from Swinburne's reasoning, corresponding to the two premises of the argument I have attributed to him. The first is a specification of the *particular* goal (G) that God is meant to be pursuing here. (This is what I mean by a lack of intentional specificity.) It is only when you have specified the divine intention in question that we can test your explanation, by asking what else would follow if God did indeed have this intention. And as we have seen (3.2.3), it will not do merely to substitute the *explanandum* for the posited goal (substituting E for G). As we have already seen, this would be a spurious kind of explanation, seriously lacking in empirical content.

The second feature that Swinburne's proposed explanations lack is a demonstration that pursuing goal G would lead God to bring about E. In the absence of laws of divine behaviour—in the absence of laws of intentional behaviour generally—I have suggested that what we should employ here is the rationality principle (5.2). We need to show that E represents the best way of bringing about goal G. But Swinburne's proposed explanations make no reference to either behavioural laws or the rationality principle. As a result, they lack a meaningful constraint. He may be right to suggest that this is how God would act, given these posited goals, but he gives us no reasoning that would support his conclusion.

7.1.2 Prediction and Retrodiction

I have spoken of a hypothesis being corroborated by successful predictions. But the term "prediction" is ambiguous. In its strict sense, it refers to the deduction of hitherto unobserved facts. When Albert Michelson and Edward Morley set up their famous experiment in 1887, they did not yet know what its outcome would be. All they knew is that if there were a luminiferous aether, you would expect a difference in the speed of light when measured parallel to and at right angles to the movement of the earth through the aether. Their failure to observe this difference constituted strong evidence against the theory. But the term "prediction" is sometimes used in a looser sense. We have seen that to test his theory of the electron, J. J. Thomson "predicted" that if cathode rays were negatively charged particles, they would carry their charge into an enclosure. But he already knew the outcome of the experiment that tested the prediction, which had been performed in 1895 by Jean Perrin.[9]

The Popperian view. The question that arises here is: Do we need successful "predictions" in the strict sense of that word? That is to say, is it necessary that the confirming observation should occur only *after* the formulation of our hypothesis? Could a theory be corroborated by facts that are already known? A strictly Popperian view of testability denies this; it insists that the facts that corroborate a theory must be previously unknown. For Popper, what counts is a *severe test*, and a severe test of a theory is one whose outcome is unlikely to be observed, given background knowledge alone.[10] A theory is corroborated insofar as it has passed severe tests. But if the outcome of the test is already part of our background knowledge, then a "prediction" of that outcome can hardly constitute a severe test.

The problem with the Popperian view is one at which I have already hinted. It is simply too demanding, given actual scientific practice. As John Worrall points out, the facts concerning the perihelion of Mercury—the rate at which its elliptical orbit around the sun rotates—were known well in advance of Einstein's theory of general relativity. (The apparent anomaly here, on a Newtonian view, had been noted as early as 1859.) But the fact that Einstein's physics could explain this movement while Newton's could not has generally been taken as evidence in support of general relativity.[11] On a Popperian view, this conclusion would be illegitimate.[12]

In addition to this, there appear to be good theoretical reasons to allow a theory to be corroborated by known facts. After all, it could be argued, what matters when we are testing a theory is that its consequences are true.

> If the evidence shows that some consequence of a theory is true, then this cannot depend on whether the evidence came to be known before the theory was proposed or afterwards. Such historical considerations, interesting as they may be, ought not to affect questions of confirmation or evidential support.[13]

So on logical grounds alone, it would seem reasonable to allow a theory to be corroborated by facts that are already known.

But does this mean that *just any* known fact could corroborate a theory, given that it is an observed consequence of that theory? This view—the idea that any positive case of a hypothesis would corroborate it[14]—is sometimes referred to as "Nicod's criterion" (named after the logician Jean George Pierre Nicod [1893–1924]). But if Popper's criterion is too restrictive, Nicod's criterion, without further qualification, is too permissive. Firstly, it would allow corroboration by observed facts that differ from one another in ways that are irrelevant to the hypothesis being tested.[15] Secondly, it would allow a hypothesis to be corroborated by citing further instances of the same phenomenon we are seeking to explain. And thirdly, it leads to Carl Hempel's notorious "raven paradox."[16] So this criterion needs to be tightened up a little.

A heuristic account. There are a number of ways in which one might tighten up Nicod's criterion. The first is John Worrall's "heuristic view" of corroboration: the idea that the facts that are considered to corroborate a theory should not be those that were used to construct it.[17] There is much to be said for this view, which would at least help to eliminate the accumulation of irrelevant instances. A theory cannot be corroborated by citing further instances of the phenomena of the type it was devised to explain; it can be corroborated only by citing *other kinds* of facts. But this view, too, faces difficulties. The first is that of deciding which facts *were* used in the construction of a theory, which is by no means as simple a task as it might appear.[18] And the heuristic view does not avoid the raven paradox,[19] which Popper's original view has the virtue of solving. (If background knowledge already "predicts" that my yellow cup is a non-black non-raven, then observing the cup cannot count as a severe test of the theory that "all ravens are black."[20])

An historical account. There is, however, a second way of tightening up Nicod's criterion, namely by taking into account competing theories. I will call this an "historical" (as opposed to purely logical) account of corroboration. When our background knowledge includes another potential explanation of the fact in question, then our hypothesis can be corroborated if it is able to "predict" some fact that cannot be explained by, or that apparently falsifies, its predecessor.[21] Whether that fact is known or unknown is irrelevant.

What if the theory we wish to test has no predecessor? In particular, what if it is the only hypothesis on offer, with regard to a particular fact? As we have seen (4.3.2), proposed theistic explanations are often like this. When Richard Swinburne argues that the theistic hypothesis would explain the very existence of laws of nature,[22] he is claiming to explain a fact which— as Elliot Sober notes—"no other hypothesis really engages as a problem. This is an instance of inference to the 'best' explanation only in the Pickwickian sense that just one explanation has been suggested."[23] Assuming that this proposed theistic explanation is a potential explanation, could it be corroborated by "predicting" some fact we already know?

In advocating an historical view of confirmation, Alan Musgrave argues that it could. Even a solitary hypothesis, he insists, could be corroborated by reference to known facts. One can still think of a theory as being tested against a competitor, except that in this case the competitor is "the empty or tautologous theory."[24] In these circumstances, Musgrave argues, "the first testable theory in any field will be confirmed by all the phenomena which it explains (whether or not they were known in advance)."[25] If one accepts this view, then a theistic explanation that has no competitor would be corroborated by a consilience of explanatory successes, even in the absence of successful predictions (in the sense of predictions of hitherto unknown facts). And if it has competitors, it could be corroborated by its ability to explain some known fact which they are unable to explain.[26]

This solution seems to me a good one. Indeed I shall refer to a similar suggestion shortly (7.1.3), when discussing the "null hypothesis." It is not clear to what extent, if at all, it avoids the raven paradox, at least in the case of a solitary hypothesis. But that's a general problem I cannot hope to resolve here.[27] And an historical approach—one that measures corroboration against competing theories—has other advantages. It explains, for instance, why lists of explanatory virtues often include "explanatory power." There is no doubt that we do value theories of broad scope, which "make sense of what would otherwise be a dissociated collection of facts."[28] But the fact that a theory may have a narrow scope—in the sense that it purports to explain only a small range of phenomena—should not count against it. Narrowness of scope is not necessarily an explanatory vice. What might make us favour a theory is its capacity to explain facts that its competitor *should* be able to explain, but cannot. In this sense, and in this sense alone, is explanatory power a suitable criterion of theory choice.

At what conclusion, then, have I arrived? Should we demand of proposed theistic explanations that they predict in the strict sense, allowing us to deduce facts that had been hitherto unobserved? No, we should not. It seems that a proposed theistic explanation, like any other kind of proposed explanation, could be corroborated by facts that are already known. But it must be the *actual* theistic hypothesis that is being corroborated, in all its intentional specificity, not some very general statement about divine action. And in this respect most proposed theistic explanations fall short; they do not even attempt to meet the required standard.

7.1.3 The Solitary Potential Explanation

It is tempting to leave the issue of testability there. But one philosopher of science, Elliot Sober, has vigorously rejected the idea that a solitary hypothesis can be tested. Sober argues against at least one class of proposed theistic explanations on the grounds that the explanations in question have no

Successful Theistic Explanations 123

competitors. This means, he argues, that they are untestable. And if they are untestable, then they fail to meet the standards of at least a scientific explanation. If this were true, it would be a conclusion which the atheist would welcome. On the assumption that testability is at least a highly desirable feature of any theory (scientific or otherwise), Sober's argument would practically eliminate a whole class of proposed theistic explanations at a single stroke. But is Sober correct?

Elliot Sober's argument. As we have seen (5.1.1), Sober argues that an explanation that makes merely probable predictions can be tested only over against its competitors. If O is an observation, and H_1 is a hypothesis, then we can draw no conclusion from the mere fact that the likelihood of O given H is low. To reject H_1, Sober argues, we need an alternative, H_2, which would render the outcome more likely. We need to be able to show that

$$Pr(O|H_2) > Pr(O|H_1).$$

Why is this? It is, as Sober writes, because there is no probabilistic equivalent of *modus tollens*.[29] There is no valid argument which runs:

(1) If H were true, O would be highly improbable.
(2) But O.
(3) Therefore H is not true.

It is easy to see why, for to adopt this line of argument would lead to unacceptable consequences. If you win the national lottery, this is a highly improbable outcome, given that the lottery was fair and that you bought just one ticket. But it does not cast doubt on the hypothesis that the lottery was fair. And if we have a line which is 1000 miles long, onto which we drop a pin at random, the chance that it will fall just where it does is very small. But that does not cast doubt on the hypothesis that it was dropped at random.[30] It follows, Sober writes, that there is no "Law of Improbability that begins with the premise that Pr(O|H) is very low and concludes that H should be rejected."[31]

If Sober is correct, if probabilistic theories can only be tested comparatively, it would seem that a solitary proposed theistic explanation can receive short shrift. If there is no alternative against which to test it, then it cannot be tested. And if it cannot be tested, it lacks one of the most important *desiderata* of a satisfactory explanation. Sober illustrates this by referring to Swinburne's proposed theistic explanation of the existence of laws of nature. Whatever else may be said about this argument, Sober writes,

> it is not a *scientific* argument for the existence of God. Science is in the business of testing alternative hypotheses against each other, where these alternatives make different predictions. In the present example,

the theistic hypothesis allegedly predicts that the universe will contain laws. But what is the competing hypothesis and what does it predict? It might be thought that if there were no God, then there probably wouldn't be laws of nature. I don't know how a probability can be assigned in this case.[32]

If this is correct, it is an important conclusion. I have argued in the previous section that even a solitary potential explanation can be corroborated, if it predicts facts other than the fact to be explained, and that for this purpose it can "predict" facts that are already known. But Sober's argument suggests that this is impossible, that such a test requires an alternative potential explanation, so that we can compare the likelihood of what we observe on the two hypotheses. So is Sober right? And if he is, what are the implications for proposed theistic explanations?

A response to Sober. My first response is to note that the theistic explanations in which I am interested are not probabilistic, in the sense of assigning a certain probability to the *explanandum*. They are a species of intentional explanation and intentional explanations are best thought of as deductive arguments (2.1.4). We may have varying degrees of confidence about the truth of their premises. Those premises may enjoy only a moderate degree of evidential support, so that the most we can say is that they are probably true. It follows that we may not be confident that our argument has explanatory force (5.5). But this does not mean it is a probabilistic argument. If the premises of our deductive argument are true, the conclusion cannot be false; its probability is 1.0.[33]

But not everyone who offers a theistic explanation takes this view. In particular, Richard Swinburne, whose argument Sober is attacking, regards theistic explanations as probabilistic. So let's grant Sober this assumption, for the sake of the argument, and see what follows. One response is that even if a probabilistic theistic account *is* the only proposed explanation on offer, it may be possible to test one or more of its elements comparatively. One can do so by choosing some fact about the world and inventing a rival, natural hypothesis, to see which of these hypotheses—the theistic one and its secular rival—would render this fact more likely. Paul Draper's restatement of the evidential argument from evil illustrates this procedure. What Draper does is to focus on the distribution of pleasure and pain in the world, and offer a natural explanation of that phenomenon. He calls this the hypothesis of indifference:

> (HI) Neither the nature nor the condition of sentient beings on earth is the result of benevolent or malevolent actions performed by non-human persons.[34]

He then challenges the theist to come up with an alternative, theistic account that would render these facts more likely or (if you prefer) less surprising.

Another possible response would be to point out, as I did in the previous section, that even a solitary theistic explanation can be tested by invoking what statisticians call the "null hypothesis." What do I mean? If an experimenter is wanting to test the efficacy of a drug, then the null hypothesis is that there will be no statistically significant difference in outcome between a test group and a control group. More precisely, the null hypothesis predicts that any differences between the two groups will be attributable to chance.

In this situation, there is only one hypothesis being tested—that the drug will be effective. Can we say that it is being tested comparatively? In a certain sense, yes. The hypothesis will be corroborated to the extent that the null hypothesis is disproved. And it will be disproved to the extent that the result is significantly more likely to have occurred on the hypothesis under test than by chance. If the result is represented as E, the hypothesis under test as H, and the null hypothesis as C, then the hypothesis is corroborated if (to some significant degree)

$$Pr(E|H) > Pr(E|C).$$

How can this observation be applied to a proposed theistic explanation? Well, where a rival proposed explanation does exist—say, Darwin's theory as opposed to the creationist account—then we can ask which of these would render a range of observations more likely. We can test the theistic hypothesis comparatively, in precisely Sober's sense. But where there is no rival potential explanation—where the proposed theistic explanation is the only one on offer—one could argue that there does exist a default null hypothesis over against which it can be tested. It is the claim that the fact in question occurred by chance.[35]

But while this seems a legitimate argument, it is not my preferred response. My preferred response is simply to deny Sober's conclusion. If corroboration by the passing of independent tests is a *desideratum* in any explanation, then a repeated failure to pass such tests will count against the explanation in question. Sober's point is that no one failure would *falsify* such an explanation. If the prediction it makes is merely probable, then the failure of a prediction does not show that the hypothesis is false. This is surely true. But it need not mean that no solitary proposed explanation is testable. If we can use it to predict facts other than that which it was introduced to explain, then it is testable. And even if repeated failures to pass such tests do not, strictly speaking, falsify the theory, they should at least arouse our suspicions. I have argued (2.1.3.2) that we do not need to demonstrate that an explanation is true in order to have reason to accept it. But by the same token we do not need to prove that an explanation is false in order to have reason to reject it, or at least to seek an alternative. If a proposed explanation is not corroborated by independent tests, it does not necessarily follow that it is false. (To this extent, Sober is correct.) But it does follow that we have less reason to regard it as a good explanation, one we are entitled to accept.

7.2 BACKGROUND KNOWLEDGE

A second *desideratum* for any explanation has to do with its relationship to our background knowledge. What I wish to argue is that consistency with background knowledge is an explanatory virtue, one that should contribute to our willingness to accept a proposed explanation. And proposed theistic explanations are no exception to this rule. They will score poorly when measured against this criterion, precisely because the agent they posit is so dissimilar to any other with which we are familiar.

But first, what do I mean by "background knowledge"? Background knowledge is best thought of as those facts of which we are aware independently of the explanation in question. More precisely, it consists of all the propositions we have reason to regard as true other than the proposed *explanans*. But we should also exclude from background knowledge the fact we are trying to explain, for to appeal to the *explanandum* in support of the *explanans* is to ask about the latter's explanatory force. It is to ask whether the hypothesis is, in fact, a potential explanation of the fact to be explained. And that is a prior question to the one I am asking here, which I dealt with in Chapter 6. The point I am making here is this: When the mechanisms posited by potential explanation are consistent with what we already know about the world, this can (and should) contribute to our willingness to accept it. And when they are not consistent with what we already know about the world, this gives us a reason to treat it with suspicion.

Background knowledge, so defined, includes successful theories. The point I am making here is that we should (other things being equal) prefer those proposed explanations that are consistent with what we already know about the world. And this means they are consistent not only with observable facts, but also with our best existing theories. One could apparently explain the operation of electric light bulbs (and even candles) by proposing that they "suck dark" rather than "emit light."

> Take for example, the dark suckers in the room where you are. There is less dark right next to them than there is elsewhere. The larger the dark sucker, the greater its capacity to suck dark. Dark suckers in a parking lot have much greater capacity than the ones in this room. As with all things, dark suckers don't last forever. Once they are full of dark, they can no longer suck. This is proven by the black spot on a full dark sucker. A candle is a primitive dark sucker. A new candle has a white wick. You will notice that after the first use, the wick turns black, representing the dark which has been sucked into it. If you hold a pencil next to the wick on an operating candle, the tip will turn black, because it got in the way of the dark flowing into the candle. Unfortunately, these dark suckers have a very limited range. There are also portable dark suckers. The bulbs in these units can't handle all of the dark by themselves, and must be aided by a dark storage unit. When the dark storage unit is full, it must be either emptied or replaced

before the portable dark sucker can operate again. If you break open one of these filled canisters, one will see that there is indeed a great quantity of stored dark on the inside.[36]

And so on. Intriguingly, this account of an outrageous proposed explanation—let's call it "Dark Sucker Theory" (DST)[37]—also includes facts that, at first sight, might appear to corroborate it. There are, of course, many facts that count against it. But one of these is that DST is so radically at variance with what we already know about the world.[38] This is already sufficient reason not to take it seriously.

"But DST," you might respond, "is nothing more than an internet joke." And that is true. So let me illustrate the importance of background knowledge with a well-known, real-life example.[39] When Darwin set out his theory of biological evolution, a major difficulty facing his theory was that we could not directly observe the process of natural selection. So a key question was: Do we know of any mechanism of this kind to which we can appeal, which would give natural selection the status of a *vera causa*, a "true cause"?[40] Darwin found such a mechanism in artificial selection, the process by which plant and animal breeders select favourable characteristics.[41] As it happens, Darwin was disappointed to see his theory rejected by the chief exponent of the *vera causa* doctrine, John Herschel.[42] But the point is that Darwin felt it was important to point to some mechanism, with which we were already familiar, which was analogous to the one he was positing.

To say we should prefer theories that are consistent with what we already know is not to embrace the view that explanation consists of "reduction to the familiar."[43] After all, much recent scientific explanation has been what we might call reduction to the *un*familiar, the principles and entities posited by both relativity theory and quantum physics being very strange indeed.[44] Rather, what I am advocating is the view that

> other things being equal, the explanations afforded by a theory are better explanations if the theory is familiar, that is, introduces mechanisms, entities, or concepts that are used in established explanations. The use of familiar models is not essential to explanation, but it helps.[45]

And if we must depart from what is familiar, we are safest to do so by way of a series of conservative steps, rather than by taking a grand leap into the dark. For as Quine and Ullian remark, "the longer the leap . . . the more serious an angular error in the direction."[46]

7.2.1 Theism and Background Knowledge

How would a theistic hypothesis rate, when assessed against this *desideratum*? The problem here is that the theistic hypothesis posits a mechanism—the action of a spiritual being within the material world—that is entirely unlike any other mechanism with which we are familiar. Not only does this mechanism lack analogy; it is also wholly mysterious. It is true that if you hold to some kind of substance dualism—if you believe that the human mind is a kind of immaterial substance—you might argue that there *does* exist an analogy to God's relationship to the world. It is the relationship of an immaterial mind to a material body. On this view, God's relationship to the world is no more or less mysterious than my relationship to my body. But this alleged analogy is a tenuous one. For we know that certain features of our bodies seem to be at least *closely related* to the workings of the mind. Even substance dualists attribute a particular role to the brain, which functions as the means by which body and soul can communicate. So even on a dualist view, the relationship of mind and body is not quite as mysterious as God's relationship to the world.

My argument at this point resembles that offered by J. L. Mackie against Swinburne's cosmological argument. Mackie concedes that "*if* there were a god with the traditional attributes and powers, he would be able and perhaps willing to create such a universe as this."[47] But he goes on to argue that

> we have to weigh in our scales the likelihood or unlikelihood *that* there is a god with these attributes and powers. And the key power . . . is that of fulfilling intentions *directly*, without any physical or causal mediation, without materials or instruments. There is nothing in our background knowledge that makes it comprehensible, let alone likely, that anything should have such a power. All our knowledge of intention-fulfilment is of *embodied* intentions being fulfilled *indirectly* by way of bodily changes and movements which are *causally* related to the intended result, and where the ability thus to fulfil intentions itself has a *causal history*, either of evolutionary development or of learning or of both.[48]

In setting out his argument. Mackie refers to the prior probability of the theistic hypothesis. But there is no need to do so. The same conclusion could be reached by arguing that the theistic hypothesis lacks an explanatory virtue, one that would contribute to its acceptance.

7.2.2 The Relevance of Background Knowledge

Swinburne, it should be noted, had already attempted to ward off this objection.[49] He did so by simply denying the relevance of background knowledge to an assessment of the theistic hypothesis. Swinburne concedes that in normal circumstances, the prior probability of a theory is a function of our background knowledge, as well as the theory's simplicity and scope. And a theory is consistent with our background knowledge "in so far as the kinds of entities and laws that it postulates are similar to those that probably (on our evidence) exist and operate in other fields."[50] I have already examined Swinburne's example of the poltergeist (3.2.2). He argues that in certain circumstances one could be justified in positing the existence of an unembodied agent, in this case a poltergeist. But the prior probability of this hypothesis will be diminished by the fact that such an agent is very different from the other agents with which we are familiar.[51] And one of these differences is precisely the fact that a poltergeist would be an unembodied agent.[52] So far, so good. Up to this point, Swinburne and Mackie are in agreement. But Swinburne also argues that the theistic hypothesis is an exception to this rule: in this case, he suggests, we do not need to take such considerations into account.

Why not? With regard to any theory, Swinburne argues that the significance of background knowledge decreases as the scope of our theories increases. "More and more of the observational evidence falls into the category of data that the theory needs to explain, rather than data that it takes for granted in explaining other things."[53] In the case of a theory of wide scope, we should not demand that the entities whose existence it posits resemble those that the theory is meant to explain. As Swinburne writes, "it is no objection to some theory of physics postulating fundamental particles and purporting thereby to explain the physical and thereby chemical behaviour of medium-sized objects that it postulates particles quite unlike those medium-sized objects."[54] But as a hypothesis that seeks to explain the very existence of universe, theism is a hypothesis of the widest possible scope.[55] It follows that there is no background knowledge, other than purely logical knowledge, with which it has to fit. The theist does not need to worry about the fact that his posited personal agent is so different from any other with which we are familiar.

This is a very odd argument. It is made still more puzzling by the revelation that Swinburne has *stipulated* what is to count as background knowledge. Within the framework of confirmation theory that Swinburne employs, the relevant distinction is not (as it is for me) between the *explanandum* and background knowledge, but between new evidence and background evidence.[56] And Swinburne argues that

> the division between new evidence [e] and background evidence [k] can be made where you like—often it is convenient to include all evidence derived from experience in *e*, and to regard *k* as being what is called in confirmation theory mere "tautological evidence," that is, in effect all our other irrelevant knowledge.[57]

Well, it may well be "convenient" to make the division in this way. (For one thing, it makes it easier to set aside considerations that might lower the prior probability of theism.) But given that we are apparently free to choose, is this the most natural way to divide the evidence?

No, it is not.[58] The key question here is: Which facts about the world fall within the scope of the proposed explanation? Those that do fall within the scope of the explanation constitute the relevant evidence (*e*); those that do not constitute background knowledge (k). As we have seen, Swinburne's argument tacitly concedes this point, since he justifies his position by arguing that the theistic hypothesis covers everything that exists (other than its own *explanans*). More precisely, he holds to the view that "the theist argues from all the phenomena of experience, not from a small range of them."[59] But is this true? Well, there is a sense in which the theistic hypothesis *could* cover all the phenomena of experience. For since *ex hypothesi* God is the cause of all that is, then if theism were true, any fact at all could be explained by reference to God. If God exists and if he is the cause of all that occurs, presumably he has some reason for acting as he does and the theist could (in principle) identify this reason. So it is true that, on the theistic hypothesis, the existence of God could explain everything. If we take p to represent any true proposition about the world, then the existence of God could explain not merely $p_1, p_2, p_3 \ldots p_n$, taken disjunctively. It could also explain the conjunction of all these true propositions.

Now if the theist *were* explaining the conjunction of all true propositions about the world, then what Swinburne says about background knowledge might be correct. But no theist ever does this, nor is it conceivable that any theist could. For even assuming that it makes sense to speak of "explaining everything"—that the world can be divided into discrete, independently existing states of affairs, waiting to be explained—we could never know the vast, conjunctive proposition that would describe everything. In practice, all the theist can do is to offer an explanation of *some particular fact* or relatively restricted set of facts about the world. And even if we restrict $p_1, p_2, p_3 \ldots p_n$ to all those propositions we *know* to be true, the theist does not argue from all these propositions either. What he does is to appeal to *particular facts* about the world in support of his hypothesis. So it is simply not true that: "the theist argues from all the phenomena of experience, not from a small range of them."[60]

Once we grasp this, we can see that it is always possible to distinguish between those facts about the world that the theist claims to be explaining (e) and those facts about the world that his proposed explanation takes for granted (k). It is, I have argued, the latter that constitute the relevant background knowledge. For instance, when arguing that the existence and action of God explains the existence of "a complex physical universe," the theist is not trying to explain why there exist embodied agents. Perhaps he thinks he can offer *another* theistic explanation, which explains this fact, too. But that explanation will posit a different divine intention—it will be a different explanation—and in so doing it will take the existence of the universe for granted.

In fact this is precisely what Swinburne does. He offers a series of reasons (not just one reason) why God would create a complex physical universe, morally free agents, morally embodied agents, animals, a beautiful universe, and so on.[61] For as he implicitly recognises, these are distinct facts about the world requiring distinct divine intentions. He may not specify just which intention lies behind each creative act (7.1.1), but he implicitly recognises that different intentions are required. And in explaining, for instance, the existence of animals, Swinburne takes for granted the existence of a universe. Only if we subsume all of these intentions under the catch-all category of "reasons God would have to do x"—a strategy I have already argued is unhelpful—would this appear to be one explanation.

In a word, Mackie is right. While positing the existence of an unembodied agent might be warranted, if that hypothesis possessed other explanatory virtues, the fact that it posits an otherwise unknown kind of mechanism counts against it. The theist may not neglect this fact.

7.3 PAST EXPLANATORY SUCCESS

There is another explanatory virtue that could be classed under background knowledge, but which is significant enough to be listed separately. It is the previous explanatory success (or lack of it) of the kind of hypothesis that is on offer. Some care is required here. I am not speaking of what we might call the "track record" of the *same* hypothesis. For given that a hypothesis can be corroborated by known facts (7.1.2), considerations of past explanatory success would come under the heading of corroboration. But hypotheses cannot be fully understood, nor should they be evaluated, in isolation from one another. Any particular hypothesis can be seen as part of a research programme or a research tradition, which unites a series of proposed explanations sharing certain common assumptions. And we can include under background knowledge the past successes or failures of the research programme to which our hypothesis belongs.

It is true that to speak of "research programmes" raises some difficult issues. For any particular classification of hypotheses into research programmes can be contested. What we may regard as distinct research programmes often overlap: they share common assumptions.[62] And within a single research programme there may exist fierce disputes about the assumptions being employed.[63] But I argued in Chapter 1 that we can distinguish the naturalistic research programme of the modern sciences—which proceeds as if there were no God—from the tradition of proposed theistic explanations. Insofar as they sometimes seek to offer mutually exclusive explanations of the same phenomena (4.3.3.2), these two programmes are in competition.

Not only are they in competition, but a comparison of their track records will count against theism. For the naturalistic research programme of the modern sciences has been stunningly successful since its inception in the seventeenth century. Again and again, it has shown that postulating the existence of a deity is not required in order to explain the phenomena. Sir Isaac Newton (1642–1727) still required God to fine-tune the mechanics of his solar system, but by the time of Pierre Simon de Laplace (1749–1827), the astronomer notoriously had no need of that hypothesis. Until 1859, it seemed that the diversity of living organisms could not be accounted for without reference to God, but Charles Darwin offered us a more successful, natural alternative.

In the face of such successes, many religious thinkers simply abandoned the natural world to the secular sciences. Shortly after reading Darwin's *Origin of Species*, the geologist Charles Lyell wrote in his diary: "It is not from enquiries in to the physical world, present or past, that we gain an insight into the spiritual; we may arrive at conclusions unwelcome to our speculations."[64] As Michael Bartholomew writes,

> it is a revealing comment. Before 1859 natural philosophers in Britain had confidently believed precisely the opposite. They were certain that enquiries into the physical world were bound to elicit clear insights into "the spiritual," insights so unambiguous that they could be used as a foundation for a defence of the Christian faith. In 1859 that foundation turned to dust, and Lyell's brief statement can stand as an emblem of his recognition of that disaster.[65]

Indeed, the "intelligent design" and creationist movements of today can be seen as, in part, a reaction to Lyell's counsel of despair.

One might argue that this history is just that, history. Past failure does not, strictly speaking, preclude future success. Who knows? We may yet require the theistic hypothesis. That is true. But it is also true that any proposed theistic explanation comes out of a stable whose horses have previously performed badly. A prudent punter will be reluctant to put money on its future success. From a Bayesian point of view, you might argue that the past failure of the tradition of theistic explanation lowers the prior probability of any proposed theistic hypothesis. But even from the explanationist perspective which I have chosen (2.1.3.2), you can argue that past failure counts against present acceptance. It establishes what one might describe as a defeasible presumption in favour of natural explanations.[66]

One recent writer, Richard Carrier, defends this view by offering an inductive argument for the scientist's presumption of naturalism. "Natural explanations," he writes, "have had a flawless track record: every time we get to the bottom of things, it is always a natural explanation that ends up being true."[67] We need not share Carrier's complacent view that the record of modern science has been "flawless." All we need note is that it has been successful, flaws and all. Belonging to a successful research tradition of this kind is an explanatory virtue. And it is a virtue that proposed theistic explanations clearly lack.

7.4 SIMPLICITY

What about the criterion of simplicity, to which I have already had reason to refer? A key issue here is that of definition. What makes a theory simple?

Swinburne adopts what we may call a "metaphysical" conception of simplicity.[68] The simplicity of a theory, he writes,

> is a matter of its postulating few (logically independent) entities, few properties of entities, few kinds of entities, few kinds of properties, properties more readily observable, few separate laws with few terms relating few variables, the simplest formulation of each law being mathematically simple.[69]

This is a very broad definition indeed, and its application to theism is problematic.[70] Is God really, as Swinburne argues, "the simplest kind of person there could be?"[71] As we have seen (3.3.1), there does exist a theistic doctrine of divine simplicity, which in some form or other Swinburne wishes to endorse.[72] But one could argue, with Cleanthes (and Plantinga),[73] that this doctrine is incompatible with the idea that God is a personal agent. And what about the doctrine of the Trinitarian nature of God? Is this compatible with the idea that God is "the simplest kind of person there is?"[74] Perhaps it is, but the theist at least has a case to answer here.

7.4.1 Auxiliary Hypotheses

Swinburne's criterion of simplicity is closely related to what I shall call "ontological economy," and which I shall discuss in a moment (7.5). I favour a rather different definition of simplicity, which is broadly Popperian in flavour and which is most clearly expressed in the work of Paul Thagard. Karl Popper offers what at first sight seems an idiosyncratic definition of simplicity. The simplicity of a theory, he suggests, is equivalent to its empirical content or degree of falsifiability.[75] Building on this foundation, Thagard argues that simplicity has to do with the number of auxiliary hypotheses that a theory requires in order to explain the fact in question. The fewer the auxiliary hypotheses, the simpler the theory.

Note how Thagard's conception of simplicity differs from Swinburne's. Thagard does not argue that one theory (T_1) should be preferred to another (T_2) simply because T_1 postulates the existence of fewer entities. In fact, he argues that we may prefer a theory that postulates more entities than its competitors if it has greater explanatory power or, in Thagard's terms, if it contributes to consilience.[76] The important fact—that which makes a theory simple in Thagard's sense—is that it contributes towards consilience "without making a host of assumptions with narrow application."[77]

At first sight, Thagard's conception of simplicity may seem different from Popper's, but in fact the two are closely related. For a theory that is preserved from refutation only with the aid of auxiliary hypotheses loses empirical content. It is, in Popper's terms, less falsifiable and to this extent more complex.[78] This account of simplicity, as developed by Thagard, seems more workable than Swinburne's conception, which requires us to count the number of entities or principles a theory employs. Any such count will

134 *Theism and Explanation*

inevitably be arbitrary, for the entities posited by a theory can be identified in different ways.

7.4.2 Van Inwagen's Defence

How would a proposed theistic explanation rate, when assessed against this view of simplicity? This is a difficult question to answer, since an account of divine action lacks the precision of a scientific theory (7.6) and it is hard to distinguish the core of such an account from its auxiliary hypotheses. But let me look at just one case where this distinction can be made, which I have adapted from an example given by Peter van Inwagen. I should begin by clarifying van Inwagen's position. He believes he does not need to show that theism is the best explanation (or even a potential explanation) of any fact about the world. He is apparently convinced, along with Alvin Plantinga, that belief in God can be a matter of warranted, undefeated, basic belief.[79] It follows, he thinks, that the theist requires no arguments in support of her belief in God. However, van Inwagen is countering the argument that theism is *not* the best explanation of what we observe, since there is a better explanation, namely the hypothesis of indifference. And the way in which van Inwagen develops his defence is by offering scenarios that function, in effect, as auxiliary hypotheses, bridging the gap between his theistic beliefs and the observable data.

As the reader will have guessed, van Inwagen's particular target is Paul Draper's evidential argument from evil. As we have seen (5.4.4 and 7.1.3), Draper argues that the distribution of pain and pleasure which we observe in the world (E) is more likely given what he calls the "hypothesis of indifference" (HI) than given theism (T). According to Draper's hypothesis of indifference, "neither the nature nor the condition of sentient beings on earth is the result of benevolent or malevolent actions performed by nonhuman persons."[80] So Draper's argument arrives at the conclusion that the likelihood of what we observe given the hypothesis of indifference is greater than the likelihood of what we observe given theism:

$Pr(E|HI) > Pr(E|T)$.

This would lend support to the hypothesis of indifference. How does van Inwagen counter this argument? Well, as we have already seen (5.4.3.1), he defends theism by expressing scepticism about the premises of Draper's argument. Van Inwagen's scepticism takes two forms.[81] I have already described his modal scepticism. But he also adopts what he calls a "moral scepticism," by which he means a scepticism about our capacity to judge the comparative moral value of states of affairs.

To lend force to his scepticism, van Inwagen offers a number of theistic scenarios that would account for the existence of evil. He is not suggesting that any of these is probably true. (He is not offering a theodicy, but merely a defence, to use a distinction much favoured by contemporary theistic philosophers.[82]) Rather, he is suggesting that "for all we know" such scenarios *could* be true. In doing this, he is hoping to counter the assessment of relative probability that forms the basis of Draper's evidential argument. Van Inwagen's "for all we know" scenarios are intended to show that we cannot safely make that judgement. The procedure here is parallel to that of the lawyer who offers a series of possible scenarios which would exonerate her client, not in order to suggest that any of them is true, but in order to suggest that he cannot safely be convicted.[83]

So far, so good.[84] But as van Inwagen recognises, many thinkers will be unwilling to accept the legitimacy of this strategy. How can he make it more plausible? He can do so, he argues, by offering a parallel argument,[85] which has to do with a hypothetical ancient Greek atomist. Such a person, he writes, might be faced with the objection that if air were made of tiny solid particles, as he asserts, then it "would behave like fine dust. It would eventually settle to the ground and become a mere dusty coating on the surface of the earth."[86] But, the objector continues, this does not happen. It apparently follows that air is probably not made of fine particles. The objection here is parallel to that of the atheist who argues that if theism were true, we would not expect to observe the distribution of pleasure and pain that actually exists. It follows, the atheist argues, that theism is probably not true.

How might the atomist respond? He might do so, van Inwagen argues, by offering a defence parallel to van Inwagen's own, that is to say, a scenario regarding atoms that is true "for all anyone knows."[87] Here's one. Atoms, he might suggest, are (for all we know) covered with invisible long flexible spikes, which keep them apart and prevent them falling to the ground. Since this (or any number of other possible scenarios) might be true, the objector is in no position to judge what would occur if the atomic hypothesis were correct. It follows that the atomist's belief is undefeated.

This is an interesting argument, in a number of ways. Van Inwagen's argument assumes that we already have reason to regard theism as true, irrespective of its explanatory force. As I have already noted, he rejects what we might call an "evidentialist" defence of Christian faith. But I shall suppose for a moment that this underlying assumption is wrong, that theism must prove itself as a hypothesis, having some explanatory force. It is not just atheists who believe this to be true; there are theistic philosophers, such as Richard Swinburne, who hold to an evidentialist view. The evidentialist assumption also underlies Paul Draper's argument, to which van Inwagen is responding.

So let's assume, for the sake of the argument, that the theist is offering his belief in God as an explanatory hypothesis. In these circumstances, he could offer a defence against Draper's evidential argument: a possible scenario that would account for the existence of evil. This would, as van Inwagen himself notes, function as an auxiliary hypothesis, allowing the theist to explain an apparent anomaly (the existence of evil).[88] But if the theist's defence resembled the atomist's spike hypothesis, its defects would be clear. The atomist apparently has no independent reason to believe in the existence of such spikes: his auxiliary hypothesis, as van Inwagen describes it, is entirely *ad hoc*. Yes, it might be true, but we have no independent reason to accept it.[89] *Pace* van Inwagen,[90] the fact that the spikes resemble the electromagnetic forces for which *we* have independent evidence is neither here nor there. The point is that van Inwagen's ancient atomist had no independent support for this auxiliary hypothesis. Even if his belief were true, in his situation he would have been acting irrationally in maintaining it. A hypothesis that could be saved from refutation only in this way lacks the virtue of simplicity. Unless it exhibits a range of other virtues, it would be unworthy of our acceptance.

7.5 ONTOLOGICAL ECONOMY

I outlined a moment ago Richard Swinburne's definition of "simplicity" (7.4). There exists an explanatory virtue which closely resembles his conception of simplicity, but I shall deal with it under a different heading, that of ontological economy. This resembles the classic principle of economy-in-explanation attributed to William of Ockham: *entia non sunt multiplicanda praeter necessitatem* (entities are not to be multiplied beyond necessity). But it is a little more specific, and avoids some of the difficulties inherent in Swinburne's view. It is most accurately described as a principle of "ontological type-economy," which suggests that we should not posit *new kinds* of entities without sufficient reason. Such a principle is not unrelated to the issue of background knowledge. When discussing background knowledge (7.2), I argued that we would have more reason to accept a hypothesis positing unobservable entities if we could point to familiar mechanisms that bore some analogy to it. My principle of ontological type-economy could be regarded as another way of expressing this idea. It suggests that we should not posit a hitherto unknown type of cause without sufficient reason.

Something akin to this principle appears to underlie the actualism of Charles Lyell's *Principles of Geology*[91]—the idea that "*no causes whatever* have from the earliest time to which we can look back, to the present, ever acted, but those *now acting*; and that they never acted with different degrees of energy from that which they now exert."[92] What inspired this principle? It was, certainly, a desire to posit only *verae causae* of the kind John Herschel had espoused,[93] that is to say, "causes which experience has shown to exist, and to be efficacious in producing similar phenomena."[94] But underlying this *vera causa* principle is a desire to avoid positing new kinds of entities when familiar ones will suffice. For Lyell argues that if we abandon this actualist principle, then we open the door to "the utmost license of conjecture in speculating on the causes of geological phenomena."[95] The implication of Lyell's position seems to be clear. It is better to posit even a vast number of "minute, but incessant mutations" of the kind with which we are familiar,[96] than to appeal to a lesser number of actions on the part of what he calls a "mysterious and extraordinary agency."[97]

I have already noted that this principle at least resembles Ockham's razor. But it is worth noting that principles of this kind predate Ockham. Indeed a very similar principle is to be found at the beginning of Aquinas's discussion of the existence of God. Following the pattern of the medieval *disputatio*, Aquinas begins by outlining two arguments in support of atheism. The first is the existence of evil. If God is infinite goodness, it is suggested, there would be no evil. "But," writes Aquinas, "there is evil in the world. Therefore God does not exist."[98] It is the second argument which anticipates Ockham's razor.

> What can be accomplished by a few principles is not effected by many. But it seems that everything we see in the world can be accounted for by other principles, supposing God did not exist. For all natural things can be reduced to one principle, which is nature, and voluntary things can be reduced to one principle, which is human reason, or will. Therefore there is no need to suppose God's existence.[99]

The implication here is that if what we observe *can* be explained without reference to God, then it *ought* to be so explained. Such a fact, if it were a fact, would render theistic explanations redundant, and would be an argument for atheism. If even Aquinas was happy to accept this principle, one would expect it to be relatively uncontroversial.

Of course, the reason Aquinas was happy to accept this principle is that he thought there *were* facts about the world that cannot be explained without invoking a divine agent. After all, he follows this argument by spelling out his famous five "proofs" of God's existence. And even my revised version of Ockham's razor suggests that we should not posit new kinds of entities *without sufficient reason*. It follows that if there is sufficient reason to do so, positing new kinds of entities is acceptable. (Herschel's *vera causa* doctrine, if taken at face value, implies that we can never posit a new kind of entity. But this is surely wrong.) In the case of theism, we would be warranted in positing the existence of a new kind of entity, namely God, if the theistic hypothesis possessed, to a sufficiently high degree, other explanatory virtues. But one of those virtues is that the hypothesis in question should be informative. And I shall argue in a moment (7.6) that the theistic hypothesis is less than informative, precisely because it posits what Lyell calls a "mysterious and extraordinary agency." If this is true, then the principle of ontological economy will have an important role to play in theory choice. We could, conceivably, have sufficient reason to accept a theistic hypothesis, despite its lack of ontological economy. But if there is an alternative and more economical hypothesis, we would have good reason to prefer it. And if there is not, we would have good reason to seek it.

7.6 INFORMATIVENESS

My final *desideratum* is that a theory be informative. By "informativeness" here I mean something close to what Peter Lipton describes as the "loveliness" (as opposed to the "likeliness") of a proposed explanation. A "lovely" explanation, he writes, is one that specifies "some articulated causal mechanism . . . whose description allows us to deduce the precise details of the effect."[100] There are two aspects to this definition: the first has to do with the description of a mechanism, while the second has to do with our ability to deduce what would follow if the proposed explanation were true. I have already noted that a proposed theistic explanation will often lack an *intermediate* causal mechanism—one that would mediate between the divine will and its effect—and I have suggested that this fact is not necessarily a fatal objection to a hypothesis of this kind (3.4.2). What I want to focus on here is the second aspect of Lipton's definition: the idea that we should prefer a hypothesis that enables us to "deduce the precise details of the effect." Such a hypothesis will not only have empirical content—it will exclude certain states of affairs—but it will specify in some detail just what it does and does not predict.[101] How does theism fare when measured against this *desideratum*?

7.6.1 Quantifiable Predictions

One objection that might be put forward here is that a theistic explanation does not make *quantifiable* predictions. The natural sciences have been able to make such spectacular progress partly because of their assumption, since the time of Galileo, that "the book of nature" is "written in the language of mathematics."[102] This is one of the factors that allows the sciences to have precise empirical content: it enables them to spell out exactly what does and does not follow if a scientific theory were true. Thus while physicists, for example, speak of entities that are both unobservable and very different from those which we encounter every day, they can do so with some precision because they have a language distinct from our everyday language in which to describe such realities. That "language" (speaking metaphorically) is mathematics. By way of contrast, theism lacks a precise language with which to speak of God; it must use our everyday language. And this language lacks precision.

A theist might respond that in this respect proposed theistic explanations are not alone. Our everyday intentional explanations also fail to make quantitative predictions. Worse still, they use notoriously vague terms such as "belief," "desire," "hope," and "fear." We use such terms to explain and to predict people's behaviour, even when we lack any clear idea of what mental states they denote or the mechanisms by which they are expressed (3.2.1). So measured by this criterion, our everyday intentional explanations are also less than "lovely." Yet they can still be useful; they still have explanatory force and can still enable us to make some rough-and-ready predictions. And unless you are prepared to reject all forms of intentional explanation, the fact that a proposed theistic explanation lacks precision does not seem a fatal objection.

7.6.2 The Mysteriousness of the Divine Agent

This is, at first sight, a good response. But it fails to take into account a key fact about proposed theistic explanations, namely the mysteriousness of the posited divine agent. We have very little idea just what would be denoted by the predicates that we use of God. In discussing this difficulty, it is useful to distinguish two types of predicates, namely *mental* and *action* predicates.[103] I have already discussed the difficulty of using mental predicates—terms such as "belief," "desire," "love," or "anger"—in reference to God (3.3.3). What I wish to focus on here are the difficulties associated with using action predicates in reference to God. What could it mean to say that God *creates* something, or that he *speaks* to us? In what sense can we say that God *commands, forgives, comforts,* or *guides*?[104] There are two options here. The theist might argue that both mental and action predicates are used of God analogically. But on the received theological view of analogy (3.3.1), what does this mean? It means that we are simply unable to grasp just what these terms would mean when applied to God; their proper meaning in this context exceeds human comprehension. So our language will lack precision. We will be unable to specify precisely what it would mean for God to "speak" or to "guide" or to "comfort."

The second option is to argue, with William Alston, that we *can* use such terms of God in their literal sense. Would this mean that our action predicates had a more precise meaning? No, it would not. For how does Alston argue for this conclusion? He suggests we can abstract some core meaning from these terms and distinguish this meaning from the particular way in which such actions are performed by creatures like us. We "create" things, for instance, by way of bodily movements, but it is at least conceivable that a being could "create" things even if he does not engage in any bodily movement.[105] This may be true, but precisely because this "creating" is not done in the manner in which we are familiar, we are left with the difficulty of specifying what we might expect to observe, if he did.

7.6.3 Divine Actions as Basic Actions

The theist might respond that we *can* specify how God would act, in order to create. We would expect God's creative act to be a basic action (3.4.2),[106] so that whatever God wills should simply come into existence, "by magic," as it were. There are no means that he need employ. If this is true, then what we would expect of a divine agent would be precisely a series of miracles (4.4), perhaps akin to those narrated in the first chapter of Genesis (5.3.3).

This may be true, and it may constitute a good argument against belief in theistic evolution, but it does not answer the objection. For a theistic explanation proposes that God is bringing about the *explanandum* in order to achieve some goal.[107] If a proposed theistic explanation does not specify the divinely-willed goal, the purpose God has in acting in this way, it will have little empirical content (3.2.3). But to specify a goal in order to explain an action (even a basic action) is to say how we would expect the agent to act, given that goal. If we posit that God sent the Boxing Day tsunami in order to punish sinners (4.1.2), then we must be able to say that an event such as a tsunami is how we would expect God to "punish" sinners.

Here's another way of making the same point. Matthew Ratcliffe has recently argued that much of our everyday social interaction is guided by our shared understanding of the social norms governing human behaviour. We know from experience "what is to be done" in a particular situation and this is (often, at least) sufficient to enable us to understand other people's actions. If we ask, for instance, why someone is standing outside a building, on a cold day, it is sufficient to be told "he's a security guard."[108] We don't need to attribute certain beliefs and desires to the person in question in order to understand his behaviour. Similarly, as James Baillie writes,

> I enter a café and my eyes meet those of the person behind the counter. I need not assume "He believes that I want attention, and he desires to help me," etc. Rather, given the context, he takes me as a customer and I take him as a barista. What we want, and what we do, flows from this mutual understanding.[109]

One can accept this point without denying what I have been assuming so far: that positing beliefs and desires does have explanatory force and that we sometimes explain human behaviour in precisely this way.[110] But all I want to note here is the difficulty Ratcliffe's account poses for proposed theistic explanations. When it comes to a posited divine agent, we lack anything analogous to the shared social norms that can help us to understand human behaviour. Even if we are told, with regard to a divine agent, that he is (for instance) a "loving father," it is unclear what such a role would entail, in the case of a divine agent. We will often know "what is to be done" by a human parent, in a particular situation, but there are no social norms that would guide us in predicting the behaviour of a divine agent.

A believer might counter this objection by arguing that she already knows how the divine agent will act, in this situation, for she knows how God has acted in the past, in similar situations. Indeed, this is how believers often reason, by appealing to what they take to be paradigmatic instances of divine action, often found in sacred scripture.[111] But this, of course, merely begs the question: it assumes that the believer already has a successful theistic explanation, either of these past events themselves or of the scriptures in which these divine actions are revealed.

Successful Theistic Explanations 141

These considerations bring me back to the point I made when discussing theological scepticism (5.5). Given the mysteriousness of the posited divine agent, we can never be confident that the *explanandum* is, in fact, how we would expect God to act. The rationality principle may enable us to make some predictions (5.2), but we can never be confident about the judgements we make. The point I am making here is a closely related one, namely that any predictions we make—however provisionally—will lack precision. We have a pretty good idea how a human being might go about "comforting" or "punishing" a fellow creature, so given this posited intention, we can predict just how she will and will not act. But how would God go about comforting someone? Or punishing someone? Or speaking to her? An omnipotent being will presumably have a practically infinite range of choices open to him, only a few of which we can begin to comprehend. Since we do not know the full range of divine options, we cannot know with any degree of confidence how God would or would not act, in order to achieve his goals. Once again, it seems, the theological sceptic has a point.

7.6.4 The Danger of Accommodation

What follows from these considerations? It seems that any proposed theistic explanation will lack something, when measured against this *desideratum* of informativeness. It will be, at best, an "unlovely" explanation, which will not allow us to "deduce the precise details of the effect."[112] In itself, this fact counts against proposed theistic explanations. But it also means that they face a particular danger, that of "making things fit." More technically, they face the danger of *accommodation* as distinct from *prediction*. It will be all too easy for the theist to redescribe the *explanandum*, perhaps in all innocence, so that it appears to fit her description of divine action. But the "explanation" in question may be nothing more than a kind of verbal coincidence.

Here's an example of how this might occur. Let's say I experience a sense of confidence and joy when reading a particular passage of scripture. How am I to explain this? The believer might appear to explain this feeling by saying that what I am experiencing is the voice of God.[113] More precisely, she may suggest that what I am experiencing is the "internal testimony of the Holy Spirit" of which John Calvin wrote.[114] And this "explanation" of my feelings might be taken to corroborate some other theistic claim, perhaps one having to do with the authority of scripture. While there are many problems with a proposed explanation of this kind,[115] one of them arises from the difficulty of knowing just what this claim means. What would it mean to "hear" the "voice of God" when God is an incorporeal being who does not "speak" in our everyday sense of that word? Precisely because this claim is less than informative, it is easy for the believer to suggest it is true, that what I am experiencing is indeed the Holy Spirit. (We might regard this as a variant on Kitcher's "spurious unification" problem [3.2.3.1].)

The theist could reply that this is no more than a danger, and one that faces many proposed explanations. It could, in principle, be countered by a sufficiently robust process of testing. The problem is that this would require us to make further predictions, each of which would be equally "unlovely." It follows that this weakness in proposed theistic explanations seems inescapable. We can never be confident that we are not being deceived by a clever use of words. So once again, we have reason to prefer a natural explanation, which has at least the capacity to be more informative. And even if we had no natural explanation to hand, we would always be justified in seeking one.

8 Conclusion

> Miss Binney spoke as if this explanation ended the matter, but the kindergarten was not convinced.
>
> Beverly Cleary

Let me end this enquiry by stating my conclusions, before returning to the question with which I began, that of the methodological naturalism of the modern sciences.

8.1 A SILVER BULLET?

In Chapters 1 to 4 of this study, I examined a number of the objections that might be raised against proposed theistic explanations. Those objections will by now be familiar. The first is that proposed theistic explanations exclude no possible state of affairs; the second is that the actions of an agent capable of miracles would be unpredictable; the third suggests that the very concept of God is incoherent; the fourth maintains that the will of God cannot be a cause. I have argued that while these objections raise some serious issues with which a theist philosopher ought to grapple, they do not, in themselves, rule out the possibility of a successful theistic explanation.

In Chapter 5, I set out the circumstances in which invoking a divine agent would constitute a *potential* explanation of some state of affairs. It would do so, I argued, only if we could conceive of no better way in which a divine agent could have brought about his posited intention. This optimality condition constitutes a powerful constraint upon any proposed theistic explanation. Given the existence of apparently pointless evils, the theist will have a difficult task showing that his proposed explanation meets this condition. But let's assume that the theist could do so. Let's say that we could be warranted in regarding an account of divine agency as a potential explanation of some state of affairs.

What would follow? Well, not very much. The theist would still need to show that his proposed explanation was a successful one, that we had sufficient reason to accept it. Chapter 7 set out the conditions that a potential theistic explanation would have to meet in order to be regarded as the actual explanation of some state of affairs. It has shown that measured against a list of accepted explanatory virtues, a theistic hypothesis is simply incapable of achieving a high score. It is not (as things stand) consistent with the rest of our knowledge, it comes from a tradition whose proposed explanations have previously scored poorly, it is ontologically extravagant, and it does not enable us to predict the precise details of the effect. It other words, it lacks many of the qualities we would normally demand of successful explanations.

What conclusion, then, have I reached? If, on a number of key points, we give the theist the benefit of the doubt, we cannot exclude the *bare possibility* that there might one day exist a successful theistic explanation. The reason for this is that at least some of these criticisms represent *contingent* (rather than *necessary*) failings. As things stand, for instance, proposed theistic explanations are not consistent with the rest of our knowledge. But we can imagine things being otherwise. It follows that we cannot be certain that *no* account of divine agency could *ever* warrant acceptance as the explanation of some state of affairs. But if a proposed theistic explanation must meet the conditions set out above—which are no more onerous than those we demand of other explanations—then that possibility seems remote. Many if not all proposed theistic explanations can be shown to be not even *potential* explanations of the facts to be explained, since they fail to meet the optimality condition (5.3.3). And even if they met this first condition, they will (at present) score poorly when ranked against key explanatory virtues. They are unlikely to be the best explanations of any state of affairs. And even if they were the only potential explanations on offer, we would have good reason to seek natural alternatives.

Many atheists will regard this as an unsatisfying conclusion. For it does not exclude the possibility that we could, one day, have sufficient reason to accept a proposed theistic explanation. The possibility may be remote, but it remains "on the books" (as it were). It follows, they might argue, that my arguments do not provide what is needed: a "silver bullet," which could "put a merciful end to all the nonsense." There is no *in principle* argument which would exclude any proposed theistic explanation, *a priori* (as it were). Applied to the debate regarding scientific naturalism, my discussion fails to offer a principled reason for excluding (once and for all) talk of divine agency from the sciences.

8.2 Methodological Naturalism?

Does this matter? I suspect not. At the very beginning of my discussion I distinguished between two senses of the term "naturalism." The first, which I attributed to Quine, holds that there are certain standards which any successful explanation must meet. If a proposed theistic explanation met these standards, then we should embrace it. It is a further question, albeit one much debated in the literature, whether we choose to call such an explanation "scientific." Politically and legally, it may be an important issue, but nothing of any philosophical importance rests on the answer we give. My own view is that it would be odd to exclude from the sciences any explanation that met the standards I have outlined. Any adequate explanation deserves, *ipso facto*, to be classed as scientific. But if you want to adopt a narrower definition of the "scientific," and argue that a successful theistic explanation would be a satisfactory explanation, but not a scientific one, then this is merely a dispute about words. The important philosophical question we should ask of any proposed explanation is not, "Does this invoke a supernatural agent?" The important question is, "Is it a satisfactory explanation?"

A Quinean naturalist might hold that (in the words of Susan Haack) "the only means we have of figuring out what the world is like, is our experience of the world and our explanatory theorizing about it."[1] The question then becomes whether our "explanatory theorizing" could include reference to a divine agent. As should be clear by now, I have no argument with a naturalism of this kind. Indeed, my argument has presupposed it. My only qualification is that I see no reason to call such a position "naturalistic." But the naturalism with which I began, the methodological naturalism of the sciences, is of a different kind. This entails something closely resembling an ontological claim. More precisely, it is a procedural rule which demands that in offering explanations we should posit only natural entities, however those are defined. Such a rule would certainly exclude proposed theistic explanations. (It would exclude other kinds of proposed explanations as well, but it would certainly exclude theistic ones.) It is this kind of naturalism that is invoked and defended by many of the opponents of intelligent design theory. Does my analysis lend it any support?

If methodological naturalism is taken to mean that no proposed theistic explanation could ever have any explanatory force, then no, my analysis does not support this conclusion. Such a claim would correspond to a general *in principle* objection, one which applies to *all* proposed theistic explanations. It would hold that for *any* statement about divine agency, there could exist *no fact* of which it would be even a potential explanation. Such a sweeping dismissal, I have argued, cannot be justified. What my analysis suggests is that if we want to argue that proposed theistic explanations lack explanatory force, we need to do so on case-by-case basis, by showing (for instance) that a proposed theistic explanation fails to meet the optimality condition. We would need to show that *for this particular statement* about divine agency, then even if it were true, it would not explain the particular *explanandum* to which it is being applied. Or even if it would, the proposed explanation would be less than satisfactory on other grounds. It might (for instance) be formulated in a way that lacks empirical content or lacks corroboration by independent tests. I am confident that such arguments would be often, if not always, decisive. But a sweeping, *in principle* dismissal of proposed theistic explanations is unwarranted.

What about a more modest methodological naturalism? My analysis does support the view that we ought to have a *preference* for natural explanations, since these have a better chance of exhibiting the features that characterise an adequate explanation. But this is a very modest position. After all, none of the features I have discussed—testability, consistency with background knowledge, simplicity, ontological economy, and informativeness—rule out proposed theistic explanations *a priori*. A proposed theistic explanation formulated with the requisite degree of intentional specificity would be testable (7.1.1). Whether it survives the test is another question, but it is not a question which we can decide in advance. Consistency with background knowledge is a contingent matter: if we already had a tradition of successful theistic explanations, then there would be no reason to reject yet another. Ontological economy is a *ceteris paribus* condition. It suggests that we should not posit new kinds of entities unless these are required and it is at least conceivable that positing a divine agent might be required, to explain some phenomenon. And while a proposed theistic explanation may not be a "lovely explanation," which would allow us to deduce the precise details of the effect, this does not seem (by itself) a fatal objection, if it were to score highly on our other criteria.

So yes, my arguments might give us reason to prefer natural explanations when these are available, and to seek natural explanations when they are not. It follows that a proposed theistic explanation should be, at best, an explanation of last resort.[2] One might argue that this view—that we should abandon the search for natural explanations only *in extremis*—represents a kind of "presumption of naturalism." And so it does. But my point is that such a presumption would be (in principle) defeasible. And it falls short of what most people mean by the "methodological naturalism" of the sciences.

My own view is that the naturalistic research tradition of the sciences has been stunningly successful and must rank as of one of the greatest of human achievements. But I think it is poorly served by attempts to define science in such a way as to exclude the supernatural. The debate over intelligent design is instructive in this regard. One might win a legal victory by insisting that this proposed theistic explanation is not what we customarily call "science." And this is true, for contingent historical reasons. But it would be much more effective to show that this particular proposed theistic explanation, with its deliberately vague appeal to an unspecified "designer," is practically vacuous. It lacks the first and most important virtue of any proposed explanation, namely that of testability. It follows that this *particular* proposed theistic explanation should be rejected.

Could the theist produce a better one? I doubt it, but then it would be most regrettable if we were to forbid him to try. Nothing could be more antithetical to the spirit of free enquiry than this kind of censorship. If proposed theistic explanations are to be defeated, as they have been so often in the past, it will be by way of the free contest of ideas. The contribution which I hope this study has made is to show how this could be done, by outlining the standards against which any proposed theistic explanation should be measured.

Appendix
Intentional Explanations

> Motivation is a central human concern ... And the "scientific" way to understand it is, as with everything else, is to take it on its own terms and find concepts for bringing out its typical patterns.
>
> Mary Midgley

As I noted earlier (3.2.1), intentional explanations have long been a contested issue among both philosophers and psychologists. If, as is sometimes suggested, any proposed explanation of this form is fatally flawed, then theistic explanations are also fatally flawed. End of discussion. As it happens, I do not think that intentional explanations are fatally flawed. But since none of the relevant arguments are specific to theistic explanations, it seemed best to relegate discussion of this topic to an appendix.

Before I begin, a qualification seems in order. My analysis will employ concepts such as "belief," "desire," and "intention." As I noted earlier (3.2), these are often described as "folk psychological" concepts, and it is the use of such concepts that is philosophically controversial. I have already made reference to Matthew Ratcliffe's recent challenge to the role of folk psychology in social interaction (7.6.3). Ratcliffe argues that there are many circumstances in which we do not need to posit beliefs and desires in order to make sense of other people's behaviour. It is sufficient that we understand the shared social norms governing human behaviour in particular situations. To illustrate his point, Ratcliffe cites Alfred Schutz's analysis of "ideal types":

> If I observe, or even hear about, a man tightening a nut, my first interpretive scheme will picture him as joining together two parts of an apparatus with a wrench. The further information that the event is taking place in an automobile factory permits me to place the operation within the total context of "automobile" manufacturing. If I know in addition that the man is an auto worker, then I can assume a great deal about him, for instance, that he comes to work every morning and goes home every night, that he picks up his check every payday, and so on. I can then bring him into a wider context of meaning by applying to him the ideal type "urban worker" or, more specifically, "Berlin worker of the year 1931." And once I have established the fact that the man is a

German and a Berliner, then all the corresponding interpretive schemes become applicable to him.[1]

In this situation, Ratcliffe argues, the man's behaviour is entirely explicable without attributing to him any mental states such as beliefs, desires, and intentions.

There is much in Ratcliffe's analysis that is worthy of discussion. It is not clear that an explanation by reference to social norms would be a *causal* explanation,[2] but there can be little doubt that we often understand the actions of others by reference to such norms. Indeed, I have already argued that his account provides a further reason to be sceptical of proposed theistic explanations, since in the case of such proposed explanations we cannot appeal to shared social norms or anything analogous to them (7.6.3). All we can do in the case of a posited divine agent is to attribute to that agent certain beliefs and desires and to see what explanatory force this attribution would offer. But precisely for this reason, I have restricted myself to a traditional folk-psychological account of intentional explanations. There may be other factors that enter into the explanation of human behaviour, but it is the folk-psychological account that offers the most helpful way of thinking about proposed theistic explanations.

A.1 ACTIONS, REASONS, AND CAUSES

The starting point for much of the contemporary discussion has been Donald Davidson's 1963 paper "Actions, Reasons, and Causes." That paper begins by discussing what it means for something to be a *reason* for an action. It goes on to discuss whether a reason is also a *cause*. Davidson answers these question by defending two theses, which following G. F. Schueler I shall refer to as the "belief-desire" thesis (BD) and the "causal thesis" (CT).[3]

> BD: R is a primary reason why an agent performed the action A under the description d only if R consists of a pro attitude of the agent towards actions with a certain property, and a belief of that agent that A, under the description d, has that property.[4]
>
> CT: A primary reason for an action is its cause.[5]

It is the second (causal) thesis that is the particular focus of Davidson's attention and much of his paper responds to objections to it. So what are we to make of these two theses? Are they defensible?

A.1.1 The Causal Thesis

While Davidson's second, causal thesis has been the subject of some debate,[6] I have no quarrel with it. I have already touched on the difficulties that attend any discussion of causation, let alone one that posits a divine agent (3.4.3). But as Davidson argues, if we do not recognize a reason as a cause, in some sense of that word, it is hard to make any sense of the idea that I am acting *for* a reason. In particular, it would seem impossible to distinguish the reason for which I acted from a reason which I had but which was incidental to my acting as I did. (Being hungry, I had a reason to go to the kitchen, namely to find something to eat, but the reason I actually went to the kitchen was to make a coffee. So among the reasons I had for performing this action, only one actually brought it about.)

To say that a reason can be a cause is to leave open the question of what kind of cause it is.[7] It may be a very different kind of cause from that which we find elsewhere in the natural world, perhaps one that does not operate according to strict laws (Appendix 3.3). And to say that a reason is a cause is not to eliminate the agent herself from the process. It is the agent who is acting (Appendix 1.2); what we are trying to explain is why she is acting in this particular way. There are philosophers who continue to reject Davidson's causal thesis,[8] but I shall not attempt to answer them here. Rather, I shall simply assume that the casual thesis is defensible and shall develop its implications in the course of the discussion.

A.1.2 The Belief-Desire Thesis

What about Davidson's first thesis, namely his belief-desire thesis (BD)? There are two points which may be made here. Let me start with the less controversial, which is a mere matter of clarification. It relates to the term "desire." While "belief-desire thesis" is a convenient shorthand, "desire" needs to be understood in the broadest possible sense. Davidson's own preferred term is *pro attitude*, and he makes it clear that a pro attitude can be (for example) an evaluative belief. As he writes, under pro attitudes

> are to be included desires, wantings, urges, promptings, and a great variety of moral views, aesthetic principles, economic prejudices, social conventions, and public and private goals and values in so far as these can be interpreted as attitudes of an agent directed towards actions of a certain kind.[9]

This is a significant point, for not every desire constitutes a reason to act.[110] An agent may have a desire, but in the light of some evaluative belief may choose not to act on it (Appendix 2.2).

Let me approach this point obliquely, by way of an apparent objection to Davidson's belief-desire thesis. The objection has to do with what it means to act intentionally. It might seem that to cite an agent's beliefs and desires is not yet to offer an adequate account of intentional action. For a desire may cause an action without that action being intentional. It may be caused by the appropriate mental states—by beliefs and desires that make it reasonable—but in a way that is causally "deviant."[11] Davidson himself offers an example of this causal deviance.

> A climber might want to rid himself of the weight and danger of holding another man on a rope, and he might know that by loosening his hold on the rope he could rid himself of the weight and danger. This belief and want might so unnerve him as to cause him to loosen his hold, and yet it might be the case that he never *chose* to loosen his hold, nor did he do it intentionally.[12]

It follows, the objection runs, that we cannot analyse an intentional action simply in terms of the agent's beliefs and desires.

Richard Swinburne considers this objection to be fatal to Davidson's belief-desire thesis. He argues that on Davidson's view what causes an intentional action is some "passive state" of the agent or "some event involving him."[13] But, he continues, "if an intention (or wish or desire) of P to bring about E is some passive event or state, it could bring about E without P's having intentionally brought about E. Causation by an intention (so understood) does not guarantee intentional action."[14] Swinburne illustrates his objection with another example of causal deviance, this time from the work of Richard Taylor.

> Suppose . . . that a member of an audience keenly desires to attract a speaker's attention, but, being shy, only fidgets uncomfortably in his seat and blushes. We may suppose, further, that he does attract the speaker's attention by his very fidgeting; but he did not fidget *in order* to attract the speaker's attention, even though he desired that result and may well have realised that such behaviour was going to produce it.[15]

Swinburne's objection seems correct. Surely, we might argue, it is the agent who brings about the action, not some mental state which the agent might happen to have. As Swinburne writes, "having an intention is not something that happens to an agent, but something she does."[16] There is an insight here that should be preserved. But does it rule out Davidson's analysis? Can these two perspectives be reconciled?

I believe they can. They can be reconciled by recognising the existence of a distinct kind of mental state, which I shall describe as an "intention,"[17] and a distinct kind of mental event, which I shall describe as the "formation of an intention."[18] An intention is a kind of pro attitude,[19] but it differs from the pro attitudes that may contribute to its formation. It is not merely a judgement that something is desirable, all things being equal; it is the judgement that something *is to be done*.[20] As I argued earlier (3.2 and 5.2), an intentional explanation operates by positing an intention, understood in this sense, and by showing that the action to be explained is a rational one, given that intention. It follows (as Davidson argues) that an intentional explanation is a causal explanation. For an intention is a mental state—a species of pro attitude—which can rightly be described as the cause of the agent's behaviour. And just as the act of accepting a proposition can be a voluntary act, even though forming a belief is not, so the act of forming an intention can be a voluntary act, even though having a desire is not.[21]

An intentional explanation explains an act as the most rational way of enacting an intention, given a certain set of beliefs. But our desire for explanation may go further than this. I have argued that an explanation that posits an intention and explains the agent's behaviour in the light of it is an intentional explanation. It doesn't need to do anything else (1.3.3): the action is explained by invoking the relevant intention. But we might want to go further and to explain its *explanans*. After all, the formation of an intention is a mental event, and the resulting intention a mental state. So it is perfectly reasonable to ask after the causes of this event.[22] At that point, *pace* Swinburne, it does seem appropriate to cite "some . . . state of the agent or some event involving him."[23] Even if an intention is a *sui generis* mental state, and even if the formation of an intention is an act on the part of the agent, we can still ask why an agent formed this intention rather than another. It is at this point that we will need to invoke the agent's beliefs and desires.[24] How would invoking his beliefs and desires explain his intention? That's a question I shall address shortly (Appendix 2.2).

A.1.3 The Rationality Principle

So an intentional explanation posits an agent having a particular intention, as well as a set of beliefs relevant to its attainment, and shows that the action in question is a rational one, given that intention. And if we want to explain the *explanans*, then we will need to show that this was a reasonable intention to form, given the agent's other beliefs and desires. This talk of what is "rational" or "reasonable" highlights a central feature of intentional explanations, namely their reliance upon what I have called the *rationality principle* (5.2). This principle is best thought of as a *presumption of rationality*, comparable to the legal presumption of innocence or what I have called the scientist's "presumption of naturalism" (7.3 and 8.2). We explain an agent's action by positing a particular intention and by offering a practical syllogism that has a description of that action as its conclusion. But to do this is to presume that the agent is acting rationally. If that presumption turns out to be false, then an intentional explanation cannot be given.

Let me examine this rationality principle a little more closely. A useful place to start is with Dan Dennett's discussion of what he calls "the intentional stance." Dennett argues that there are three strategies we can adopt when attempting to predict the behaviour of any system. The first of these is the *physical stance*: "if you want to predict the behavior of a system, determine its physical constitution . . . and the physical nature of the impingements upon it, and use your knowledge of the laws of physics to predict the outcome for any event."[25] The second is the *design stance*: here "one ignores the actual . . . details of the physical constitution of an object, and, on the assumption that it has a certain design, predicts that it will behave *as it is designed to behave* under various circumstances."[26] It is the third strategy that is the focus of Dennett's attention, namely the *intentional stance*. When adopting this strategy, we treat the system in whose behaviour we are interested as a rational agent, and by attributing to it certain beliefs and desires, we predict how it *ought* to behave.

What beliefs and desires do we attribute to the system in question, in order to arrive at our prediction? And what does it mean to treat something as a rational agent? Dennett's answer is admirably concise.

(1) A system's beliefs are those it *ought to have*, given its perceptual capacities, its epistemic needs, and its biography. . . .
(2) A system's needs are those it *ought to have*, given its biological needs and the most practicable means of satisfying them. . . .
(3) A system's behavior will consist of those acts that *it would be rational* for an agent with those beliefs and desires to perform.[27]

The first two of Dennett's points are relatively uncontroversial, provided we understand that the "ought" here has no moral connotations. It means simply that we attribute to the subject the beliefs and desires (or beliefs and pro attitudes) that we would *expect* her to have, given the kind of being she is and her particular history. The third requirement, namely that we treat the subject as a rational agent, is more controversial. But it is, I want to argue, at the heart of such explanations.

This rationality principle is also central to the work of Donald Davidson, in whose writings it is sometimes referred to as "the principle of charity." At times, Davidson seems to offer a particularly strong version. When discussing, for instance, the impossibility of incommensurable conceptual schemes, Davidson argues that in order to understand other people "we must count them right in most matters."[28] But he offers what is apparently a weaker version of the principle when discussing intentional explanations. In this context, Davidson argues, the principle of charity demands that we find "a large degree of rationality and consistency" in the behaviour of those whose actions we are explaining.[29] For Davidson, this presumption of rationality is not something imported from outside as it were; it is implicit in the very concepts we use to explain behaviour intentionally.[30] In other words, without the rationality principle (or principle of charity), there can be no intentional explanations.

Why do we employ such a principle? One answer would be, "because it works." If we treat people *as if* they were rational agents we can often understand and even predict their behaviour. Dennett, for one, seems tempted by this instrumentalist view, arguing at one point that the rationality which we assume is a "myth," since human beings often act irrationally. But he adds that the rationality principle "works very well" for the simple reason that "we are *pretty* rational."[31] So the simplest explanation of the utility of the rationality principle would seem to be that it is (more or less) true: we often do act rationally. And when we become aware that we are not acting rationally, we try to adjust our beliefs or actions so as to act more rationally.[32] In this sense, the rationality principle is at least an approximation to the truth.[33] Remember, too, that we adopt this principle only as a presumption; it *is* defeasible. We may find that the agent in question reasons badly about how she should act. Or we may find that she is not, in fact, acting in accordance with the intention she has formed, since she suffers from weakness of will (Appendix 2.3).

What does "rationality" imply, in this context? In Chapter 5 (5.3.3), I identified three criteria of rationality in action, although my list makes no claim to be exhaustive. A first and minimal requirement is that of *consistency*. Given certain beliefs and desires, we would expect a rational agent to act in a way which is consistent with those beliefs and desires. If we posit that a particular agent desires to express affection for her partner, this would explain her purchasing a gift. Her purchasing a gift would be consistent with her desire to express affection. It would not be consistent with her stirring rat poison into his coffee. A closely related requirement is that of *perceived efficacy*. Given a particular goal, a rational agent will act in a way which (if her beliefs were true) would bring about that goal. She may, of course, be mistaken. She may think that purchasing a boldly striped tie for her beloved will successfully convey her feelings of affection, when in fact he loathes ties in general, let alone striped ones. But given her (mistaken) beliefs, this might still be a rational way to act. Finally, there is the requirement of *efficiency*. Given a posited goal, we would expect a rational agent, all other things being equal, to choose the most efficient way of attaining that goal. If she intends to go to the supermarket, then we would expect her to take the most direct route, unless she has some other goals whose attainment demands otherwise.

A.2 EXPLANATION AND ARGUMENTS

To what point has this discussion led? Intentional explanations explain an agent's behaviour by positing a particular reason for acting, an intention which (it is claimed) motivates her behaviour. What our explanation needs to show is that, given this intention, it would be reasonable for the agent to act in this way.[34] This means that our attempt to offer an intentional explanation may be defeated. There may be no intention that we can plausibly attribute to this agent that would make her behaviour rational, even by her own lights. In this situation, we would have to seek some other kind of explanation.

A.2.1 The Practical Syllogism

I suggested earlier that an intentional explanation is best thought of as an argument (2.1.4). We can now see why this is the case. For to show that a course of action is reasonable, given the circumstances, is to show that it follows, by some process of logic, from certain premises. To demonstrate this, we need to offer an argument, most commonly a practical syllogism (4.4.3), which has a posited intention as its premise and the action as its conclusion. To what extent will this syllogism reflect the agent's actual process of reasoning? That will differ from case to case. An intentional explanation assumes that the agent has engaged in *some* process of reasoning, of which our practical syllogism is a more or less full expression. But the reasoning in which the agent actually engages may be enthymematic: it may fail to articulate some of its premises. And on some occasions, an agent may judge that a particular action is the best course of action without being aware of having engaged in any reasoning at all. An intentional explanation will make explicit the process of reasoning that led to my action, even if I was not conscious of engaging in any such deliberative process.

That last claim requires illustration, but illustrations are not difficult to find. If I am walking down a bush track and I push aside a branch in order to pass through, then my action is intentional, but it is hardly based on any conscious process of deliberation.[35] If on arrival at the library desk, I hand the librarian the book I am holding, my action is intentional, but it also involves little, if any conscious deliberation.[36] When I drive from the university to my home, I may be acting in ways that are entirely unreflective. I may be engaged in animated conversation with a friend while also stopping for traffic lights, taking the correct turn, and reacting to other drivers. When I decide to stop for a traffic light, I may be engaging in no conscious process of deliberation. But I am nonetheless acting for a reason and my actions could be explained intentionally. To say this is to assume that agents can engage in reasoning without being aware of the fact, but in an age when cognitive psychologists speak freely about "unconscious reasoning,"[37] this does not seem an unreasonable assumption to make.

In brief, then, an intentional explanation explains an action by way of a practical syllogism. But what form does this practical syllogism take? Let me begin with Robert Audi's schema, which he describes as "the simplest basic schema for practical reasoning."[38] I have merely shifted its syntax into the third person, to make its explanatory use clear.

Major premise—the motivational premise: the agent wants ϕ.
Minor premise—the cognitive premise: her A-ing would contribute to realizing ϕ.
Conclusion—the practical judgment: the agent should A.

Will this suffice as a description of an intentional explanation? It suffers from two weaknesses. The first lies in its first premise, which states merely that the agent has a desire for ϕ. I have already argued that having a desire is not the same as having an intention. The second is that this syllogism moves from two facts about the agent to a conclusion about what the agent "should" do. Even if we can clarify what it means to say that the agent "should" perform action A—in the sense that this is the most reasonable way for her to act—what we are wanting to explain is the agent's action. So ideally our conclusion should describe the action itself, while making it clear how it flows from the premises.

Georg Henrik von Wright offers us a form of practical syllogism that addresses both of these issues.

(1) A intends to bring about p.
(2) A considers that he cannot bring about p unless he does a.
(3) Therefore A sets himself to do a.[39]

Note how this differs from Audi's schema. The initial premise now posits an intention rather than a mere desire, while the conclusion is a statement about the performance of the action in question. It does not merely state that it is what the agent ought to do. Will this suffice as an explanation of an action? It may be better than Audi's schema, but it still fails to make it clear how the action in question follows from the premises. Its conclusion is introduced by a "therefore," but what lies behind this "therefore" is not made explicit. So my preferred form of practical syllogism is the one I outlined earlier (4.4.3).

(1) There exists a rational agent A with intended goal G.
(2) A has beliefs $B_1, B_2, \ldots B_n$ relating to the attainment of G.
(3) If $B_1, B_2, \ldots B_n$ were true, E would be the best way of achieving G.
(4) Rational agents always choose the best way of achieving their goals.
(5) Therefore A will do E.

This introduces into the discussion the rationality principle upon which, I have argued, all intentional explanations rest. And it is this rationality principle which makes explicit the rationale behind the "should A" of Audi's formulation and the "therefore" that introduces von Wright's conclusion.

A.2.2 Explaining the *Explanans*

On the assumption that an explanation can be complete even if it does not explain its *explanans* (1.3.3), then the above syllogism represents an intentional explanation. Such an explanation posits an agent having a particular intention, along with a set of relevant beliefs, and shows the *explanandum* is how we would expect such an agent to act. But we may, of course, ask a further question. We may ask why this agent formed this particular intention. For an agent possessing a particular set of beliefs and desires may often have more than one possible reason to act.[40] And those reasons may be such that, considered individually, they would lead the agent to form quite different intentions.[41] Take, for instance, the situation in which I form the intention to accept a job offer in a different city.[42] One could apparently explain my having this intention by citing those factors which would favour it. The new position represented a promotion, the university department to which I am moving is larger and livelier than my present one, the city to which I am moving has a warmer climate, and so on. The problem is that there are other factors that would count against my accepting the job. House prices in this new city are higher, my wife will have to leave her job, the children will need to move school, and so on. So whether I accepted the job or refused it, an onlooker could have posited sets of beliefs and desires that would apparently explain the intention I formed.

What is happening in a case such as this? In this situation, there exists a variety of possible intentions, a variety of potential reasons for acting, none of which is irreconcilable with my having the beliefs and desires I do. If you want to know why I formed the intention I eventually had, then you will need to explain why I favoured one set of potential reasons rather than another. Once again, it is important to note that this represents a new intentional explanation having a new *explanandum*. Let's say the original explanation set out to explain some particular action on my part—perhaps why my wife and I sold our house. It may have explained this fact by positing a particular intention—namely, that I intend to take up a job in another city. That explanation has now done its job. But one can then ask why I formed this particular intention, and in many situations the answer to that new question will be far from obvious. So it is worth reflecting for a moment on how we might answer it.

My suggestion is this. We can explain why an agent acted on one set of potential reasons rather than another by forming a new argument, a new syllogism (if you like), which has a description of the agent's beliefs and desires for its premises, and a description of her intention as its conclusion. What will be distinctive about this argument is that it will explain how the agent weighed up the various potential reasons for action to which her beliefs and desires could have given rise. It will include what we can call an "evaluative" premise,[43] as long we understand that it is the *agent's* evaluation it expresses, not that of the observer. As observers, we do not need to share the agent's evaluative judgements. We might choose differently, in his situation. But what we are trying to explain is his choice, not ours.

Among recent authors, it is G. F. Schueler who has most clearly highlighted this point; one of his examples illustrates it. The example has to do with a voter, faced with the decision about whether to vote for a tax increase. The tax increase will make possible subsidized childcare, but it will also mean that the agent will experience a loss of income. The following line of reasoning, Schueler suggests, would explain why such an agent would form the intention to vote for a tax increase.

(1) Subsidized day care is a good thing.
(2) This proposed tax increase is necessary if there is to be subsidized day care in my community.
(3) At the same time, it will cost me some money, which I would like to use elsewhere, if this tax increase is passed.
(4) Still, it is more important that my community have subsidized day care than that I keep for my own use the few dollars it will cost me each year.
(5) So, I should vote for this tax increase.[44]

Premises (2) and (3) give reasons that would, considered individually, lead to different actions. So it is premise (4) which plays the key role here. It shows why the agent acted as she did, favouring one set of reasons over another.

The importance of the evaluative premise (4) is shown by looking at an explanation of why someone might *not* vote for the tax increase. It could be identical to the first, except for the fourth premise (and, of course, the conclusion).

(1) Subsidized day care is a good thing.
(2) This proposed tax increase is necessary if there is to be subsidized day care in my community.
(3) At the same time, it will cost me some money, which I would like to use elsewhere, if this tax increase is passed.
(4) It is more important that I keep for my own use the few dollars it will cost me each year than that my community have subsidized day care.[45]
(5) So, I should not vote for this tax increase.

Both agents might agree that subsidized childcare is valuable. Both agents might recognise the cost to themselves of voting for the increase. Both might wish to keep the money for themselves. To this extent they have the same beliefs and desires. Where they differ is in the relative weight which they assign to these considerations. And it is this which is captured by the evaluative premise (4).

A.2.3 The Problem of *Akrasia*

In the discussion to this point, I have made a couple of key distinctions. The first is that between a desire and an intention (Appendix 1.2). The second is between what we might call a "first-order" intentional explanation, which takes us from posited intention to action, and a "second-order" explanation, which explains why the agent formed this particular intention (Appendix 2.2).

Let me illustrate the importance of these distinctions by way of a brief discussion of "weakness of will," the problem of *akrasia* to which Aristotle refers.[46] If we follow Davidson's original formulation, and understand a (first-order) intentional explanation as one that cites an agent's beliefs and desires, then weakness of will becomes a problem. For the fact is that agents do not always act in the way in which it would be reasonable for them to act, given their beliefs and desires. Yet their "incontinent" actions (as Davidson calls them[47]) are still intentional. So if we define an intentional action is one that is reasonable, given the agent's beliefs and desires, then we have lots of counterexamples: intentional actions that are *not* reasonable, given the agent's beliefs and desires.

Let me examine this issue more closely. Taking a slightly different line from that which I have advocated, Robert Audi has argued that the conclusion of a practical syllogism is most plausibly regarded as a proposition about how the agent *ought* to act, given certain beliefs and desires. It is not a description of the action itself.[48] Would this solve our difficulty? No, it would not. It merely highlights it. For if I suffer from *akrasia*, then I can decide how I ought to act and yet fail to act. Let me offer an example. After careful reflection, I have decided that animal suffering has ethical significance and that the commercial production of meat entails significant animal suffering. As an ethical agent, I want to minimise suffering, and in the light of these considerations I have decided to embrace vegetarianism. But faced with the steak option on the restaurant menu, and seeing the succulent meat being devoured by fellow diners, I can't resist. I order and eat the steak. This is surely a case of *akrasia*; my eating the steak is an "incontinent" action. The problem is that it is also an intentional act, an act performed for a reason. But the reason it is performed does not correspond to the conclusion of a practical syllogism that has my relevant beliefs and desires as its premises. How can this be?

It is at this point that we require the distinction between a desire and an intention. An intention, I argued earlier (Appendix 1.2), is an unconditional judgement that a particular course of action is to be adopted. When all is going well, an agent's intention will correspond to the conclusion of a practical syllogism that has his relevant beliefs and desires as its premises. One could, in other words, offer a successful "second-order" explanation of why he formed that particular intention. But in the case of an agent who suffers from *akrasia*, these two come apart. The incontinent act is still an intentional act, one performed for a reason. I order and eat the steak because I have formed the intention to eat meat, at least on this occasion. So one could offer a successful "first-order" explanation of why I ate the steak. The problem is that the formation of this intention was not a rational act, given my other beliefs and desires.

Weakness of will, on this account, represents a failure to act in an entirely rational way when forming an intention. So can such action be explained intentionally? Yes, it can. It can be explained by way of a first-order intentional action, one that has a description of the agent's action as its conclusion. But the attempt to create a second-order explanation—one that would explain the formation of this particular intention—will inevitably fail. The agent's action is a rational one, given his intention. But the intention is not one that he should have formed, given this beliefs and desires.[49]

Incidentally, this view of *akrasia* enables us to distinguish an incontinent action from a wicked one.[50] This distinction seems useful. One could, perhaps, describe *akrasia* as a moral fault, but we are naturally inclined to say that it represents a weakness rather than a perversity. A wicked action, on this view, enacts an intention that *is* rational, given the agent's beliefs and desires. What makes the action wicked is that the beliefs and desires on which the agent is acting are morally inappropriate. The Nazi killer, who believes that the good of humanity requires the extermination of the Jews, and who desires to serve humanity in this task, is acting rationally in forming his wicked intention. The problem is that the beliefs and desires on which he is acting rationally are, respectively, mistaken and morally perverse.

This view has an apparently paradoxical implication. A person could hold Nazi beliefs and desires yet through weakness of will fail to act on them. (If Heinrich Himmler's words are to be believed, it took some effort to overcome one's natural feelings in order to kill Jews.[51]) But this means that *akrasia* is not always a morally undesirable condition. Like Huckleberry Finn, whose feelings for Jim prevented him from acting in accordance with his (false) moral convictions,[52] we may sometimes be prevented from evil-doing precisely by weakness of will.

A.3 TESTING INTENTIONAL EXPLANATIONS

Is an intentional explanation testable? What predictions does it allow us to make? Could such an explanation be corroborated?

A.3.1 Asking the Agent

There is one prediction an intentional explanation allows us to make which is so obvious that we might overlook it. We could predict what the agent's verbal behaviour would be when asked about his intentions. If his response to our question corresponds to our proposed explanation, this will corroborate our explanation. ("Why did you pull over and stop?" "Because the policeman signaled me to do so." "Why did you vote for the tax increase?" "Because I think that subsidised childcare is more important than having a little more cash.") This would seem the most straightforward manner of testing an intentional explanation, although of course it is not always available. The agent may be dead, as in the case of historical explanations, or otherwise inaccessible. It is true that if the subject replies to our question, her doing so is itself an intentional action.[53] So if we take her reply as a corroboration of our hypothesis, we are offering a second intentional explanation, one that posits that she is telling the truth. But this is no objection to the procedure. We may have good independent reasons for assuming that our agent is telling the truth. And our assumption that her report is reliable is itself defeasible.

However, there is a further difficulty with this form of corroboration. In taking the agent's reply seriously, we are also assuming that she has an adequate grasp of her reasons for acting. She may believe she is acting for a reason, but her behaviour may be driven by some unconscious (or barely recognized) fear or desire. And even when she is acting for a reason, she may have given little or no thought to what that reason was. Even where the reasoning involved was not entirely unconscious, it may have been enthymematic (Appendix 2.1). It may have relied on premises which the agent never clearly articulated. (Her vote in favour of subsidised childcare may be motivated, at least in part, by habitual political preferences. It may seem simply obvious to her that this is the right thing to do.) In this situation, the agent may have to interpret her own actions in order to reply to our question.[54] But again, this is not a fatal objection. All that these considerations suggest is that this means of corroborating a hypothesis is fallible.[55] We may decide that we have reasons to discount the agent's own reports of her intentions. But until we do decide this, asking the agent remains one way in which we could test our hypothesis.

A.3.2 Weakness of Will

There is another objection to the idea that intentional explanations are testable. It arises, once again, from the possibility of *akrasia*, weakness of will. I have argued that an action impaired by weakness of will can still be described as an intentional action, even though it is less than fully rational (Appendix 2.3). But the possibility of weakness of will might seem to make intentional explanations untestable, at least in the sense of being tested by hitherto unobserved events. For between the prediction and the act falls the agent, who may suffer from *akrasia*. It follows that even if the agent has the posited beliefs and desires, she may fail to act in the way we would expect.

Once again, however, this does not seem to be a fatal objection. All it shows is that any such prediction must have a *ceteris paribus* ("other things being equal") clause. The "other thing" to be excluded in this case is precisely *akrasia*, weakness of will. But weakness of will is yet another feature of the agent, to be taken into account alongside her beliefs and desires. What this highlights is another feature of intentional explanations, namely that they will often appeal to the *character* of the agent.[56] They may appeal to her character to explain why she chose one apparently good reason in preference to another.[57] But they may appeal to her character in order to explain why she acted or failed to act in accordance with the reasons she had. Now if we know how an agent has acted in the past, we can form some estimate of her character. On this basis we can judge how likely it is that she will suffer from weakness of will. Predicting human behaviour is a notoriously difficult business, but it does not seem to be impossible. If it were, there could be no human social life, which relies on such predictions.

A.3.3 Intentions and Laws

There is a second, and more serious objection to the idea that intentional explanations are testable. It arises from the claim that intentional explanations are "anomalous," in the sense that they do not rely on laws. If there are no laws connecting intentions and behaviour, or if intentional explanations do not rely on laws, then on what basis could we use such explanations to make testable predictions? And if such explanations do not appeal to laws, can the causal thesis be defended? Can we have a causal explanation that does not appeal to causal laws?[58]

A.3.3.1 Causation and Laws

When discussing the relation between causation and laws (4.2.1), I suggested that we should distinguish two questions that can arise in this context.[59] The first is a metaphysical question about the nature of causation. When we say that event A causes event B, are we committed to the idea that there is a law-like relation between events of type A and events of type B? But there exists a second question, which must be distinguished from the first, having to do with the nature of explanation. In order to explain event B by citing event A, must my explanation cite a law that connects events of type A with events of type B?

Explanation without laws. It is, in the first instance, the epistemic question with which I am concerned here. Can we offer a causal explanation of an event without citing a causal law covering events of this type? My answer is that we can. And as I shall argue in a moment, an intentional explanation does precisely this. It is true that one could use an intentional explanation to construct a general law. Such a law would state that if there existed another rational agent of precisely this type (having the same beliefs and desires) then when placed in exactly the same situation he would act in the same way. (In this sense one could argue that any singular explanation entails the existence of a regularity, in the sense of a *potential* regularity.) But if this is a law, it is an unhelpful one. If we loosen this condition a little—if we argue that agents having a *similar* character, in *similar* situation, with *similar* beliefs and desires, will act in *similar* ways—we may have something a little more useful. We may be able to construct some generalisations about human behaviour.

We could also construct such generalisations inductively, by connecting reports of agent's intentions with their observed behaviour. By either method, we could identify some regular patterns in human behaviour, if that behaviour is described in broad enough terms. If a person intends to withdraw money from the bank, he will normally enter the bank and approach the teller.[60] If he intends to go for a long walk, he will normally put on comfortable shoes. If he intends to read a book, he will normally find somewhere comfortable to sit. These may not be laws in the strict sense of sustaining counterfactual claims, for they are subject to too many exceptions.[61] (We might not be prepared to say that if a person were not to put on comfortable shoes, he would not be intending to go for a walk.) But for many everyday purposes such rough and ready generalisations are reliable.[62]

What I am suggesting here is that even if such regularities exist, an intentional explanation need not cite them. For there exists another constraint on such explanations, namely the rationality principle (Appendix 1.3 and 5.2). Now one could argue that the rationality principle itself relies on a kind of generalisation, albeit one of the broadest possible scope. It presumes that intentional agents do act rationally. This can, if you like, be regarded as a law. But the point I am making is that intentional explanations do not rely on generalisations linking intentions and actions. What they rely on is a calculation of how a rational agent in this situation would be expected to act, given certain beliefs and desires. It follows that our expectation regarding an agent's behaviour is not based on any general intention–action rule, although it may gain some support from the existence of generalisations of this type. Intentional explanations do not depend on such laws, even if there are laws to which they could appeal.

Causation without laws. It would be convenient if we could answer the question regarding explanation, while remaining agnostic regarding causation. But it is not clear that this position is defensible: it may be that the two issues cannot, finally, be kept distinct. Donald Davidson certainly attempts to keep them distinct. A simple way of thinking about Davidson's view is that he is trying to maintain the following propositions, which—at first sight anyway—appear to be inconsistent.

(1) Causation involves law-like regularities.
(2) Intentional explanations do not cite laws.
(3) Intentional explanations are causal explanations.[63]

How does he reconcile these propositions? He does so by arguing, first of all, that we do not require a causal law in order to know that a singular causal statement is true.[64] So intentional explanations can be causal explanations even if they do not cite causal laws. It follow that propositions (2) and (3) are compatible. But what about proposition (1)? Is it compatible with (2) and (3)? Well, Davidson argues that although we do not require a causal law to *know* that a singular causal statement is true, there must exist such a law if it *is* true.[65] In the case of intentional explanations, such causal laws do exist. They do not cover the relevant events described as reasons, but they do cover the same events described in some other way—"neurological, chemical, or physical."[66] So propositions (1), (2), and (3) are compatible.

Against Davidson. The principal objection to Davidson's view is that it apparently reduces reasons to epiphenomena, stripping them of their causal status.[67] After all, Davidson has argued that we can speak of a cause only where there exists a law. But he has also argued that there are no laws governing events when these are described in the vocabulary of beliefs, desires, and intentions. It follows that we cannot speak of an intention as a cause. In other words, given the truth of propositions (1) and (2), proposition (3)—Davidson's causal thesis—must be false. So our three propositions really do represent an inconsistent triad. Assuming that we want to maintain (2) and (3), then we need to abandon (1). We need to abandon a nomological view of causation.

If this objection is correct, then the key question is not an epistemic one regarding explanation; it is a metaphysical question regarding causation. And we cannot answer the epistemic question without answering the metaphysical one. If we claim that there exist lawless causal explanations, we are implicitly claiming that there can be causes that do not instantiate (actual) regularities. I am inclined to think that this is not a problem, that we are not bound to a nomological view of causation (4.2.1). But do we need to say this? Is the objection correct?

In defence of Davidson. Let me restate Davidson's position. What he wants to say is that there can exist two descriptions of an event, one which is (if you like) "physical" and one which is intentional. If we describe the event using the language of the natural sciences, we can see that there exist law-like regularities, the kinds of regularities that are essential to the existence of causation. (Let's grant Davidson this latter assumption, for the sake of the argument.) But if we describe the event using the language of intentional explanations, there are no laws to which we can appeal. Does this mean that we cannot speak of an intention as a cause, given Davidson's assumption about causality? No, it does not. For both descriptions refer to the one event, and it is on the level of the event that there exists (or does not exist) a cause. After all, causation is a feature of the world, not a feature of our descriptions of it. The following argument is invalid, since it embodies a form of the representational fallacy.[68] It assumes (wrongly) that we can deduce the structure of the world from the language we use to describe it.

(1) Causation involves law-like relations.
(2) Intentional explanations do not cite causal laws.
(3) Therefore intentional explanations are not causal explanations.

If this line of criticism is correct, then the distinction both Davidson and I favour can, in fact, be maintained.

A.3.3.2 The Prediction of Behaviour

In any case, let me come back to my initial question. Does the lawlessness of intentional explanations mean that such explanations are not independently testable? No, it does not. If I have certain beliefs and desires, then—assuming I am a rational agent—this will have predictable consequences. Since those consequences extend beyond the fact to be explained, an intentional explanation will be independently testable. If you see me walking into the bank and posit that I intend to rob it, then you can form a pretty accurate idea of how I would act, on the assumption that this is true. You may predict, for instance, that I will make some effort to hide my identity, or that I will approach a teller and issue some kind of threat. And there are things you would not predict, whose occurrence would fail to corroborate the hypothesis. If I intend to rob the bank, you would not expect me to fill in a deposit form or to approach the teller and discuss the weather. The more successful predictions you make, the more we have the consilience of confirmed deductions that will corroborate your explanation. Such predictions do not depend on laws, but they are nonetheless predictions, which can be tested.

It is true that we can attribute extra beliefs and desires to our agent in order to explain why she did not act as we might expect. (This seems to be Davidson's point about the "holism of the mental."[69]) But the parallel here with the sciences is quite precise. It is always possible to amend a scientific theory by way of auxiliary hypothesis so as to prevent its falsification. This is a corollary of the Duhem-Quine thesis, which points out that hypotheses are not tested one-by-one, but in bundles (as it were). But this does not prevent scientific theories from being independently testable. On the one hand, we can often test the auxiliary assumptions independently.[70] On the other hand, the reformulated theory (that is to say, with the new auxiliary assumptions) can be used to make new predictions. At the end of the day, we may have to recognise that the theory in question represents a "degenerating research programme" and that the most rational thing (particularly if a better explanation is on offer) would be to abandon it.[71]

A.3.4 An Illustration

Let me illustrate the points I have been making by borrowing and adapting one of Jaegwon Kim's examples.[72] Let's say you are in a meeting with your colleague Sally. You see her stand up and move around the room. Since you already know that the room is stuffy, you conjecture that Sally intends to get some fresh air. If this were true, it would explain her behaviour. So it is a potential explanation. But is it the actual one? After all, many other intentions might explain her moving around the room. To conclude that this is the explanation we should accept, it needs to be corroborated. So you make a prediction.

(1) If Sally intends to get fresh air, then—all things being equal—she will open the window.

If she does open the window, your hypothesis is corroborated.

But what if she doesn't? What if Sally continues to move around the room, looking uncomfortable, but makes no move towards the window? What then? Well, you could immediately abandon your hypothesis. Or you could amend it to "save the appearances." You could, for instance, conjecture that although Sally intends to get fresh air, she does not want to let in the street noise. After all, your initial hypothesis had a *ceteris paribus* ("other things being equal") clause. So you can now argue that other things were not equal.[73] So your explanation will now read as follows.

(2) Sally is moving around the room because she intends to get fresh air. She is not opening the window because she believes this would let in the street noise and does not want to disturb her colleagues' discussion.

The second sentence represents an auxiliary hypothesis, invoked to save the appearances. But it posits new beliefs and desires, and this posit requires corroboration in turn: it should not be a merely *ad hoc* amendment in order to save your theory. Sometimes it will be possible to corroborate this new posit directly, by using it to make a new prediction that is independent of those made by the original hypothesis. Let's say, for instance, you were to explain Sally's *not* opening the window by suggesting she has a pathological fear of heights and believes that if she glanced out the window she would suffer from vertigo. This belief-desire set represents a disposition which you would expect to be operative on other occasions. So you could use it to predict how she will act on other occasions. You could predict that Sally will always avoid windows in tall buildings, so far as she can, or that she will avoid climbing ladders.

Sometimes, however, the new belief-desire set may be too closely tied to the particular situation to allow for entirely independent corroboration. Here the best you can do is to test the amended hypothesis in its entirety. You can do so by using it to make a prediction which it would not support, were it not for the newly-posited belief and desire. How could you do this, in the case in hand? Well, you could predict that Sally will find some other way of getting fresh air, perhaps by making an excuse, going downstairs, and leaving the building. The line of reasoning would then be as follows.

(3) If Sally intends to get fresh air, but believes that by opening the window she would let in the horrible street noise, she will find an excuse to leave the building.

And so on. My point is that, given an intention to get fresh air, there are ways in which we might expect Sally to act. By reconstructing how Sally might reason in this situation, you can seek corroboration of your original conjecture.

A.3.5 FALSIFICATION AND FAILURE

At this point, I can make one concession to critics of intentional explanations. It is true that, strictly speaking, no intentional explanation is falsified by the failure of a single prediction. For any intentional explanation will have *ceteris paribus* clauses, and other things may not be equal. One might argue that intentional explanations are not alone in this respect, for most explanations, even those in the natural sciences, also employ *ceteris paribus* clauses.[74] But let me rest content with the assertion that this is true of intentional explanations. There can always be some confounding factor that prevents the expected result. Sally's failure to open the window, for example, does not necessarily mean that our original hypothesis—that she intends to get fresh air—was false.

But does this mean that intentional explanations cannot be tested? No, it does not. We might, for instance, observe some further action that could be explained only by positing a new intention, one that is apparently incompatible with our original posit. Let's say, for instance, you were to observe Sally turn off the air conditioning or (being a non-smoker herself) invite her colleagues to light cigarettes. Whatever we suggest is motivating these actions, it seems incompatible with the idea that Sally is wanting fresh air. If such actions do not, strictly speaking, falsify our original hypothesis, they certainly constitute strong evidence against it.

Even in the absence of such evidence, a failure to make successful predictions will count against our proposed explanation. If we explain this failure by positing some confounding factor, then the onus is on us to produce (more or less) independent evidence of its existence. If we cannot, then the most defensible course of action would be to seek an alternative explanation of Sally's actions. If our new hypothesis receives corroboration where our initial conjecture does not, then it represents a more successful research programme—if I may use this term of so everyday and informal a process—which should be adopted. If we were motivated enough to explain Sally's actions, this is surely how we would reason. And it seems a perfectly defensible way of explaining human behaviour, or, for that matter, the behaviour of any rational agent.

Notes

NOTES TO CHAPTER 1

1. Numbers, "Science without God," 272.
2. Lyell, *Principles of Geology*, 1.76.
3. Numbers, "Science without God," 275; Brooke, *Science and Religion*, 19. As Ron Numbers notes ("Science without God," 267–69, 280), some even argued for the banishment of God from science on religious grounds.
4. Rudwick, "Introduction," xxxii; Lyell, *Principles of Geology*, 2.126.
5. Lyell, *Principles of Geology*, 2.124. When it comes to the origin of the human species (ibid., 1.156), Lyell all but abandons his famous actualism (or uniformitarianism), in his efforts to highlight the difference in kind between humans and other animals.
6. Numbers, "Science without God," 279–80.
7. Gillespie, *Charles Darwin*, 115.
8. Quine, *Theories and Things*, 21, 67.
9. Quine, "Naturalism," 252.
10. Ibid.
11. Haack, "The Two Faces of Quine's Naturalism," 353.
12. For the suggestion that even a naturalism of this kind involves no ontological claims, being merely methodological, see sect. 1.1.2.
13. Van Inwagen, "What is Naturalism?" 81.
14. Ibid., 79.
15. Ibid., 80.
16. Ibid., 81.
17. Nagel, "Naturalism Reconsidered," 8.
18. I am grateful to James Maclaurin for these examples.
19. Nagel, "Naturalism Reconsidered," 8. Paul Draper's suggestion resembles this ("God, Science, and Naturalism," 278): nature, he suggests, could be defined as "the spatiotemporal universe of physical entities together with any entities that are ontologically or causally reducible to those entities."
20. Melnyk, "A Physicalist Manifesto," 2.
21. Kanzian, "Naturalism," 90–91.
22. Compare David Papineau's statement ("Rise of Naturalism," 174) that "physicalism, as it is understood today, has no direct methodological implications."
23. Montero ("Physicalism," 187) answers "yes."
24. Nagel, "Naturalism Reconsidered," 8–9.
25. Draper, "God, Science, and Naturalism," 277.
26. Lewontin, "Billions and Billions of Demons," 26.
27. Ibid.

168   Notes

28. The sociologist Peter Berger (*Sacred Canopy*, 100) uses the phrase "methodological atheism," which more precisely describes the aspect of naturalism in which I am interested. But I shall continue to use the phrase "methodological naturalism," with the qualification that it is the exclusion of divine agency in which I am interested.
29. The cross-references throughout this study are to the numbered sections of each chapter. The first number indicates the chapter in which the relevant section is to be found. So 1.2.2 refers to the relevant subsection of Chapter 1 (the present chapter).
30. Quine, "Naturalism," 257.
31. Pennock, *Tower of Babel*, 190.
32. Ibid., 191.
33. Ruse, "The New Creationism," 180–81.
34. Johnson, *Reason in the Balance*, 211.
35. A similar point is made by Paul Draper ("God, Science, and Naturalism," 299–300).
36. Johnson, *Reason in the Balance*, 105.
37. Johnson, "Unravelling of Scientific Materialism," 23.
38. Lewontin, "Billions and Billions of Demons," 31.
39. Numbers, "Science without God," 267–69, 280.
40. Carroll, "Introduction," 29.
41. Darwin, *Origin of Species*, Chap. 13 (428–32).
42. Neal Gillespie's *Charles Darwin and the Problem of Creation* (1979) offers a philosophically aware and historically insightful account, which has yet to be bettered.
43. While some early twentieth-century philosophers took a narrower view—Otto Neurath, for instance, saw successful prediction as the primary object of science (Hempel, "Logical Positivism," 173)—the task of explanation took centre stage in the work of their successors. Carl Hempel, for example, wrote that "to explain the phenomena in the world of our experience, to answer the question 'why?' rather than only the question 'what?', is one of the foremost objectives of empirical science" (Hempel, *Aspects of Scientific Explanation*, 245).
44. Plantinga, *Warranted Christian Belief*, 386–87.
45. Fakhry, "Classical Islamic Arguments," 133–45.
46. Craig, *The Kalām Cosmological Argument*, 8.
47. There are philosophers, influenced by the later Wittgenstein (see 3.1.2), who suggest that religious beliefs should not be regarded as explanatory hypotheses. (Phillips, *Religion without Explanation*, 116; idem, *Religion and the Hermeneutics of Contemplation*, 164). If this is intended to be a descriptive rather than a prescriptive statement, it seems simply false (Banner, *Justification of Science*, 87–95). On many occasions, believers at least *think* that their beliefs are explanatory (Boyer, *Naturalness of Religious Ideas*, 43, 125–54). And some of these believers are also philosophers.
48. A similar criticism was made by Larry Laudan ("Commentary: Science at the Bar—Causes for Concern") in the wake of the 1982 McLean vs. Arkansas Board of Education creationism trial.
49. Jones, "Memorandum Opinion," 64 (emphasis mine).
50. Draper, "God, Science, and Naturalism," 288–89.
51. Swinburne, *The Existence of God*, 38–45.
52. Brauer, Forrest, and Gey, "Is it Science Yet?" 48.
53. Ibid., 48–49.
54. It may be that talk of "intuition" here is also unhelpful, for the reliability of an intuitive procedure may be intersubjectively testable. Chicken-sexing, as

James Maclaurin has reminded me, is an intuitive procedure, but its reliability is certainly testable. But let me leave that issue aside.
55. Brauer, Forrest, and Gey, "Is it Science Yet?" 53.
56. Rae, *History and Hermeneutics*, 104–5.
57. Barth, *Church Dogmatics* §19.2 (535).
58. Dawes, *Historical Jesus Question*, 241–47.
59. Dawes, "Religious Studies, Faith, and the Presumption of Naturalism," §22.
60. Reichenbach, *Experience and Prediction*, §1 (6–7), §43 (382).
61. Hardy, "Indian Mathematician Ramanujan," 139.
62. Brauer, Forrest, and Gey, "Is it Science Yet?" 58.
63. Kitcher, *Abusing Science*, 155.
64. Ibid., 125.
65. Shanks, *God, the Devil, and Darwin*, 141.
66. Ibid., 145.
67. Ibid., 148.
68. Earman, *Hume's Abject Failure*, 3. This is Earman's description of what Hume is trying to do with regard to miracles. As the title of his book suggests, he believes that Hume failed.
69. Darwin, *Origin of Species*, Chap. 14 (453); for a similar comments, see Chap. 6 (217).
70. Darwin, "Essay on Theology and Natural Selection," 417–18.
71. Huxley, "Origin of Species," 282. With regard to historical accuracy, we need to be cautious about interpreting such remarks. By Huxley's day, the religious explanations on offer consisted of little more than pious allusions to some unspecified divine activity, since it was no longer possible for an educated person to take literally the Genesis story of creation. (See Knight, "Context of Creationism," 41.) So what Darwin and Huxley were dismissing were not merely religious explanations, but religious explanations that lacked empirical content. I shall come back to the question of empirical content shortly (3.2.3).
72. Dawkins, *The Blind Watchmaker*, 141.
73. Ibid. Graham Oppy ("Hume," 523) suggests that Dawkins's argument is the same as that which David Hume puts into the mouth of Philo ("Dialogues", iv [65–66]). However, Philo's argument is a little more sophisticated. It suggests that the theistic hypothesis is unsatisfactory because it is neither simpler nor more general than the *explanandum* (the fact to be explained), simplicity and generality being regarded as explanatory virtues. (See also Hume, *Enquiry*, 4.1 §26 [30].)
74. Lawson and McCauley, *Rethinking Religion*, 165.
75. Ibid., 156.
76. Pennock, *Tower of Babel*, 195; see also ibid., 289–92.
77. Ibid.
78. Flew and MacIntyre, *New Essays*, 96–130; cf. Atran, *In Gods We Trust*, 91–93.
79. Notturno and McHugh, "Is Freudian Psychoanalytic Theory Really Falsifiable?" 308.
80. As Elliot Sober notes ("Design Argument," 42), some critics of religious explanations suggest *both* that religious explanations are unfalsifiable *and* that they have been shown to be false. But this is merely an attempt to have one's cake and eat it, too.
81. This is, notoriously, Archbishop Ussher's dating, in a work published in 1650 (McCalla, *The Creationist Debate*, 33).

82. Lipton, *Inference to Best Explanation*, 24. The same argument, as it happens, is put into the mouth of Cleanthes in David Hume's "Dialogues" (iv [65]; see Mackie, *Miracle of Theism*, 143).
83. Draper, "God, Science, and Naturalism," 297–98.
84. Ibid., 297.

NOTES TO CHAPTER 2

1. Swinburne, *Existence of God*, 7.
2. Rowe, *Can God Be Free?*, 1.
3. Boyer, *Naturalness of Religious Ideas*, 43.
4. Barrett and Keil, "Conceptualizing a Nonnatural Entity," 240.
5. I have argued elsewhere ("What *is* Wrong with Intelligent Design?" 79–80) that "intelligent design theory" also falls short of being a theory, since it is far from clear what would follow, if its vague claim of "design" were true. If any quasi-religious explanation merits Darwin's criticism (1.3.2), it is surely this one.
6. Meyer is currently the programme director of the Center for Science and Culture at the Discovery Institute in Seattle, the headquarters of the ID movement. In an admirably upfront manner, Meyer ("The Return of the God Hypothesis," 27) argues that theism can be supported by way of "inference to the best explanation" (IBE). "Theism," he writes, "explains a wide ensemble of metaphysically-significant scientific evidences and theoretical results more simply, adequately, and comprehensively than other major competing world views or metaphysical systems."
7. For another example, see Behe, *Darwin's Black Box*, 232–53.
8. Or, perhaps, "theistic *proposed* explanation," if that were not so awkward a phrase.
9. I have borrowed this phrase from Peter Lipton (*Inference to Best Explanation*, 59–60).
10. Peirce, *Collected Papers*, 5:117 (§189). Actually, Peirce offered a number of analyses of what he also called "hypothesis" or "retroduction" (Niiniluoto, "Truth-seeking by Abduction," 57–64), but this is the form upon which he finally settled.
11. Here, as in some other key respects, my account of explanation follows that of Carl Hempel (see, for instance, his *Aspects of Scientific Explanation*, 338), even though the explanations with which I am dealing do not have exactly the same form as the deductive-nomological explanations that he championed.
12. Lipton, *Inference to Best Explanation*, 60.
13. Psillos, *Causation and Explanation*, 97.
14. Perhaps Lipton is thinking of causal overdetermination (see 4.3.3.1) rather than preemption. An example would be the situation in which two assassins fire simultaneously and inflict what would be, even taken individually, fatal wounds. But I fail to see how this would count against my distinction, although it may count against the idea that a cause must be a necessary condition of its effect.
15. National Academy of Sciences, *Science and Creationism*, 2.
16. Ibid.
17. See, for instance, Collins, "God, Design, and Fine-Tuning," 123. I shall discuss Swinburne's work in some detail later (6.1.2).
18. For the thought behind this definition, I am indebted to Alan Musgrave ("Deductivism," 19), although I have reformulated it in the light of my later discussion (2.1.3.2 and 3.1.2).

19. Musgrave, "Scientific Realism," 5; Bartley, *The Retreat to Commitment*, 262–63.
20. Swinburne, *Existence of God*, 341–42.
21. Ibid., 341.
22. Swinburne (*Epistemic Justification*, 62) argues that in the case of inductive probability, no precise figures can be assigned.
23. Swinburne, *Epistemic Justification*, 56–57.
24. Swinburne, *Existence of God*, 14; *Epistemic Justification*, 57.
25. Swinburne, *Epistemic Justification*, 62.
26. Ibid., 70.
27. Ibid., 64.
28. Salmon, *Foundations of Scientific Inference*, 64.
29. Swinburne, *Epistemic Justification*, 67–68, 69.
30. Ibid., 70.
31. McGrew, "Review," para. 7.
32. Swinburne, *Existence of God*, 52–61; *Epistemic Justification*, 80–83.
33. Popper, *Logic of Scientific Discovery*, §80 (254). And assuming we can make sense of the idea of the probability of a hypothesis, Popper notes that its probability would decrease as it became more testable (*Logic of Scientific Discovery*, §34 [102–3], §83 [268–73]). So if what we are interested in is whether a hypothesis has been corroborated (7.1), assessments of its degree of "probability" would be—on Popper's view—merely a distraction.
34. Sobel, "Probabilities, Subjective and Objective," 6–7.
35. McGrew's objection is particularly interesting. Taking as an example Ptolemaic astronomy, Swinburne (*Epistemic Justification*, 73) argues that if our measure is that of epistemic probability, then the ancient Greeks may have been justified in holding to the Ptolemaic view of the cosmos. But by the standards of logical probability, they were not justified in so doing. For although they were reasoning correctly in adopting that view, they did not realise that there existed a better hypothesis. But as McGrew notes ("Review," para. 9), this "appears to entail fairly sweeping skepticism regarding the logical probability of just about everything," since for almost any theory for which we have "epistemic" justification, there may (and probably does) exist a better hypothesis.
36. Musgrave, *Essays on Realism*, 223 n. 226.
37. This assumes a distinction between acceptance and belief, similar to that defended by L. Jonathan Cohen ("Belief and Acceptance," 368; *An Essay on Belief and Acceptance*, 1–16). I shall return to this point shortly (3.1.2).
38. Gale, *Evolution Without Evidence*, Appendix (166).
39. Earman, *Bayes or Bust?*, 101.
40. Gale, *Evolution Without Evidence*, 140.
41. Ibid., 204.
42. Kitcher, *Abusing Science*, 52.
43. Quine, "Naturalism," 275.
44. Lehrer, "Justification, Explanation, and Induction," 100. William Lycan ("Explanation and Epistemology," 417) suggests that the term was first used by James Cornman in 1980, but Lehrer's paper is ten years earlier.
45. Lycan, "Explanation and Epistemology," 417. Lycan refers to this as "sturdy explanationism." A very similar position is defended by Larry Laudan ("How About Bust?" 306–8).
46. Swinburne, *Existence of God*, 48.
47. "Any sentence which is entailed by an observation report is confirmed by it" (Hempel, *Aspects of Scientific Explanation*, 31).
48. Salmon, *Foundations of Scientific Inference*, 16.
49. Ibid., 117.
50. Draper, "God, Science, and Naturalism," 297.

NOTES TO CHAPTER 3

1. Reichenbach, *Experience and Prediction*, 5.
2. Strictly speaking, of course, cathode rays are themselves theoretical entities, whose existence is inferred from certain observable, experimental facts. But that complication need not detain us here.
3. The term "electron" predates Thomson's paper, having been introduced by G. J. Stoney in 1891 as a term for a quantity of electricity. Thomson at first avoided using this term, preferring "corpuscles," since he wished to highlight the idea that these particles were components of atoms (Davis and Falconer, *J. J. Thomson*, 133).
4. McMullin, "Structural Explanation," 140; Swinburne, *Faith and Reason*, 83.
5. The literature on this topic is voluminous. A classic defence of a realist understanding of theoretical explanation is Grover Maxwell's 1962 paper "The Ontological Status of Theoretical Entities."
6. This way of describing the issue takes for granted what Stathis Psillos ("Agnostic Empiricism," 57–58) calls "semantic realism": the view that theoretical explanations are in fact making assertions about unobservable entities. What I am focusing on here is a second dimension of realism, which Psillos calls "epistemic optimism": the view that we can have adequate reason to believe that such unobservable entities exist.
7. Reichenbach, *Experience and Prediction*, 212 (§25).
8. Ibid., 116 (§14).
9. It was, in fact, Reichenbach's idea of the probability of a hypothesis to which Karl Popper was objecting (*Logic of Scientific Discovery*, §80 [254 n. 3]); cf. 2.1.3.1).
10. McMullin, "Structural Explanation," 142. Compare Hume, "Enquiry," 4.2 §29 (32–33): "It must certainly be allowed that nature has kept us at a great distance from all her secrets, and has afforded us only the knowledge of a few superficial qualities of objects; while she conceals from us those powers and principles on which the influence of those objects entirely depends."
11. Cohen, "Interview with Einstein," 72–73.
12. Mach, *Principles of Physical Optics*, viii.
13. Ayer, *Language, Truth and Logic*, 179.
14. Ayer, *Foundations of Empirical Knowledge*, 213.
15. Ibid., 231.
16. Van Fraassen, *Laws and Symmetry*, 143.
17. Le Poidevin, *Arguing for Atheism*, 107–10.
18. To speak of the Wittgensteinian view of religious language as antirealist is contestable. Some Wittgensteinians certainly use antirealist language. Speaking of the act of kneeling in thanksgiving, D. Z. Phillips writes: "Talk of God has sense in this reaction. It is not the name of an individual; it does not refer to anything" (*Religion without Explanation*, 147–48). But it is notoriously difficult to identify Wittgenstein's own views on religion. (Was Wittgenstein a Wittgensteinian?) One recent author (Vasiliou, "Wittgenstein," 36) suggests that Wittgenstein did not entirely reject a realist construal of religious language, although he did reject the idea that religious propositions are held to be true for the same kinds of reasons as scientific propositions.
19. Phillips suggests that when religious propositions are taken to be explanatory hypotheses, this represents a kind of "superstition" rather than "religion" (*Religion without Explanation*, 41; see also the same author's *Hermeneutics of Contemplation*, 162–67).
20. Among contemporary discussions of religious explanations, Michael Banner's *The Justification of Science and the Rationality of Religious Belief* is

the most explicit in its defence of realism. It combines an "inference to the best explanation" account of theism with a vigorous defence of both scientific and theological realism.
21. Musgrave, *Essays on Realism*, 284 (slightly adapted).
22. Ibid., 285.
23. Cohen, "Belief and Acceptance," 368.
24. Ibid., 369–70; Cohen, *An Essay on Belief and Acceptance*, 44–48.
25. Musgrave, "Responses," 311; Psillos, "Agnostic Empiricism," 65.
26. Bishop, *Believing by Faith*, 24–25. Bishop draws upon Cohen's work, making a very similar distinction between (a) believing to be true and (b) taking to be true in both practical (and perhaps) theoretical reasoning (ibid., 33).
27. I say "generally regarded" because there are theist philosophers who suggest that we could have direct experiences of God. Even they are reluctant to speak of such experiences as *sensory* experiences, for obvious reasons. (You may well ask what other kind of experience there is, but I cannot pursue that question here.) See, for instance, Alston, *Perceiving God*, 19–20, 59–60.
28. For a discussion of the different social and cultural contexts in which these two modes of explanation have evolved, see Horton, *Patterns of Thought*, 327–28.
29. For a discussion from the point of view of social psychology, which illuminates and overlaps the philosophical debate, see Bertram Malle's "Folk Explanations of Intentional Action," in particular Malle's discussion of "reason explanations."
30. Churchland, *Matter and Consciousness*, 44–45.
31. As it happens, I am attracted to the view that what constitutes a "natural kind" can vary from one context of enquiry to another (Griffiths, "Emotions as Natural and Normative Kinds," 905), since what we call natural kinds are "solutions to problems of disciplinary accommodation: to problems about how to sort things so as to facilitate reliable induction and explanation" (Boyd, "Kinds, Complexity, and Multiple Realization," 72). But this is not an issue I need pursue here.
32. I am grateful to Alan Musgrave for this illustration.
33. Sometimes this, too, needs to be established, as in the case of a detective investigating a crime. He must establish a list of suspects as well as a motive.
34. Danto, *Narration and Knowledge*, 177, 218. The description of the *explanans* is also important. As Mackie writes (*Cement of the Universe*, 260), "Oedipus's having married Jocasta is the same fact as his having married his mother, and if the latter caused the tragedy, so did the former. Yet the latter description helps to explain the tragedy in a way that the former does not."
35. As Georg von Wright puts it (*Explanation and Understanding*, 121), using slightly different terminology, "in order to become *teleologically explicable*, ... behavior must first be *intentionalistically understood*."
36. Swinburne, *Existence of God*, 63–64.
37. Kitcher, "Explanatory Unification," 528.
38. Popper, *Logic of Scientific Discovery*, §31 (96), §35 (103).
39. Flew, *God and Philosophy*, §2.35 (56–57).
40. Ibid., §2.36 (57–58). In a delicate balancing act, Aquinas ("De Malo" 3.1–2; in *Selected Philosophical Writings*, 296) holds that God is responsible for the sinful actions, as actions, but not for their sinful character.
41. The way of setting out the cosmological argument makes a number of contestable assumptions: that the existence of the universe is a contingent fact, that it is the sort of fact of which we can expect to have an explanation, and that nothing is simpler than something. (For a recent discussion, see Grünbaum, "Poverty of Theistic Cosmology," 561–97.) One recent author

argues that the question is simply muddled, that we are misled by the fact that "nothing" is a substantive into thinking that it is a possible state of affairs (Rundle, *Why there is Something rather than Nothing*, 113). But I am not seeking to resolve these questions here.

42. I am reminded of Sidney Morgenbesser's response to Leibniz's question, namely, "If there were nothing, you'd still be complaining!"
43. Swinburne (*Existence of God*, 151) is among those theists who try to answer this question.
44. Davidson, "Actions, Reasons, and Causes," 4.
45. Swinburne, *The Christian God*, 161.
46. Aquinas, *Summa Theologiae*, 1a 3.7; 1a 13.4.
47. Hughes, *Nature of God*, 51.
48. Hume, "Dialogues," iv (61).
49. Ibid.
50. Ibid.
51. Plantinga, *Does God Have a Nature?* 47.
52. Alston, "Speaking Literally of God," 365.
53. Schoen, *Religious Explanations*, 93.
54. Aquinas, *Summa Theologiae*, 1a 13.5.
55. Aquinas, *Summa Contra Gentiles*, 1.32.
56. Ibid., 1.14.
57. Ibid., 1.29.
58. Alston, "Speaking Literally of God," 365.
59. Ibid., 365–66.
60. Ibid., 366.
61. Ibid., 369.
62. Mascall, *Existence and Analogy*, 101–4.
63. Ibid., 113.
64. Swinburne, *Existence of God*, 62.
65. What is it like to be a cat? No one knows. But that doesn't prevent us from explaining a cat's actions intentionally. Perhaps if a cat could speak, we *could* understand it. Its form of life is not so radically different from our own.
66. This objection goes back at least as far as David Hume ("Dialogues," iv [61]) and it has been much discussed since. For a concise, recent statement of this argument against divine eternity and immutability, see Hoffman and Rosenkrantz, *The Divine Attributes*, 103–4. Swinburne (*Coherence of Theism*, 223–29) argues against the doctrine of divine eternity, and rejects a strong version of the doctrine of immutability, on similar grounds. For an opposing view, see Leftow, *Time and Eternity*, 295–97.
67. The theist could argue that God's inability to know certain future states of affairs does not compromise his omniscience, since there is no fact of the matter about what has not yet occurred. For a discussion of this option, see Swinburne, *Coherence of Theism*, 179–80. For a survey of other responses, see Helm, *Eternal God*, Chap. 7 (109–25).
68. Helm, *Eternal God*, 124.
69. Martin, *Atheism*, Chap. 12 (286–316).
70. Swinburne, *Coherence of Theism*, 71–73.
71. Swinburne, *Coherence of Theism*, 73 (cf. 306).
72. The principle is abandoned by advocates of paraconsistent logic, for reasons not unrelated to a point I am about to make (3.3.4). But let me restrict myself to classical logic for the moment.
73. This same point could be made by discussing how we might falsify our hypothesis, for although you cannot *verify* a hypothesis by deductive reasoning, you can *falsify* it (Popper, *Logic of Scientific Discovery*, §23 [71]). You can validly argue "if H, then not-E, E, therefore not-H." Now if E represents

any true proposition, then from a self-contradictory hypothesis H you can derive both E and not-E. So H could be falsified by any true proposition E simply by deriving not-E from H. This implies that if a self-contradictory hypothesis fails to explain, this is not because it has too little empirical content, but because it has too much.

74. The more radical advocates of paraconsistent logic, such as Graham Priest, argue that there *can* exist true contradictions. But I understand this to be a controversial view even among paraconsistent logicians.
75. Musgrave, *Essays on Realism*, 223. Mark Colyvan ("The Ontological Commitments of Inconsistent Theories," 119) has recently made a similar point, arguing that while consistency may be regarded as a theoretical virtue, it does not necessarily trump all other virtues.
76. Davidson, "Actions, Reasons, and Causes," 12.
77. A related question, to which I shall return (3.2.1), is whether there can exist *singular* causal explanations.
78. Grünbaum, "Creation as Pseudo-Explanation," 234–35.
79. Danto, "Basic Actions," 142; Swinburne, *Existence of God*, 35–36, 49.
80. I am grateful to Alan Musgrave for pointing out this implication of Grünbaum's argument.
81. Lewis, "Causation," 163–67.
82. Psillos, *Causation and Explanation*, 100–101.
83. Mackie, *Cement of the Universe*, 29–58.
84. Leftow (*Time and Eternity*, 292–95) applies a modified version of Lewis's counterfactual theory of causation to the question of whether a timeless God can cause temporal events. (For Leftow's modifications of Lewis's account, see ibid., 258, 294.)
85. A belief no longer universally shared by physicists: see, for instance, Steinhardt and Turok, "A Cyclic Model of the Universe," 1436–39.
86. Smith, "Causation," 169.
87. As I noted a moment ago, the belief is no longer universal: some physicists (such as Steinhardt and Turok ["A Cyclic Model of the Universe," 1436–39]) argue that our universe emerged from a pre-existing universe by way of something like a "big crunch."
88. Smith, "Causation," 171.
89. Ibid., 171–72.
90. Ducasse, *Causation and the Types of Necessity*, 79.
91. Smith, "Causation,"173.
92. Lewis, "Causation," 170.
93. Ibid.
94. Ibid.
95. Smith, "Causation," 176.
96. Ibid.
97. This is an instance of what David Stove calls, in an article of the same name, "misconditionalisation." For one could construct a valid argument for (3) $\Box E$ if the initial condition (1) were $G \supset \Box E$.
98. I am grateful to Alan Musgrave for pointing this out.
99. Smith, "Causation," 178.
100. Ibid.
101. Swinburne, *Existence of God*, 320.
102. Here I follow Swinburne (*Existence of God*, 78) and understand a complete explanation to be one which cites all the causal factors which were contributing to the production of the *explanandum* at the time it occurred.
103. Swinburne (*Existence of God*, 25, 76–77) makes precisely this point, the only difference being that he speaks of *full* explanations which are not *complete* explanations.

176 Notes

104. Dawkins, *The Blind Watchmaker*, 141.
105. Lipton, *Inference to Best Explanation*, 24.
106. To take Swinburne's example (*Existence of God*, 78), we can explain the operation of Newton's laws by reference to Einstein's theories.
107. If such an explanatory regress is to end at all, it will have to end with a brute fact, that is to say, a contingent fact of which we have no explanation. For one cannot invoke a necessary fact to explain a contingent state of affairs. (See Le Poidevin, *Arguing for Atheism*, 40–41.)

NOTES TO CHAPTER 4

1. Kim, "Events as Property Exemplifications," 160.
2. Psillos, *Causation and Explanation*, 79.
3. Swinburne, *Existence of God*, 160–66.
4. Swinburne suggests that there is much more order in the universe than a universe needs to have (*Existence of God*, 156). I have no idea how Swinburne could know this to be true. But it must be true if the question of why the universe has the amount of order it does is to be kept distinct from that of why there exists a universe.
5. Clayton, *Explanation*, 129.
6. Amar, "G–d is Angry," para. 3.
7. For a discussion of what he calls the "orgy of theodicy" that followed the tsunami, see Rosenbaum, "Disaster Ignites Debate."
8. Psillos, *Causation and Explanation*, 67.
9. For this symbolization, and its ambiguities, see Lewis, "Causation," 162.
10. Psillos, *Causation and Explanation*, 233.
11. Ducasse, "Causation: Perceivable? or Only Inferred?" 178.
12. Schoen, *Religious Explanations*, 84.
13. Astin, Harkness, and Ernst, "The Efficacy of 'Distant Healing,'" 908–10.
14. Benson, Dusek, Sherwood, et al., "Study of the Therapeutic Effects of Intercessory Prayer," 941.
15. For theological objections, see Cohen, Wheeler, Scott, et al., "Prayer as Therapy," 42–43. For a broader set of objections, see Flamm, "Faith Healing," 10–14.
16. Steven Nadler, "Malebranche on Causation," 115–16.
17. Fakhry, *Islamic Philosophy*, 53–55, 209–17.
18. Copleston, *History*, 4:196; Jolley, "Introduction," xxiii.
19. Feuerbach, *Lectures on the Essence of Religion*, 149. Thomas Aquinas anticipated this objection (*Summa Theologiae* 1a 2.3; *Selected Philosophical Writings*, 199); the "five ways" are his response.
20. Feuerbach, *Essence of Christianity*, 189. An early modern thinker such as Malebranche had further reasons for adopting the occasionalist view. For a Cartesian thinker (such as Malebranche), the Aristotelian doctrine that created beings had causal powers of their own was barely respectable. It suggested that they possessed "occult qualities," which could not be reduced to matter in motion (Jolley, "Introduction," xxii; Nadler, "Malebranche on Causation," 130).
21. Nadler, "Malebranche on Causation," 131.
22. Malebranche, *Search After Truth*, Elucidation 15 (662).
23. McCann and Kvanvig ("The Occasionalist Proselytizer," 558, 611) agree that occasionalism is incompatible with what they call "event causation," if this is understood as "a relation in which one event is responsible for the existence of another." But they claim that occasionalism is compatible with some

weaker but to their mind more defensible sense of "cause." It is not clear to me just what that weaker sense is.
24. David Hume once suggested that if you want to understand his *Treatise*, you should begin by reading Malebranche (Nadler, "Malebranche on Causation," 133). We can now begin to see why.
25. Malebranche (*Search After Truth*, Elucidation 15 [662]) does speak of searching out "the natural and particular cause of the effects in question." But he immediately adds that "since the action of these causes consists only in the motor force activating them, and since this motor force is but the will of God, they must not be said to have in themselves any force or power to produce any effects."
26. Aquinas, *Summa Contra Gentiles* 3.69.
27. Ibid., 3.77. David Hume ("Enquiry," §56 [71]) brings forward similar arguments in favour of the existence of secondary causes, although—as always with Hume—one cannot take his religious pronouncements at face value.
28. In fact, there are two views of divine action found among those who, like Aquinas, reject occasionalism (Freddoso, "God's General Concurrence," 554–55). The first can be described as "mere conservationism." It holds that God creates natural substances with their own powers and keeps them in existence. But given this underlying divine conservation, secondary causes produce their effects on their own. According to the second, which we may call "concurrentism," both God and created substances are at work in the production of some effect. But in the present context I can safely ignore this distinction.
29. This class of facts (4.3.2.1) is to be distinguished from another (4.3.3.2), namely the class of facts which have a potential natural explanation, which the atheist regards as the actual explanation, but whose truth the theist contests.
30. This assumes that attributing an event to chance constitutes an explanation; for a discussion, see Psillos, *Causation and Explanation*, 9.4 (256–59) and 11.2 (285–87).
31. Laurentin and Joyeux, *Scientific and Medical Studies*, 35–36.
32. For the first, see Swinburne, *Existence of God*, 75, 140–43; for the second, see ibid., 75, 160.
33. Note that for Swinburne the "scientifically inexplicable" is a narrower category than that of the "naturally inexplicable," since (as we have seen [1.2.2]) Swinburne distinguishes between "scientific" and "personal" (intentional) explanations. On Swinburne's definition, an explanation which invokes an embodied agent (such as a human being) would not be *scientific*, but it would be a *natural* (as opposed to supernatural) explanation. Let me, however, set this issue aside.
34. Psillos, *Causation and Explanation*, 86.
35. Bishop, *Natural Agency*, 35.
36. Moser, *Philosophy After Objectivity*, 219.
37. Paul Moser (ibid., 216–23) offers a defence of the complementarity of such explanations, although, as he notes (ibid., 221), a realist might worry that this leads to dualism. It is true that if one adopts a realist view of both intentional and natural-scientific explanations, one is committed to the existence of both mental states and brain states. How these two are related is certainly a problem, but it is hardly a new one.
38. Swinburne, *Existence of God*, 46.
39. Von Wright, *Explanation and Understanding*, 119.
40. Swinburne, *Existence of God*, 172–88.
41. Sober, "Design Argument," 43–49.
42. Swinburne speaks of "an infinity" of universes, but even a very large number of universes, having laws and initial conditions that vary at random, would make the apparent fine-tuning of our universe less surprising.

43. Swinburne, *Existence of God*, 165, 185.
44. Shanks, *God, the Devil, and Darwin*, 219.
45. Hume, "Enquiry," §90 (114). His fuller definition is, "*a transgression of a law of nature by a particular volition of the Deity, or by the interposition of some invisible agent*" (ibid., 115 n. 1).
46. An assumption that is (as I noted earlier) no longer uncontested (Steinhardt and Turok, "A Cyclic Model of the Universe," 1436–39).
47. You might argue, as does William Lane Craig (in Craig and Smith, *Theism, Atheism, and Big Bang Cosmology*, 231), that a natural explanation of the beginning of the universe violates the principle *ex nihilo nihil fit*. But, as Craig recognises, this is a metaphysical principle rather than a law of nature.
48. Craig, "Problem of Miracles," 29.
49. Quentin Smith ("The Reason the Universe Exists," 579–86) argues that the universe could have caused itself to begin to exist. I am not (yet) convinced, but I shall not address his arguments here.
50. Smith, "Historical Method," 7.
51. Pennock, *Tower of Babel*, 194–5.
52. Strauss, *The Life of Jesus*, §14 (79).
53. You might, for instance, expect such a being to create the world, as he wanted it to be, by a single divine act, merely by willing it into existence. But you might not expect that such a world would require his ongoing miraculous intervention. (On the latter point, see Quentin Smith's argument in Craig and Smith, *Theism, Atheism, and Big Bang Cosmology*, 202–6.)
54. It is true that Hume's argument applies primarily to historical reports of miracles, but I take it to be applicable even to those events which we witness first-hand.
55. Hume, "Enquiry," §86 (110).
56. Ibid., §90 (115).
57. Earman, "Bayes, Hume, and Miracles," 297.

NOTES TO CHAPTER 5

1. Earman, *Hume's Abject Failure*, 3.
2. Hume, "Dialogues," xi (107).
3. Hume, "Enquiry," §57 (72).
4. Sober, "Design Argument," 28–29.
5. See, for instance, Dembski, "Obsessively Criticized," Section 4.
6. Sober, "Design Argument," 38.
7. Sober, "Testability," 64; "Design Argument," 39.
8. Sober, "Design Argument," 38.
9. Sober, "Testability," 65.
10. Sober, "Probability Reasoning," 75.
11. Ibid. .
12. Kitcher, "Explanatory Unification," 528.
13. Sober, "Testability," 65; "Intelligent Design," 76; "Design Argument," 41–42.
14. This is not identical with the criterion of independent specification sometimes employed in discussions of causation—the idea that "*A* cannot be regarded as a cause of *B* unless *A* can be specified in some way that does not mention *B*" (Pears, "Desires as Causes," 86). As David Pears argues (ibid., 86–87), this principle is far from firmly established. But it is a different principle from the one I am defending here.

15. Hume, "Dialogues," xi (107; emphasis original).
16. Sober, "Design Argument," 41.
17. Sober, "Intelligent Design," 75.
18. Gould, *The Panda's Thumb*, 21.
19. Ibid., 20–21.
20. Sober, "Design Argument," 43.
21. Kenny, *God of the Philosophers*, 10.
22. Danto, "Basic Actions," 142. As we have seen (4.3.3.1), this raises a new question for the theist to answer. A theistic explanation, I have argued (3.2.3), views the *explanandum* as the means towards a divinely-willed end. But why should God choose any means, if he could bring about that end directly?
23. Oppy, "Hume," 522; Hume, "Dialogues", xi (111).
24. Darwin, *Origin of Species*, Chap. 13 (430).
25. Ibid., 432.
26. Pigliucci, "Design Yes, "Intelligent No," 38.
27. Grayling, "Bolus of Nonsense," para. 6.
28. Nelson, "Role of Theology," 504–5.
29. Darwin, *Origin of Species*, Chap. 6 (217); Chap. 14 (453).
30. Garcia, "Divine Freedom and Creation," 212.
31. If we understand the character of an agent to be a product of her habitual pro attitudes (or desires) and her habitual strength or weakness of will (Appendix 3.2).
32. The best known example is J. L. Mackie's 1955 article, "Evil and Omnipotence," which argues (against the free will defence) that God could have created free beings who always (freely) chose the good.
33. My optimality condition could be understood as an expression of Hume's principle, recently defended by John Beaudoin, that we should never ascribe to a cause "any qualities, but what are exactly sufficient to produce the effect" ("Enquiry," §105 [136]). It is presumably this principle that Swinburne has in mind, when he argues that the hypothesis of an infinite deity is "simpler" than that of a finite deity (*Existence of God*, pp. 97–98). In any case, the application of this principle is complicated by the possibility of a divine revelation. Let's say, for instance, that the *explanandum* is a set of sacred writings, and that we come to the conclusion that the best explanation of such writings is that they are inspired by God. (Muslim apologists regularly offer such arguments on behalf of the Qur'an.) Then the writings in question could tell us things about God which go far beyond what would be required to explain their existence. They could tell us, for instance, that he is a being whose powers are without limit.
34. Again, I am reminded of the late Sidney Morgenbesser, who once described the paradigmatic form of "Jewish logic" (particularly appropriate in this context) as "If P, why not Q?"
35. Garcia, "Divine Freedom and Creation," 212.
36. Morris, "Perfection and Creation," 236.
37. Ibid., 236–37.
38. Ibid., 237.
39. Garcia, "Divine Freedom and Creation," 200.
40. Morris, "Perfection and Creation," 237. Morris is here citing an argument proposed by Norman Kretzmann, who also offers a response. But Kretzmann's response is not an adequate one, as Morris demonstrates. Morris's own response is to deny that God is obliged by his moral perfection to create a better world. So it resembles the first objection I have discussed.
41. Garcia, "Divine Freedom and Creation," 203.
42. Rowe, *Can God Be Free?*, 89.

43. Ibid., 101.
44. Van Inwagen, "Modal Epistemology," 70.
45. Ibid., 70, 73.
46. Hume, "Enquiry," §57 (72).
47. Ibid.
48. Van Inwagen ("Modal Epistemology," 71) argues that "there is no such thing as logical possibility—not, at least, if it really is supposed to be a species of possibility." His point seems to be that while we can say when a state of affairs is logically *impossible*, it does not follow that what is not logically impossible belongs to another category, namely that of the logically possible.
49. Dembski, "Intelligent Design is not Optimal Design," para. 5.
50. Ibid., para. 9.
51. Ibid., para. 15.
52. Ibid., para. 17.
53. Hume, "Dialogues," xi (107; emphasis original).
54. Ibid., 103 (emphasis original).
55. Draper, "Pain and Pleasure," 332.
56. Hume, "Enquiry," §57 (72).

NOTES TO CHAPTER 6

1. Chap. 5, n. 33.
2. Hume, "Enquiry," §105 (136).
3. Kant, *Critique of Pure Reason*, a637/b665 (528).
4. Swinburne, *Coherence of Theism*, 71–73.
5. Swinburne, *Existence of God*, 6, 328.
6. Ibid., 4. For the sake of consistency, I have slightly altered the layout (but not the wording) of Swinburne's sample arguments.
7. Hempel, *Aspects of Scientific Explanation*, 14–20.
8. Swinburne, *Existence of God*, 4.
9. Mill, "A System of Logic" Bk. 3, Chap. 3, §1 (306).
10. Hempel, *Aspects of Scientific Explanation*, 5.
11. Chalmers, *What is This Thing?* 13.
12. Mill, "Three Essays," 447.
13. Dembski, *No Free Lunch*, 25.
14. Himma, "Application-conditions," 12.
15. Himma argues ("Application-conditions," 12–13) that the argument does not, as it stands, support the conclusion Dembski draws. I am not sure; I would rather argue that we now have a better explanation of the specified complexity of biological organisms, namely that offered by Darwin and his successors. (See my "What *is* Wrong with Intelligent Design?" 78–80.) Dembski, of course, denies that evolution by natural selection offers even a *potential* explanation of the facts.
16. In his discussion of the design argument in the first edition of *The Existence of God* (148), Swinburne claims to be offering an argument from analogy, which as Mill notes ("Three Essays," 447) is a weaker kind of argument than induction. But in the second edition of *The Existence of God* (168) Swinburne backs away from this claim. His argument, he now suggests, is "an argument from evidence that it would be probable would occur if theism were true, but not otherwise."
17. Swinburne, *Existence of God*, 151–52.
18. Ibid., 328.

19. Swinburne, *Is There a God?* 52.
20. Swinburne, *Existence of God*, 70.
21. Maher, "Confirmation Theory," 1.
22. Sober, "Design Argument," 29. It would be better to say that it is the observation that is made likely by the hypothesis rather than (as Sober does) that the hypothesis is made likely. The latter way of expressing the distinction actually confuses the two issues.
23. Varying the figures shows that the higher the prior probability of the evidence, the less significance can be attributed to a likelihood calculation. Let's say that the probability of what we observe (E) is not so surprising a fact, that its probability is, say 0.5. Then on the other figures I've given, the probability of the hypothesis (H) is raised only marginally (to 0.18). This is worth noting, since at least some of the facts which theists attempt to explain will not be particularly surprising, particularly if they have well-corroborated natural explanations (4.3.3.1).
24. In doing so, he allows the earlier arguments to lend cumulative force to the latter (*Existence of God*, 12–13), a procedure to which I have no *in principle* objection, but which I shall not discuss here.
25. Swinburne, *Existence of God*, 109.
26. Ibid., 53.
27. Ibid., 66.
28. Ibid., 341.
29. Ibid., 329. There is a person-relative aspect to Swinburne's argument from religious experience. For although it does give a role to testimony (ibid., 322–24), it largely rests on his "principle of credulity" (ibid., 303), which states that "if it seems (epistemically) to a subject that x is present (and has some characteristic), then probably x is present (and has that characteristic)."
30. Swinburne, *Existence of God*, 341.
31. Ibid., 342.
32. Plantinga, *Warranted Christian Belief*, 272–80.
33. Swinburne, *Existence of God*, 328.
34. The article in question, Meyer's "Origin of Biological Information," was published in the *Proceedings of the Biological Society of Washington* in 2004, becoming the first work advocating "design theory" to be published in a peer-reviewed scientific journal. On September 7 that year, the Biological Society of Washington published a statement repudiating both the article and intelligent design theory. (The statement is available at http://www.biolsocwash.org.) For a less than positive review, see Gishlick, Matzke and Elsberry's "Meyer's Hopeless Monster."
35. Swinburne, *Existence of God*, 23.
36. Meyer, "Return of the God Hypothesis," 27; Peacocke, *Paths from Science to God*, 32–36; Banner, *Justification of Science*, 125–53.
37. See, for example, Steinhardt and Turok, "A Cyclic Model of the Universe," 1436–39.
38. Hempel, *Philosophy of Natural Science*, 7.
39. Ayer, *Foundations of Empirical Knowledge*, 231.
40. Thomson, "Cathode Rays," 293.
41. Ibid.
42. Musgrave, *Essays on Realism*, 284. Musgrave is here adapting an example given by John Herschel (*Preliminary Discourse*, §138 [144–45]), although in support of rather a different position. Herschel is arguing that we should appeal to what we already know to be "true causes" (*verae causae*), Musgrave that we should adopt the best explanation of the phenomenon. For the relationship between the two claims, see Sects. 7.2 and 7.5.

43. Musgrave, *Essays on Realism*, 284.
44. Ibid., 285 (adapted).
45. Timothy McGrew, as we have seen (2.1.3.1), criticises Swinburne's view of justification for denying, in effect, that the ancient Greeks would have been justified in accepting Ptolemaic astronomy. No such objection can be levelled at the "explanationist" view I have adopted (2.1.3.2).
46. Musgrave, *Essays on Realism*, 285.
47. Schoen, *Religious Explanations*, 133.
48. Leibniz, "Principles of Philosophy," §32.
49. Musgrave, *Essays on Realism*, 250 n.
50. Lycan, *Judgement and Justification*, 130–31.
51. Ibid., 135, 148, 156, 158.
52. Ibid., 155, 158.
53. Ibid., 156.
54. Ibid., 158–59; see also 139–44.
55. Ibid., 143.

NOTES TO CHAPTER 7

1. As I shall argue in a moment (7.1), many philosophers regard testability as a necessary condition of at least *scientific* explanations. I would be inclined to go further and regard it as a necessary condition for accepting any proposed explanation. But I would not want to make so strong a claim for all the *desiderata* I am about to discuss.
2. . Lycan, "Explanation and Epistemology," 416.
3. Hempel, "Logical Positivism," 191.
4. Cioffi, "Freud and the Idea of a Pseudo-Science," 472.
5. Thomson, "Cathode Rays," 294.
6. Popper, *Logic of Scientific Discovery*, §31 (96), §35 (103).
7. Swinburne, *Is There a God?*, 52.
8. Ibid., 53.
9. Davis and Falconer, *J. J. Thomson*, 123.
10. Worrall, "Methodology" 46.
11. As Ian McCausland points out ("Anomalies," 283–85), this is a contestable claim, since in 1898 Paul Gerber had already offered an explanation, using classical, Newtonian mechanics, and it is still unclear whether a revised version of his proposal could be made to work. (For an on-line discussion, see Brown, "Gerber's Gravity.") But this fact needn't bother us here. What is important is that known facts could, in principle, lend support to one theory over another.
12. Worrall, "Methodology," 47.
13. Musgrave, *Essays on Realism*, 230.
14. In fact, Nicod's criterion, as discussed by Carl Hempel (*Aspects of Scientific Explanation*, 10–25), has to do with conditionals of the form "All As are B," but I am using the phrase here in an extended sense, which would make it applicable to any hypothesis.
15. Grünbaum, "Popper vs Inductivism," 120.
16. Hempel, *Aspects of Scientific Explanation*, 14–20. While not strictly a paradox, it is a puzzle. What is the puzzle? Well, if an observation confirms H_1 and if H_1 is logically equivalent to H_2, then it also confirms H_2. Let's say that H_2 is "all ravens are black" and that H_1 is "all non-black things are non-ravens," then the observation of any non-black non-raven (let's say, the yellow cup that is sitting on my desk) will confirm H_1. But the problem is that

it will also confirm H_2. So my observing a yellow cup (which is a non-black, non-raven) apparently confirms the hypothesis that all ravens are black.
17. Worrall, "Methodology," 48.
18. Musgrave, "Evidential Support," 185–86.
19. Ibid., 197 n. 17.
20. Musgrave, *Essays on Realism*, 232–33; Sober, *Reconstructing the Past*, §2.5 [61–63]).
21. Musgrave, *Essays on Realism*, 244.
22. Swinburne, *Existence of God*, 160–66.
23. Sober, "Testability," 70.
24. Musgrave, *Essays on Realism*, 246.
25. Ibid.
26. This seems to be what Paul Thagard ("The Best Explanation," 181) means by "dynamic consilience"; it is a view that finds more detailed expression in the work of Imre Lakatos ("Falsification," 134).
27. Peter Lipton's remarks (*Inference to the Best Explanation*, 95–97, 101) may offer a way ahead.
28. Timmer, "Scientists on Science," section on "Explanatory Power."
29. Sober, "Testability," 58, "Intelligent Design," 67, "Design Argument," 34.
30. Both examples are Sober's ("Design Argument," 34).
31. Sober, "Design Argument," 34.
32. Sober, "Testability," 70.
33. As I noted earlier (2.1.4), one could still employ probability calculations to decide on the posterior probability of the hypothesis in question—Pr(H|E&K)—even if the likelihood of the evidence, given the hypothesis—Pr(E|H)—is 1.0. In other words, one could employ confirmation theory in order to assess the degree of evidential support that a proposed theistic explanation enjoys, even if that explanation is deductive in form. But this does not appear to be how Swinburne is arguing.
34. Draper, "Pain and Pleasure," 332.
35. To put it this way assumes that "it happened by chance" represents an explanation. Does it? I don't know; for a discussion, see Psillos, *Causation and Explanation*, 9.4 (256–59) and 11.2 (285–87). In any case, my point is that we can always test a theistic hypothesis over against the assumption that the event in question happened by chance.
36. Hales, "Evidence and the Afterlife," 341–42, citing an anonymous internet article.
37. Wilcox, "Dark Sucker Theory."
38. As Wilcox suggests (ibid., Question 12), DST also makes no predictions that would allow one to discriminate between it and our accepted theories of light (7.1).
39. Another real-life example, highlighted by Paul Thagard ("The Best Explanation," 186), is the way in which the analogies between sound and light supported the wave theory of light.
40. Depew and Weber, *Darwinism Evolving*, 71.
41. Darwin, *Origin of Species*, Chap. 4 (132–33).
42. Depew and Weber, *Darwinism Evolving*, 148–49.
43. Thagard, "The Best Explanation,"188.
44. Hempel, *Philosophy of Natural Science*, 83–84.
45. Thagard, "The Best Explanation," 188.
46. Quine and Ullian, *Web of Belief*, 67.
47. Mackie, *Miracle of Theism*, 100.
48. Ibid.
49. Swinburne, "Mackie, Induction, and God," 387.

184 Notes

50. Swinburne, *Existence of God*, 53.
51. Ibid., 65.
52. Ibid., 64.
53. Ibid., 60. Note that Swinburne's definition of background knowledge effectively restricts it to observational evidence. By excluding our best theories, Swinburne significantly (and conveniently) narrows its scope.
54. Swinburne, *Existence of God*, 146.
55. Ibid., 65–66.
56. Ibid., 16.
57. Ibid., 17.
58. Sobel, "Probabilities, Subjective and Objective," 9.
59. Swinburne, *Existence of God*, 71.
60. Ibid.
61. Ibid., 112–31.
62. Musgrave, "Kuhn's Second Thoughts," 292.
63. Ibid., 290.
64. Bartholomew, "Lyell and Evolution," 294.
65. Ibid., 294–95.
66. Draper, "God, Science, and Naturalism," 295–96.
67. Carrier, "Argument from Biogenesis," 742.
68. Prevost, "Swinburne, Mackie and Bayes's Theorem," 181.
69. Swinburne, *Existence of God*, 53.
70. Mackie, *Miracle of Theism*, 100.
71. Swinburne, *Existence of God*, 97.
72. Swinburne, *The Christian God*, 160.
73. Hume, "Dialogues," iv (61); Plantinga, *Does God Have a Nature?*, 47.
74. Banner, *Justification of Science*, 152–53.
75. Popper, *Logic of Scientific Discovery*, §43 (126–28).
76. Thagard, "The Best Explanation," 186.
77. Ibid., 184. As Thagard notes, auxiliary hypotheses, introduced in an *ad hoc* manner, do not detract from simplicity if they are themselves corroborated, if they help to explain new facts, or are "shared by competing theories."
78. Popper, *Logic of Scientific Discovery*, §46 (131).
79. Van Inwagen, "Problem of Evil," 162 n. 6.
80. Draper, "Pain and Pleasure," 332.
81. Van Inwagen, "Problem of Evil," 151.
82. Ibid., 139–40; Plantinga, *God, Freedom and Evil*, 28.
83. Van Inwagen, "Problem of Evil," 140–43. Van Inwagen speaks of an historian defending the character of Richard III, but I have transposed it into that of a lawyer defending a client, to make his point clearer.
84. I have already suggested (5.4.3.2) that such scepticism undermines the theist's explanatory claims as much as the atheist's argument from evil. But that's not the point I'm making here.
85. Van Inwagen, "Problem of Evil,"136. In fact, van Inwagen offers two parallel arguments, but I shall examine just the first, since the issues raised by the second are no different.
86. Van Inwagen, "Problem of Evil,"153.
87. Ibid., 155.
88. Ibid., 139.
89. Would it suffice to show that the auxiliary hypothesis is likely, given the central hypothesis? Would it be enough to show that if theism were true, the proposed scenario is plausible (ibid., 139). Well, it would help. But the atomist's spike hypothesis doesn't seem to have even this much in its favour.
90. Ibid., 153.

91. I am grateful to George Couvalis for this insight.
92. Lyell, *Life, Letters, and Journals*, 1.234.
93. Rudwick, "Introduction," ix.
94. Herschel, *Preliminary Discourse*, §141 (148).
95. Lyell, *Principles of Geology*, 1.86.
96. Ibid., 3.3.
97. Ibid., 1.75.
98. Aquinas, *Summa Theologiae*, 1a 2.3.
99. Ibid.
100. Lipton, *Inference to Best Explanation*, 118.
101. One of Thomson's reasons for preferring the electron hypothesis over the aether hypothesis was that the former was "definite and its consequences can be predicted" ("Cathode Rays," 293).
102. Galileo, *The Assayer*, 183–84.
103. Alston, "Speaking Literally of God," 371.
104. Ibid., 379.
105. Ibid., 383–84.
106. Ibid., 383.
107. Once again, I note that God could, for precisely the same reason, achieve that goal directly (4.3.3.1), but I am assuming that the theist can give some reason why he does not do so.
108. Ratcliffe, *Rethinking Commonsense Psychology*, 95.
109. Baillie, "Review" 173. For a similar example, see Ratcliffe, *Rethinking Commonsense Psychology*, 94.
110. See the introduction to the Appendix.
111. Dawes, "Paradigmatic Explanation,"64–77.
112. Lipton, *Inference to Best Explanation*, 118.
113. See, for instance, Plantinga, *Warranted Christian Faith*, 250. To call this inner feeling "the internal testimony of the Holy Spirit" is, of course, to make an explanatory claim, even if—like Plantinga—you are not justifying your Christian faith by arguing that it is the best explanation. The theist cannot escape offering theistic explanations merely by renouncing his dependence on them.
114. Calvin, *Institutes*, 1.7.4 (78–79).
115. Not least among these is that it could be made by believers of differing persuasions in support of radically incompatible claims—for instance, both that the Bible is the Word of God and that the Qur'an is divinely revealed. In fact, the Book of Mormon makes a very similar claim (Moroni 10:4) in support of its authority, a fact which should make more orthodox Calvinist Christians uncomfortable.

NOTES TO CHAPTER 8

1. Haack, "The Two Faces of Quine's Naturalism," 353.
2. Draper, "God, Science, and Naturalism," 297.

NOTES TO THE APPENDIX

1. Ratcliffe, *Rethinking Commonsense Psychology*, 150, citing Schutz, *Phenomenology of the Social World*, 192–93. Schutz, it should be noted, is here indicating the *variety* of ideal types which an individual can employ in understanding a social situation.

2. Schutz himself (*Phenomenology of the Social World*, 233) appears to be working with a very minimal notion of "causal adequacy": "an ideal-typical construct," he writes, "is causally adequate when it turns out to predict what actually happens, in accord with all the rules of frequency."
3. Schueler, *Reasons and Purposes*, 9.
4. Davidson, "Actions, Reasons, and Causes," 5.
5. Ibid., 12.
6. Davidson ("Actions, Reasons, and Causes," 12 n. 1) lists as opponents of the causal thesis Gilbert Ryle, G. E. M. Anscombe, Stuart Hampshire, H. L. A. Hart and A. M. Honoré, A. I. Melden, and William Dray. But William Dray, at least, does not belong on this list, for he explicitly affirms that "reasons, too, can be causes" (Dray, *Laws and Explanations*, 153).
7. Schueler, *Reasons and Purposes*, 16.
8. Carl Ginet, for instance, apparently rejects the causal thesis, arguing that an intentional explanation does not require a "causal connection between the explaining factor (cited or implied) and the action" (Ginet, "In Defense," 229). Ginet offers a sophisticated but very different account of human agency (see, for instance, his *On Action*, 140–41), which I cannot hope to evaluate here. For an initial critical response, see the review by Lawrence Davis in *Mind* (1991): 393. Taking a slightly different line, Cohen (*An Essay on Belief and Acceptance*, 63–67) argues that while explanations appealing to beliefs and desires can be causal, explanations that appeal to acceptances (or, I would say, intentions) are not. But this seems untenable: it would mean that "appeals to acceptance and intention can at best rationalize one's behaviour, not explain it" (Bezuidenhout, "An Essay on Belief and Acceptance," 394–95).
9. Davidson, "Actions, Reasons, and Causes," 4.
10. This is one of the points made by T. M. Scanlon in his criticism of what he takes to be "the standard desire model" (Scanlon, *What We Owe to Each Other*, 43).
11. Bishop, *Natural Agency*, 125.
12. Davidson, "Freedom to Act," 79.
13. Swinburne, *Existence of God*, 42.
14. Ibid.
15. Cited in Swinburne, *Existence of God*, 42.
16. Swinburne, *Existence of God*, 43.
17. Davidson eventually comes to the same conclusion, in "Intending" (1978), in order to deal with (*inter alia*) the problem of *akrasia* (weakness of will). He is followed in this respect by a number of authors. Michael Bratman, for instance (*Intention, Plans, and Practical Reason*, 10) argues that "we have as much reason to speak of an agent's intentions to act as we have to talk of her desires and beliefs." Similarly, Cohen's distinction between "desires" and "acceptances" ("Belief and Acceptance," 380; *An Essay on Belief and Acceptance*, 40–49) parallels my distinction between desires and intentions.
18. Davidson ("Intending," 89) concedes that one could lay stress on the formation of the intention, seeing this as a mental event, but argues that this "provides . . . little illumination." So he chooses to think of an intention as a mental state, already formed.
19. Davidson, "Intending," 102.
20. Bishop, *Natural Agency*, 114. Alfred Mele (*Motivation and Agency*, 27) describes intentions as "executive attitudes towards plans."
21. This point closely resembles one made by Cohen ("Belief and Acceptance," 381–82; *An Essay on Belief and Acceptance*, 44–49).
22. It might be objected that this way of posing the question assumes a compatibilist rather than libertarian view of freedom. Perhaps it does, but would

this be a fatal objection? In any case, it does so only if we think that a cause must be both a necessary *and sufficient* condition of its effect. But as Mackie argues (*Cement of the Universe*, 62), a cause may contribute to an effect without being a sufficient condition of it. It may be merely an INUS—"an *insufficient* but *non-redundant* part of an *unnecessary* but *sufficient*"—condition.

23. Swinburne, *Existence of God*, 42.
24. Does this solve the causal deviance problem? I think it does, since it means that an act is not intentional unless it is caused by the agent's unconditional judgement that this "is to be done." But a further solution might start with the idea that intentional behaviour is sensitive to certain facts, and that causally deviant action lacks this sensitivity (Bishop, *Natural Agency*, 148–50).
25. Dennett, *Intentional Stance*, 16.
26. Ibid., 16–17.
27. Ibid., 49.
28. Davidson, "On the Very Idea of a Conceptual Scheme," 197.
29. Davidson, "Psychology as Philosophy," 237.
30. Ibid., 236–37.
31. Dennett, *Intentional Stance*, 50.
32. Føllesdal, "Rationality Assumptions," 316.
33. Popper, "Models, Instruments, and Truth," 178.
34. The rationality principle, as we have seen, acts as a constraint on such explanations, for as Schueler writes (*Reasons and Purposes*, 130 n.), "there will almost always be numerous, conflicting, or even inconsistent interpretations of any action, each of which will make *some* sense of it." What we are looking for is the interpretation that assumes the highest degree of rationality (Dennett, *Intentional Stance*, 21).
35. Audi, *Practical Reasoning*, 116.
36. The example is based on one of Audi's illustrations (*Practical Reasoning*, 114).
37. For a summary of the literature, see Allen and Reber's article of the same name.
38. Audi, *Practical Reasoning*, 99.
39. Von Wright, *Explanation and Understanding*, 96.
40. Davidson ("Actions, Reasons, and Causes," 16) makes essentially the same point, arguing that an intentional explanation must evaluate "the relative force of the various desires and beliefs in the matrix of decision." He concludes that the practical syllogism cannot perform this explanatory role, since it "exhausts its role in displaying an action as falling under one reason." This is true, but it does not prevent us from asking, and attempting to answer, the broader question.
41. Audi (*Practical Reasoning*, 88) does recognise the possibility of "conflicting reasons." But his basic schema does not allow us to deal with them. One could represent the different reasons by way of different practical syllogisms, but the question then arises as to how these can be integrated to produce a single intention.
42. My example is loosely based on Nagel, *The View from Nowhere*, 115–16.
43. More precisely, it will need to include a *comparative* evaluative premise, since some of the other premises may also express judgements of value, as we shall see in a moment.
44. Schueler, *Reasons and Purposes*, 69.
45. Ibid., 70.
46. Aristotle, *Nicomachean Ethics*, Bk. 7; see Audi, *Practical Reasoning*, 19–24.
47. Davidson, "How is Weakness of Will Possible?" 21–22.

48. Audi, *Practical Reasoning*, 99.
49. Ibid., 42.
50. Bishop, *Natural Agency*, 109; Davidson, "How is Weakness of Will Possible?" 41.
51. Bennett, "The Conscience of Huckleberry Finn," 127–29.
52. Ibid., 125–27.
53. As von Wright puts it (*Explanation and Understanding*, 113), "verbal behavior does not in principle afford more direct access to the inner states [of an agent] that any other (intentional) behavior."
54. The fact that we often engage in intentional explanations of our own behaviour has been highlighted by von Wright (*Explanation and Understanding*, 114) and Dennett (*Intentional Stance*, 91).
55. Von Wright, *Explanation and Understanding*, 113.
56. I understand the *character* of the agent to be a product of her habitual pro attitudes along with the strength or weakness of will that she regularly displays.
57. Schueler, *Reasons and Purposes*, 69–87.
58. At least some of those who reject Davidson's causal thesis do so because they assume that there can be no causal explanation that does not cite causal laws (Thalberg and Levison, "Are There Non-Causal Explanations of Action?," 84). It is this view that I am about to reject.
59. Psillos, *Causation and Explanation*, 233.
60. Of course, if a person intends to rob the bank, he will normally do the same thing. There are often, if not always, a number of intentions which could give rise to the same action. So our identification of the cause on the basis of the action must be provisional, subject to further verification. This is, of course, the problem of abduction (6.2.1), the fact that *on its own* abductive reasoning looks like the fallacy of affirming the consequent.
61. Let me offer an example. Danto (*Narration and Knowledge*, 221) argues that we can subsume the behaviour of the inhabitants of Monaco—putting out American flags on the occasion of their national holiday—by citing a law, namely "whenever a nation has a sovereign of a different national origin than its own citizens, those citizens will, on the appropriate occasions, honour that sovereign in some acceptable fashion." But as Michael Scriven asks (Olafson, "Narrative History," 272 n. 12), when have the inhabitants of England shown any tendency to honour the Greek origin of Prince Philip?
62. For a defence of the reliability of such predictions, see Ran Lahav's "The Amazing Predictive Power of Folk Psychology."
63. This is my interpretation of Davidson's position, although I think it is a defensible one. My proposition (1) corresponds to Davidson's "principle of the nomological character of causality" ("where there is causality, there must be a law"); my proposition (2) is an application of Davidson's principle of the "anomalism of the mental" ("there are no strict deterministic laws on the basis of which mental events can be predicted and explained"); and my proposition (3) is an application of Davidson's "principle of causal interaction" ("at least some mental events interact causally with physical events"). See Davidson, "Mental Events," 208.
64. Davidson, "Causal Relations," 159–60.
65. Davidson, "Causal Relations," 160; "Mental Events," 215–23.
66. Davidson, "Actions, Reasons, and Causes," 17.
67. Hutto, "Davidson's Identity Crisis," 47–49.
68. Dyke, *Metaphysics and the Representational Fallacy*, 7–8.
69. Davidson, "Mental Events," 217.
70. Sober, "Testability," Sect. 1.

71. Lakatos, "Falsification," 155.
72. Kim, *Philosophy of Mind*, 34.
73. A controlled experiment is, of course, designed to test a hypothesis by removing such confounding factors, although even here we cannot guarantee they have been eliminated. But I am assuming that we cannot perform a controlled experiment, whether for practical reasons or because the explanation being offered is a singular one (4.2.1).
74. Sober, "Testability," 57.

Bibliography

Allen, Rhianon and Arthur S. Reber. "Unconscious Intelligence." In *A Companion to Cognitive Science*, edited by William Bechtel and George Graham, 314–23. Blackwell Companions to Philosophy, vol. 13. Oxford: Blackwell, 1998.
Alston, William P. *Perceiving God: The Epistemology of Religious Experience*. Ithaca, NY: Cornell University Press, 1991.
———. "Speaking Literally of God" [1981]. In *Philosophy of Religion: Selected Readings*, edited by Michael Peterson, William Hasker, Bruce Reichenbach, David Basinger, 365–86. New York: Oxford University Press, 1996.
Amar, Shlomo. "G–d is Angry." Published in the on-line Arutz Sheva, http://israelnationalnews.com/news.php3?id=74503, 31 December 2004.
Aquinas, Thomas. *Selected Philosophical Writings*, edited by Timothy McDermott. The World's Classics. Oxford: Oxford University Press, 1993.
———. *Summa Contra Gentiles*. Turin: Marietti, 1914.
———. *Summa Theologiae [Summa Theologica]*. Turin: Marietti, 1915.
Astin, John A., Elaine Harkness, Edzard Ernst. "The Efficacy of 'Distant Healing': A Systematic Review of Randomized Trials." *Annals of Internal Medicine* 132 (2000): 903–10.
Atran, Scott. *In Gods We Trust: The Evolutionary Landscape of Religion*. Evolution and Cognition. Oxford University Press, 2002.
Audi, Robert. *Practical Reasoning*. The Problems of Philosophy: Their Past and Present. London: Routledge, 1989.
Ayer, A. J. *The Foundations of Empirical Knowledge*. London: Macmillan, 1940.
———. *Language, Truth and Logic* [1936]. Harmondsworth: Penguin, 1971.
Baillie, James. "Review of *Rethinking Commonsense Psychology* by Matthew Ratcliffe." *Philosophical Books* 49:2 (April 2008): 172–75.
Banner, Michael C. *The Justification of Science and the Rationality of Religious Belief*. Oxford Philosophical Monographs. Oxford: Clarendon Press, 1990.
Barrett, Justin L. and Frank C. Keil. "Conceptualizing a Nonnatural Entity: Anthropomorphism in God Concepts." *Cognitive Psychology* 31 (1996): 219–47.
Barth, Karl. *Church Dogmatics*, vol. 1, part 2: *The Doctrine of the Word of God*. Translated by G. T. Thomson and Harold Knight. Edinburgh: T. & T. Clark, 1956.
Bartholomew, Michael. "Lyell and Evolution: An Account of Lyell's Response to the Prospect of an Evolutionary Ancestry for Man." *The British Journal for the History of Science* 6 (1972–73): 261–303.
Bartley, William Warren. *The Retreat to Commitment*. 2nd edition. La Salle, IL: Open Court, 1984.
Beaudoin, John. "On Some Criticisms of Hume's Principle of Proportioning Cause to Effect." *Philo* 2 (1999): 26–40.

Behe, Michael J. *Darwin's Black Box: The Biochemical Challenge to Evolution.* New York: Free Press, 1996.

Bennett, Jonathan. "The Conscience of Huckleberry Finn." *Philosophy* 49 (1974): 123–34.

Benson, Herbert, Jeffery A. Dusek, Jane B. Sherwood, et al. "Study of the Therapeutic Effects of Intercessory Prayer in Cardiac Bypass Patients: a Multicenter Randomized Trial of Uncertainty and Certainty of Receiving Intercessory Prayer." *American Heart Journal* 151 (2005): 934–42.

Berger, Peter L. *The Sacred Canopy: Elements of a Sociological Theory of Religion* [1967]. Anchor Books. New York: Doubleday, 1969.

Bezuidenhout, Anne. "An Essay on Belief and Acceptance." *The Review of Metaphysics* 50 (1996): 392–95.

Bishop, John. *Believing by Faith: An Essay in the Ethics and Epistemology of Religious Belief.* Oxford: Oxford University Press, 2007.

———. *Natural Agency: An Essay on the Causal Theory of Action.* Cambridge Studies in Philosophy. Cambridge: Cambridge University Press, 1989.

Boyd, Richard N. "Kinds, Complexity and Multiple Realization: Comments on Millikan's 'Historical Kinds and the Special Sciences.'" *Philosophical Studies* 95 (1999): 67–98.

Boyer, Pascal. *The Naturalness of Religious Ideas: A Cognitive Theory of Religion.* Berkeley: University of California Press, 1994.

Bratman, Michael E. *Intentions, Plans, and Practical Reason* [1987]. The David Hume Series of Philosophy and Cognitive Science Reissues. Palo Alto, CA: CSLI Publications, 1999.

Brauer Matthew J., Barbara Forrest, and Steven G. Gey, "Is it Science Yet? Intelligent Design Creationism and the Constitution" *Washington University Law Quarterly* 83 (2005): 1–149.

Brooke, John Hedley. *Science and Religion: Some Historical Perspectives.* Cambridge History of Science Series. Cambridge: Cambridge University Press, 1991.

Brown, Kevin. "Gerber's Gravity," http://www.mathpages.com/home/k-math527/kmath527.htm, 26 October, 2006.

Calvin, John. *Institutes of the Christian Religion.* Translated by Ford Lewis Battles. Library of Christian Classics, vols. xx and xxi. London: SCM, 1961.

Carrier, R. C. "The Argument from Biogenesis: Probabilities Against a Natural Origin of Life." *Biology and Philosophy* vol. xix (2004): 739–64.

Carroll, Joseph. "Introduction." In *On the Origin of Species by Means of Natural Selection* by Charles Darwin, 9–72. Peterborough, ON: Broadview Press, 2003.

Chalmers, A. F. *What is This Thing Called Science? An Assessment of the Nature and Status of Science and Its Methods.* 2nd edition. St Lucia: University of Queensland Press, 1982.

Churchland, Paul M. *Matter and Consciousness: A Contemporary Introduction to the Philosophy of Mind.* A Bradford Book. Cambridge, MA: MIT Press, 1984.

Cioffi, Frank. "Freud and the Idea of a Pseudo-Science." In *Explanation in the Behavioural Sciences*, edited by Robert Borger and Frank Cioffi, 471–515. Cambridge: Cambridge University Press, 1970.

Clayton, Philip. *Explanation from Physics to Theology: An Essay in Rationality.* New Haven, CT: Yale University Press, 1989.

Cohen, Cynthia B., Sondra E. Wheeler, David A. Scott, et al., "Prayer as Therapy." *The Hastings Center Report* 30 (May 2000): 40–43.

Cohen, I. Bernard. "An Interview with Einstein." *Scientific American* 193:1 (July 1955): 68–73.

Cohen, L. Jonathan. "Belief and Acceptance." *Mind* 98 (July 1989): 367–89.

———. *An Essay on Belief and Acceptance.* Oxford: Clarendon Press, 1992.

Collins Robin. "God, Design, and Fine-Tuning." In *God Matters: Readings in the Philosophy of Religion*, edited by Raymond Martin and Christopher Bernard, 119–35. New York: Longman Press, 2003.

Colyvan, Mark. "The Ontological Commitments of Inconsistent Theories." *Philosophical Studies* 141 (2008): 115–23.

Copleston, Frederick, S.J. *A History of Philosophy*. 9 vols. Image Books. Garden City, NY: Doubleday, 1963.

Craig, William Lane. *The Kalām Cosmological Argument*. Library of Philosophy and Theology. London: Macmillan, 1979.

———. "The Problem of Miracles: A Historical and Theological Perspective." In *Gospel Perspectives*, vol. 6, *The Miracles of Jesus*, edited by David Wenham and Craig Bloomberg, 9–48. Sheffield: JSOT Press, 1986.

Craig, William Lane and Quentin Smith. *Theism, Atheism, and Big Bang Cosmology*. Oxford: Clarendon Press, 1993.

Danto, Arthur C. "Basic Actions." *American Philosophical Quarterly* 2 (1965): 141–48.

———. *Narration and Knowledge*. New York: Columbia University Press, 1985.

Darwin, Charles. "Essay on Theology and Natural Selection" [1838]. Notes on John Macculloch's *Proofs and Illustrations of the Attributes of God*, transcribed and annotated by Paul H. Barrett. In *Darwin on Man: A Psychological Study of Scientific Creativity together with Darwin's Early and Unpublished Notebooks* by Howard E. Gruber, 414–22. New York: E. P. Dutton, 1974.

———. *The Origin of Species by Means of Natural Selection* [1859]. Pelican Classics. Harmondsworth, UK: Penguin, 1968.

Davidson, Donald. "Actions, Reasons, and Causes" [1963]. In *Essays on Actions and Events*, 3–19. Oxford: Clarendon Press, 1980.

———. "Causal Relations" [1967]. In *Essays on Actions and Events*, 149–62. Oxford: Clarendon Press, 1980.

———. "Freedom to Act" [1973]. In *Essays on Actions and Events*, 63–81. Oxford: Clarendon Press, 1980.

———. "How is Weakness of the Will Possible?" [1970]. In *Essays on Actions and Events*, 21–42. Oxford: Clarendon Press, 1980.

———. "Intending" [1978]. In *Essays on Actions and Events*, 83–102. Oxford: Clarendon Press, 1980.

———. "Mental Events" [1970]. In *Essays on Actions and Events*, 207–25. Oxford: Clarendon Press, 1980.

———. "On the Very Idea of a Conceptual Scheme" [1974]. In *Inquiries into Truth and Interpretation*, 183–98. Oxford: Clarendon Press, 1984.

———. "Psychology as Philosophy" [1971]. In *Essays on Actions and Events*, 229–44. Oxford: Clarendon Press, 1980.

Davis, E. A. and I. J. Falconer. *J. J. Thomson and the Discovery of the Electron*. London: Taylor & Francis, 1997.

Davis, Lawrence D. "Review of *On Action* by Carl Ginet." *Mind* 100 (1991): 390–94.

Dawes, Gregory W. *The Historical Jesus Question: The Challenge of History to Religious Authority*. Louisville, KY: Westminster John Knox, 2001.

———. "Paradigmatic Explanation: Strauss's Dangerous Idea." *Louvain Studies* 32 (2008): 64–77.

———. "Religious Studies, Faith, and the Presumption of Naturalism." *Journal of Religion and Society* 5 (2003). http://www.creighton.edu/JRS

———. "What *is* Wrong with Intelligent Design?" *International Journal for Philosophy of Religion* 61 (2007): 69–81.

Dawkins, Richard. *The Blind Watchmaker* [1986]. London: Penguin, 1988.

194 Bibliography

Dembski, William A. "Intelligent Design is not Optimal Design." 2000. http://www.designinference.com/documents/2000.02.ayala_response.htm

———. *No Free Lunch: Why Specified Complexity Cannot Be Purchased Without Intelligence*. Langham, MD: Rowman & Littlefield, 2002.

———. "Obsessively Criticized but Scarcely Refuted: A Response to Richard Wein." 2002. http://www.designinference.com/documents/05.02.resp_to_wein.htm

Dennett, Daniel C. *The Intentional Stance*. A Bradford Book. Cambridge, MA: MIT Press, 1987.

Depew, David J. and Bruce H. Weber. *Darwinism Evolving: Systems Dynamics and the Genealogy of Natural Selection*. A Bradford Book. Cambridge, MA: MIT Press, 1995.

Draper, Paul R. "God, Science, and Naturalism." In *The Oxford Handbook of Philosophy of Religion*, edited by William J. Wainwright, 272–303. New York: Oxford University Press, 2005.

———. "Pain and Pleasure: An Evidential Problem for Theists." *Noûs* 23 (1989): 331–50.

Dray, William. *Laws and Explanations in History*. Oxford: Oxford University Press, 1957.

Ducasse, Curt John. *Causation and the Types of Necessity* [1924]. New York: Dover Publications, 1969.

———. "Causation: Perceivable? or Only Inferred?" *Philosophy and Phenomenological Research* 26 (1965): 173–79.

Dyke, Heather. *Metaphysics and the Representational Fallacy*. Routledge Studies in Contemporary Philosophy. London: Routledge, 2007.

Earman, John. "Bayes, Hume, and Miracles." *Faith and Philosophy* 10 (1993): 293–310.

———. *Bayes or Bust? A Critical Examination of Bayesian Confirmation Theory*. A Bradford Book. Cambridge, MA: MIT Press, 1992.

———. *Hume's Abject Failure: The Argument Against Miracles*. Oxford University Press, 2000.

Fakhry, Majid. "Classical Islamic Arguments for the Existence of God." *The Muslim World* 47 (1957): 133–45.

———. *A History of Islamic Philosophy*. 2nd edition. New York: Columbia University Press, 1983.

Feuerbach, Ludwig. *The Essence of Christianity* [1843]. Translated by Marian Evans. London: Trübner, 1881.

———. *Lectures on the Essence of Religion* [1851]. Translated by Ralph Mannheim. New York: Harper & Row, 1967.

Flamm, Bruce L. "Faith Healing Confronts Modern Medicine." *The Scientific Review of Alternative Medicine* 8:1 (Spring/Summer 2004): 9–14.

Flew, Antony and Alasdair MacIntyre. *New Essays in Philosophical Theology*. London: SCM, 1955.

Flew, Antony. *God and Philosophy*. Amherst, NY: Prometheus Books, 2005.

Føllesdal. Dagfinn "The Status of Rationality Assumptions in Interpretation and in the Explanation of Action." *Dialectica* 36 (1982): 301–16.

Freddoso, Alfred J. "God's General Concurrence with Secondary Causes: Why Conservation is Not Enough" in *Philosophical Perspectives V: Philosophy of Religion*, edited by James E. Tomberlin, 553–85. Atascadero, CA: Ridgeview Publishing, 1991.

Gale, Barry G. *Evolution without Evidence: Charles Darwin and The Origin of Species*. Brighton: Harvester, 1982.

Galilei, Galileo. *The Assayer* (1623). In *The Controversy on the Comets of 1618*. Translated by Stillman Drake and C. D. O'Malley, 151–336. Philadelphia: University of Philadelphia Press, 1960.

Garcia, Laura L. "Divine Freedom and Creation." *The Philosophical Quarterly* 42 (1992): 191–213.
Gillespie, Neal C. *Charles Darwin and the Problem of Creation*. Chicago: University of Chicago Press, 1979.
Ginet, Carl. "In Defense of a Non-Causal Account of Reasons Explanations" *Journal of Ethics* 12 (2008): 229–37.
———. *On Action*. Cambridge Studies in Philosophy. Cambridge: Cambridge University Press, 1990.
Gishlick, Alan, Nick Matze, and Wesley R. Elsberry. "Meyer's Hopeless Monster." 2004. http://www.pandasthumb.org/archives/2004/08/me-yers_hopeless_monster.html
Grayling, A. C. "Bolus of Nonsense." *New Humanist* Web Exclusive Articles, 2008. http://newhumanist.org.uk/1881
Gould, Stephen Jay. *The Panda's Thumb: More Reflections on Natural History*. New York: Norton, 1980.
Griffiths, Paul E. "Emotions as Natural and Normative Kinds." *Philosophy of Science* 71 (2004): 901–11.
Grünbaum, Adolf. "Creation as a Pseudo-Explanation in Current Physical Cosmology" *Erkenntnis* 35 (1991): 233–54.
———. "Popper vs Inductivism." In *Progress and Rationality in Science*, edited by Gerard Radnitzky and Gunnar Andersson, 117–142. Boston Studies in the Philosophy of Science 58 / Synthese Library 125. Dordrecht: D. Seidel, 1978.
———. "The Poverty of Theistic Cosmology." *The British Journal for the Philosophy of Science* 55 (2004): 561–614.
Haack, Susan. "The Two Faces of Quine's Naturalism." *Synthese* 94 (1993): 335–56.
Hales, Steven D. "Evidence and the Afterlife." *Philosophia* 28 (2001): 335–46.
Hardy, G. H. "The Indian Mathematician Ramanujan." *The American Mathematical Monthly* 44 (1937): 137–55.
Helm, Paul. *Eternal God: A Study of God Without Time*. Oxford: Clarendon Press, 1988.
Hempel, Carl G. *Aspects of Scientific Explanation*. New York: Free Press, 1965.
———. "Logical Positivism and the Social Sciences." In *The Legacy of Logical Positivism: Studies in the Philosophy of Science*, edited by Peter Achinstein and Stephen F. Barker, 163–94. Baltimore, MD: Johns Hopkins Press, 1969.
———. *Philosophy of Natural Science*. Foundations of Philosophy. Englewood Cliffs, NJ: Prentice-Hall, 1966.
Herschel, John Frederick William. *A Preliminary Discourse on the Study of Natural Philosophy* [1830]. The Sources of Science 17. New York: Johnson Reprint Corporation, 1966.
Himma, Kenneth Einar. "The application-conditions for design inferences: Why the design arguments need the help of other arguments for God's existence." *International Journal for Philosophy of Religion* 57 (2005): 1–33.
Hoffman, Joshua and Rosenkrantz, Gary S. *The Divine Attributes*. Exploring the Philosophy of Religion. Oxford: Blackwell, 2002.
Horton, Robin. *Patterns of Thought in Africa and the West: Essays on Magic, Religion and Science*. Cambridge: Cambridge University Press, 1993.
Hughes, Gerard J. *The Nature of God*. The Problems of Philosophy. London: Routledge, 1995.
Hume, David. "Dialogues Concerning Natural Religion" [1779]. *Principal Writings on Religion*, edited by J. C. A. Gaskin, 29–130. Oxford World's Classics. Oxford University Press, 1993.
———. "An Enquiry Concerning Human Understanding" [1777]. In *Hume's Enquiries*, edited by L. A. Selby-Bigge, 5–165. 2nd edition. Oxford: Clarendon Press, 1902.

———. *A Treatise of Human Nature* [1740], edited by L. A. Selby-Bigge. 2nd edition. Oxford: Clarendon Press, 1978.
Hutto, Daniel D. "Davidson's Identity Crisis." *Dialectica* 52 (1998): 45–61.
Huxley, Thomas Henry. "The Origin of Species" [1860]. In *Lay Sermons, Addresses, and Reviews*, 255–98. New Edition. London: Macmillan, 1883.
Johnson, Phillip E. *Reason in the Balance: The Case Against Naturalism in Science, Law, and Education*. Downers Grove, IL: InterVarsity, 1995.
———. "The Unravelling of Scientific Materialism." *First Things* 77 (November 1997): 22–25.
Jolley, Nicholas. "Introduction." In *Malebranche: Dialogues on Metaphysics and Religion*, edited by Nicholas Jolley and David Scott, viii–xxiv. Cambridge Texts in the History of Philosophy. Cambridge: Cambridge University Press, 1997.
Jones, John E. "Memorandum Opinion." Kitzmiller et al. vs Dover Area School District. U.S. District Court for the Middle District of Pennsylvania, 20 December 2005. http://www2.ncseweb.org/wp.
Kant, Immanuel. *The Critique of Pure Reason* [1787]. Translated by Norman Kemp Smith. London: Macmillan Press, 1929.
Kanzian, Christian. "Naturalism, Physicalism, and Some Notes on 'Analytical Philosophy.'" In *Analytic Philosophy Without Naturalism*, edited by Antonella Corradini, Sergio Galvan, and E. Jonathan Lowe, 89–93. Routledge Studies in Twentieth-Century Philosophy. London: Routledge, 2006.
Kenny, Anthony. *The God of the Philosophers*. Oxford: Clarendon Press, 1979.
Kim, Jaegwon. "Events as Property Exemplifications." In *Action Theory: Proceedings of the Winnipeg Conference on Human Action, 9–11 May 1975*, edited by Myles Brand and Douglas Walton, 159–77. Dordrecht: Reidel, 1976.
———. *Philosophy of Mind*. Dimensions of Philosophy. Boulder, CO: Westview [HarperCollins], 1996.
Kitcher, Philip. *Abusing Science: The Case Against Creationism*. Cambridge, MA: MIT Press, 1996.
———. "Explanatory Unification." *Philosophy of Science* 48 (1981): 507–31.
Knight, David. "The Context of Creationism in Darwin's England." In *The Cultures of Creationism: Anti-Evolutionist in English-Speaking Countries*, edited by Simon Coleman and Leslie Carlin, 29–43. Aldershot: Ashgate, 2004.
Lahav, Ran. "The Amazing Predictive Power of Folk Psychology." *Australasian Journal of Philosophy* 70 (1992): 99–105.
Lakatos, Imre. "Falsification and the Methodology of Scientific Research Programmes." In *Criticism and the Growth of Knowledge*, edited by Imre Lakatos and Alan Musgrave, 91–189. Cambridge: Cambridge University Press, 1970.
Laudan, Larry. "Commentary: Science at the Bar—Causes for Concern" *Science, Technology, and Human Values*, 7:41 (1982): 16–19.
———. "How About Bust? Factoring Explanatory Power Back into Theory Evaluation." *Philosophy of Science* 64 (1997): 306–16.
Laurentin, René and Henri Joyeux, *Scientific and Medical Studies on the Apparitions at Medjugorje* [1985]. Translated by Luke Griffin. Dublin: Veritas, 1987.
Lawson, E. Thomas and Robert N. McCauley. *Rethinking Religion: Connecting Cognition and Culture*. Cambridge: Cambridge University Press, 1990.
Leftow, Brian. *Time and Eternity*. Cornell Studies in the Philosophy of Religion. Ithaca, NY: Cornell University Press, 1991.
Lehrer, Keith. "Justification, Explanation, and Induction." In *Induction, Acceptance, and Rational Belief*, edited by Marshall Swain, 100–133. Synthese Library. Dordrecht: D. Reidel, 1970.
Leibniz, Gottfried Wilhelm. "The Principles of Philosophy, or, the Monadology" [1714]. In *Philosophical Essays*, edited and translated by Roger Ariew and Daniel Garber, 213–25. Indianapolis, IN: Hackett, 1995.

Le Poidevin, Robin. *Arguing for Atheism: An Introduction to the Philosophy of Religion*. London: Routledge, 1996.
Lewis, David. "Causation" [1973]. In *Philosophical Papers* vol. ii, 159–213. New York: Oxford University Press, 1986.
Lewontin, Richard C. "Billions and Billions of Demons." *The New York Review of Books* 44:1 (January 9, 1997): 24–33.
Lipton, Peter. *Inference to the Best Explanation* Philosophical Issues in Science. London: Routledge, 1991.
Lycan, William G. "Explanation and Epistemology." In *The Oxford Handbook of Epistemology*, edited by Paul K. Moser, 408–37. Oxford: Oxford University Press, 2002.
———. *Judgement and Justification*. Cambridge Studies in Philosophy. Cambridge: Cambridge University Press, 1988.
Lyell, Charles. *Life, Letters, and Journals of Sir Charles Lyell, Bart*, edited by Katharine M. Lyell. London: John Murray, 1881.
———. *Principles of Geology*. 3 vols. [1st edition 1830]. Chicago: University of Chicago Press, 1990.
Mach, Ernst. *The Principles of Physical Optics: An Historical and Philosophical Treatment* [1921]. Translated by John S. Anderson and A. F. A. Young [1926]. New York: Dover Publications, 1953.
Mackie, J. L. *The Cement of the Universe*. Oxford: Clarendon Press, 1974.
———. "Evil and Omnipotence." *Mind* 64 (1955): 200–12.
———. *The Miracle of Theism*. Oxford: Clarendon Press, 1982.
Maher, Patrick. "Confirmation Theory." In *The Encyclopedia of Philosophy*. 2nd edition. Edited by Donald M. Borchert. MacMillan Reference Books. Woodbridge, CT: Macmillan, 2005. patrick.maher1.net/ctk.pdf, 24 May 2006.
Malebranche, Nicolas. *The Search After Truth*, edited by Thomas M. Lennon and Paul J. Olscamp. Cambridge Texts in the History of Philosophy. Cambridge: Cambridge University Press, 1997.
Malle, B. F. "Folk Explanations of Intentional Action." In *Intentions and Intentionality: Foundations of Social Cognition*, edited by B. F. Malle, L. J. Moses, and D. A. Baldwin, 265–86. Cambridge, MA: MIT Press, 2001.
Martin, Michael. *Atheism: A Philosophical Justification*. Philadelphia: Temple University Press, 1992.
Mascall, E. L. *Existence and Analogy* [1949]. London: Darton, Longman & Todd, 1966.
Maxwell, Grover. "The Ontological Status of Theoretical Entities." In *Scientific Explanation, Space, and Time*, edited by Herbert Feigl and Grover Maxwell, 3–27. Minnesota Studies in the Philosophy of Science, vol. iii. Minneapolis, MN: University of Minnesota Press, 1962.
McCalla, Arthur. *The Creationist Debate: The Encounter between the Bible and the Historical Mind*. London: Continuum, 2006.
McCann, Hugh J. and Jonathan L Kvanvig. "The Occasionalist Proselytizer: A Modified Catechism." In *Philosophical Perspectives V: Philosophy of Religion*, edited by James E. Tomberlin, 587–615. Atascadero, CA: Ridgeview Publishing, 1991.
McCausland, Ian. "Anomalies in the History of Relativity." *Journal of Scientific Exploration* 13 (1999): 271–90.
McGrew, Timothy. "Review of Richard Swinburne, *Epistemic Justification*" [2002]. Notre Dame Philosophical Reviews. http://ndpr.nd.edu/re-view.cfm?id=1094
McMullin, Ernan. "Structural Explanation." *American Philosophical Quarterly* 15 (1978): 139–47.
Mele, Alfred R. *Motivation and Agency*. New York: Oxford University Press, 2003.

Melnyk, Andrew. *A Physicalist Manifesto: Thoroughly Modern Materialism.* Cambridge Studies in Philosophy. Cambridge: Cambridge University Press, 2003.

Meyer, Stephen C. "The Origin of Biological Information and the Higher Taxonomic Categories." *Proceedings of the Biological Society of Washington* 117 (2004): 213–39.

———. "The Return of the God Hypothesis." *Journal of Interdisciplinary Studies* 11 (1999): 1–38.

Mill, John Stuart. "A System of Logic Ratiocinative and Inductive" [1843]. In *Collected Works of John Stuart Mill*, vols. vii–viii, edited by J. M. Robson. Toronto: University of Toronto Press, 1973–74.

———. "Three Essays on Religion" [1874]. In *Collected Works of John Stuart Mill*, vol. x, edited by J. M. Robson, 369–489. Toronto: University of Toronto Press, 1969.

Montero, Barbara. "Physicalism in An Infinitely Decomposable World." *Erkenntnis* 64 (2006): 177–91.

Morris, Thomas V. "Perfection and Creation." In *Reasoned Faith: Essays in Philosophical Theology in Honor of Norman Kretzmann*, edited by Eleonore Stump, 234–47. Ithaca, NY: Cornell University Press, 1993.

Moser, Paul K. *Philosophy After Objectivity: Making Sense in Perspective* [1993]. New York: Oxford University Press, 1999.

Musgrave, Alan. "Deductivism." Unpublished paper, Computer and Information Science Seminar, University of Otago, 2007.

———. *Essays on Realism and Rationality.* Studies in the Philosophy of Karl R. Popper and Critical Rationalism 12. Amsterdam: Editions Rodopi, 1999.

———. "Evidential Support, Falsification, Heuristics, and Anarchism." In *Progress and Rationality in Science*, edited by Gerard Radnitzky and Gunnar Andersson, 181–201. Boston Studies in the Philosophy of Science 58 / Synthese Library 125. Dordrecht: D. Seidel, 1978.

———. "Kuhn's Second Thoughts." *British Journal of Philosophy and Science* 22 (1971): 287–306.

———. "Responses." In *Rationality and Reality: Conversations with Alan Musgrave*, edited by Colin Cheyne and John Worrall, 293–333. Studies in History and Philosophy of Science, vol. xx. Dordrecht: Springer, 2006.

———. "Scientific Realism and the Miracle Argument." Unpublished paper, Philosophy Seminar, University of Otago, 2005.

Nadler, Steven. "Malebranche on Causation." In *The Cambridge Companion to Malebranche*, edited by Steven Nadler, 112–38. Cambridge: Cambridge University Press, 2000.

Nagel, Ernest. "Naturalism Reconsidered." *Proceedings and Addresses of the American Philosophical Association* 28 (1954–55): 5–17.

Nagel, Thomas. *The View from Nowhere.* New York: Oxford University Press, 1986.

National Academy of Sciences. *Science and Creationism.* Washington, DC: National Academy Press, 1999.

Nelson, Paul A. "The Role of Theology in Current Evolutionary Reasoning." *Biology and Philosophy* 11 (1996): 493–517.

Niiniluoto, Ilkka. "Truth-seeking by Abduction." *Induction and Deduction in the Sciences*, edited by Friedrich Stadler, 57–82. Vienna Circle Institute Yearbook, vol. xi. Dordrecht: Kluwer, 2003.

Notturno, M. A. and Paul R. McHugh. "Is Freudian Psychoanalytic Theory Really Falsifiable?" *Metaphilosophy* 18 (1987): 306–20.

Numbers, Ronald L. "Science without God: Natural Laws and Christian Beliefs." In *When Science and Christianity Meet*, edited by David C. Lindberg and Ronald L. Numbers, 265–85. Chicago: University of Chicago Press, 2003.

Olafson, Frederick A. "Narrative History and the Concept of Action." *History and Theory* 9 (1970): 265–89.
Oppy, Graham. "Hume and the Argument for Biological Design." *Biology and Philosophy* 11 (1996): 519–34.
Papineau, David. "The Rise of Physicalism." In *The Proper Ambition of Science*, edited by M. W. F. Stone and Jonathan Wolff, 174–208. London: Routledge, 2000.
Peacocke, Arthur. *Paths from Science Towards God: The End of All Our Exploring*. Oxford: Oneworld, 2001.
Pears, David. "Desires as Causes of Actions." In *The Human Agent*—Royal Institute of Philosophy Lectures 1: 1966–67, 83–97. London: Macmillan, 1968.
Peirce, Charles Sanders. *Collected Papers of Charles Sanders Peirce*, vol. v, *Pragmatism and Pragmaticism*, edited by Charles Hartshorne and Paul Weiss. Cambridge, MA: Harvard University Press, 1934.
Pennock, Robert T. *Tower of Babel: The Evidence Against the New Creationism*. A Bradford Book. Cambridge, MA: MIT Press, 2000.
Phillips, D. Z. *Religion and the Hermeneutics of Contemplation*. Cambridge: Cambridge University Press, 2001.
———. *Religion without Explanation*. Oxford: Basil Blackwell, 1976.
Pigliucci, Massimo. "Design Yes, Intelligent No. A Critique of Intelligent Design Theory and Neocreationism." *Skeptical Inquirer* 25:5 (September/October 2001): 34–39.
Plantinga, Alvin. *Does God Have a Nature?* The Aquinas Lecture 1980. Marquette, WI: Marquette University Press, 1980.
———. *God, Freedom and Evil*. Essays in Philosophy. London: George Allen & Unwin, 1975.
———. *Warranted Christian Belief*. New York: Oxford University Press, 2000.
Popper, Karl R. *The Logic of Scientific Discovery* [1959]. Routledge Classics. London: Routledge, 2002.
———. "Models, Instruments, and Truth: The Status of the Rationality Principle in the Social Sciences." In *The Myth of the Framework: In Defence of Science and Rationality*, edited by M. A. Nottorno, 154–84. London: Routledge, 1994.
Prevost, Robert. "Swinburne, Mackie and Bayes's Theorem." *International Journal for Philosophy of Religion* 17 (1985): 175–84.
Psillos, Stathis. "Agnostic Empiricism versus Scientific Realism: Belief in Truth Matters." *International Studies in the Philosophy of Science* 14 (2000): 57–75.
———. *Causation and Explanation*. Montreal: McGill-Queen's University Press, 2002.
Quine, W. V. "Naturalism; Or, Living Within One's Means." *Dialectica* 49 (1995): 251–61.
———. *Theories and Things*. Cambridge, MA: Harvard University Press, 1981.
Quine, W. V. and J. S. Ullian. *The Web of Belief*. 2nd edition. New York: Random House, 1978.
Rae, Murray A. *History and Hermeneutics*. Edinburgh: T. & T. Clark, 2005.
Ratcliffe, Matthew. *Rethinking Commonsense Psychology: A Critique of Folk Psychology, Theory of Mind and Simulation*. London: Palgrave Macmillan, 2007.
Reichenbach, Hans. *Experience and Prediction: An Analysis of the Foundations and the Structure of Knowledge*. Chicago: University of Chicago Press, 1938.
Rosenbaum, Ron. "Disaster Ignites Debate: 'Was God In the Tsunami?'" *The New York Observer* 10 January 2005, Front Page 3.
Rowe, William L. *Can God Be Free?* Oxford: Clarendon Press, 2004.
Rudwick, Martin J. S. "Introduction." In *Principles of Geology* by Charles Lyell, vols. vii–lviii. [1st edition 1830]. Chicago: University of Chicago Press, 1990.

Rundle, Bede. 2004. *Why there is Something rather than Nothing*. Oxford: Clarendon Press.

Ruse, Michael. "The New Creationism: Its Philosophical Dimension." In *The Cultures of Creationism: Anti-Evolutionism in English-Speaking Countries*, edited by Simon Coleman and Leslie Carlin, 175–92. Aldershot: Ashgate, 2004.

Salmon, Wesley C. *The Foundations of Scientific Inference*. Pittsburgh, PA: University of Pittsburgh Press, 1966.

Scanlon, T. M. *What We Owe to Each Other*. Cambridge, MA: Belknap Press (Harvard University Press), 1998.

Schoen, Edward L. *Religious Explanations: A Model from the Sciences*. Durham, NC: Duke University Press, 1985.

Schueler, G. F. *Reasons and Purposes: Human Rationality and the Teleological Explanation of Action*. Oxford: Clarendon Press, 2003.

Schutz, Alfred. *The Phenomenology of the Social World* [1932]. Translated by George Walsh and Frederick Lehnert. Northwestern University Studies in Phenomenology and Existential Philosophy. Evanston, IL: Northwestern University Press, 1967.

Shanks, Niall. *God, the Devil, and Darwin: A Critique of Intelligent Design Theory*. Oxford: Oxford University Press, 2004.

Smith, Morton. "Historical Method in the Study of Religion" [1968]. In *Studies in the Cult of Yahweh*, vol. i, *Studies in Historical Method, Ancient Israel, Ancient Judaism*, edited by Shaye J. D. Cohen, 3–14. Religions in the Greco-Roman World 130/1. Leiden: E. J. Brill, 1996.

Smith, Quentin. "Causation and the Logical Impossibility of a Divine Cause." *Philosophical Topics* 21 (1996): 169–91.

———. "The Reason the Universe Exists is that it Caused itself to Exist." *Philosophy* 74 (1999): 579–86.

Sobel, Jordan Howard. "Probabilities, Subjective and Objective, Dividing the Evidence, and Fine-Tuning: to Comments Made by Richard Swinburne." 29 May 2006. http://www.scar.utoronto.ca/~sobel/OnL_T/

Sober, Elliott. "The Design Argument." In *God and Design: The Teleological Argument and Modern Science*, edited by Neil A. Manson, 27–54. London: Routledge, 2003.

———. "Intelligent Design and Probability Reasoning." *International Journal for Philosophy of Religion* 52 (2002): 65–80.

———. *Reconstructing the Past: Parsimony, Evolution, and Inference*. A Bradford Book. Cambridge, MA: MIT Press, 1988.

———. "Testability." *Proceedings and Addresses of the American Philosophical Association* 73 (1999): 47–76.

Steinhardt, Paul J. and Neil Turok. "A Cyclic Model of the Universe." *Science* 296 (2002): 1436–39.

Stove, D. C. "Misconditionalisation." *Australasian Journal of Philosophy* 50 (1972): 173–83.

Strauss, David Friedrich. *The Life of Jesus Critically Examined* [1840]. Translated by George Eliot. Lives of Jesus Series. Philadelphia: Fortress Press, 1972.

Swinburne, Richard. *The Christian God*. Oxford: Clarendon Press, 1994.

———. *The Coherence of Theism*. Revised edition. Clarendon Library of Logic and Philosophy. Oxford: Clarendon Press, 1993.

———. *Epistemic Justification*. Oxford: Clarendon Press, 2001.

———. *The Evolution of the Soul*. Revised edition. Oxford: Clarendon Press, 1997.

———. *The Existence of God*. 2nd edition. Oxford: Clarendon Press, 2004.

———. *Faith and Reason*. Oxford: Clarendon Press, 1981.

———. *Is There a God?* Oxford: Oxford University Press, 1996.

———. "Mackie, Induction, and God." *Religious Studies* 19 (1983): 385–91.
Thagard, Paul R. "The Best Explanation: Criteria for Theory Choice" [1976]. In *Theory, Evidence and Explanation*, edited by Peter Lipton, 173–89. International Research Library of Philosophy. Aldershot: Dartmouth, 1995.
Thalberg, Irving and Arnold B. Levison. "Are There Non-Causal Explanations of Action?" In *Enigmas of Agency: Studies in the Philosophy of Human Action*, by Irving Thalberg, 73–86. Muirhead Library of Philosophy. London: George Allen & Unwin, 1972.
Thomson, J. J. "Cathode Rays." *Philosophical Magazine* 44 (1897): 293–317.
Timmer, John. "Scientists on Science." *Nobel Intent*. The Science Journal of *Ars Technica*. http://arstechnica.com/journals/science.ars/2006/8/31/5164
Tylor, Edward B. *Primitive Culture*. 5th edition. London: John Murray, 1913.
van Fraassen, Bas C. *Laws and Symmetry*. New York: Oxford University Press, 1989.
van Inwagen, Peter. "Modal Epistemology." *Philosophical Studies* 92 (1998): 67–84.
———. "The Problem of Evil, the Problem of Air, and the Problem of Silence." In *Philosophical Perspectives*, vol. v, *Philosophy of Religion*, edited by James E. Tomberlin, 135–65. Atascadero, CA: Ridgeview Publishing, 1991.
———. "What is Naturalism? What is Analytical Philosophy?" In *Analytic Philosophy Without Naturalism*, edited by Antonella Corradini, Sergio Galvan, and E. Jonathan Lowe, 74–88. Routledge Studies in Twentieth-Century Philosophy. London: Routledge, 2006.
Vasiliou, Iakovos. "Wittgenstein, Religious Belief, and *On Certainty*." In *Wittgenstein and Philosophy of Religion*, edited by Robert L. Arrington and Mark Addis, 29–50. London: Routledge, 2001.
von Wright, Georg Henrik. *Explanation and Understanding*. International Library of Philosophy and Scientific Method. London: Routledge & Kegan Paul, 1971.
Wilcox, Roger M. "The Dark Sucker Theory Page." Revised December 18, 2003. http://home.netcom.com/~rogermw/darksucker.html#energy
Worrall, John. "The Ways in Which the Methodology of Scientific Research Programmes Improves on Popper's Methodology." In *Progress and Rationality in Science* edited by Gerard Radnitzky and Gunnar Andersson, 45–70. Boston Studies in the Philosophy of Science 58 / Synthese Library 125. Dordrecht: D. Seidel, 1978.

Index

A

abduction: and induction, 102–8; Peirce's schema for, 21, 23, 28, 30, 50, 73, 80–81, 86, 98, 108–9, 118; problem of, 36–38, 108–10, 112–13, 188 n.60
acceptance and belief, 37–38, 125, 171 n.37, 173 n.26
accommodation and assimilation, 141–42
actual explanations. *See* explanations: proposed, potential, and actual.
actualism, in geology, 136. *See also vera causa* doctrine.
adequacy, causal. *See* causal adequacy.
adequate explanations. *See* explanations: standards of adequacy.
ad hoc explanations. *See* explanations: *ad hoc*.
affirming the consequent, 109
Agassiz, Louis, 12
akrasia. See weakness of will.
al-Farabi, Abu Nasr, 8
Alston, William P., 47–48, 139, 173 n.27
Amar, Shlomo, 60
analogy, argument from, 180 n.16. *See also* God: analogical language regarding
Anscombe, G. E. M., 186 n.6
antirealism. *See* realism and antirealism.
anthropomorphism in God-concepts, 20
apparitions. *See* Medjugorje.
Aquinas, Thomas: on analogical language, 47–48; on concepts of God, 46; on God and evil, 173 n.40; on ontological economy, 137; on theistic explanations, 8, 176 n.19.

argument: from analogy (*see* analogy: argument from); from design (*see* design argument); from evil (*see* evil: argument from)
arguments and explanations. *See* explanations: and arguments; practical syllogism; intentional explanations: as arguments.
Aristotelian philosophy, 176 n.20
assimilation. *See* accommodation and assimilation
astronomy, Ptolemaic. *See* Ptolemaic astronomy.
atheism, methodological, 168 n.28. *See also* methodological naturalism.
atomism, 135, 184 n.89
Audi, Robert, 154–55, 187 n.41
auxiliary hypotheses. *See* explanations: and auxiliary hypotheses.
Ayer, A. J., 35–36

B

Babylonian Exile, 67–68
background knowledge, 39, 126–31, 184 n.53
Banner, Michael C., 114, 172 n.20
barber paradox, 94
Barth, Karl, 10
Bartholomew, Michael, 132
basic actions, 52, 85, 139–40, 179 n.22, 185 n.107
Bayes's theorem, 24, 106, 111, 115, 181 n.23. *See also* confirmation theory.
Beaudoin, John, 179 n.33
belief and acceptance. *See* acceptance and belief.
belief-desire thesis. *See* intentional explanations: belief-desire thesis.

Bentham, Jeremy, 113
Berger, Peter L., 168 n.28
best explanation. *See* inference to the best explanation.
best possible world, 91–94
biblical prophets *See* prophets, biblical.
big bang hypothesis, 53, 56–57, 72, 175 nn.85, 87, 178 n.47
Bishop, John, 38, 173 n.26
Book of Mormon. *See* Mormon, Book of.
Bosnia-Herzegovina. *See* Medjugorje.
boson. *See* Higgs boson.
Boxing Day tsunami. *See* tsunami, Boxing Day.
Brauer, Matthew J., 9–11
brute facts, 67, 111, 176 n.107
Buckland, William, 12

C

Calvin, John, 141
Carrier, R. C., 132
Cartesian philosophy, 176 n.20
cathode rays, 34, 172 n.2
causal adequacy, 186 n.2
causal deviance. *See* intentional explanations: and causal deviance.
causal overdetermination, 170 n.14
causal preemption, 22–23, 170 n.14
causal thesis. *See* intentional explanations: causal thesis.
causation: counterfactual definitions of, 54–55; divine, 53–58; event, 176 n.23; Humean definitions of, 53–54, 61–62, 161–64; and independent specification criterion, 178 n.14; and laws, 53–54, 161; and mechanism, 52–53; and occasionalism (*see* occasionalism); regularity definitions of, 53–54, 61–62, 161–64; singularist definitions of, 61–63, 108; ubiquity of divine, 45, 57–58. *See also* explanations: causal; intentional explanations: causal thesis.
causes, primary and secondary, 57, 64–65
chance. *See* explanations: and chance.
character. *See* intentional explanations: and character of the agent.
Cioffi, Frank, 116
Clayton, Philip, 60
Cohen, L. Jonathan, 37, 173 n.26, 186 nn.8, 17, 21

coherence of theism. *See* theism: coherence of
Collins, Robin, 23, 79
Colyvan, Mark, 175 n.75
concurrentism, 177 n.28. *See also* occasionalism.
confirmation theory: and explanationism, 111–12; and theism, 79, 82, 124, 132; and theory acceptance, 23–26, 105–6, 111–12, 115, 183 n.33. *See also* justificationism.
conservationism, 177 n.28. *See also* occasionalism.
consilience, dynamic, 183 n.26
context: of discovery, 10; of justification, 10
Cornman, James. 171 n.44
corroboration: heuristic account of, 121; historical account of, 121–22; and Nicod's criterion, 121
cosmological argument, 45–46, 173 n.41
Couvalis, George, 185 n.91
Craig, William Lane, 72, 178 n.47
creation story, 89–90, 139–40
creationism, 8, 12, 16, 89–90. *See also* intelligent design theory.
credulity, principle of. *See* principle of credulity.
Cupitt, Don, 36.

D

Danto, Arthur C., 188 n.61
Dark Sucker Theory, 126–27, 183 n.38
Darwin, Charles: objections to theistic explanations, 13–14, 88, 169 n.71; on the origin of species, 1, 11, 26–27, 180 n.15; and suboptimality arguments, 86; on the *vera causa* doctrine, 127
Davidson, Donald: belief-desire thesis of, 149–51; causal thesis of, 51, 148–49, 186 n.6; on differing reasons for action, 187 n.40; on explanations and laws, 62, 162–64, 188 n.63; on intentions, 186 nn.17, 18; on principle of charity, 152; on pro attitudes, 46, 149; on weakness of will, 158
Davis, Lawrence D., 186 n.8
Dawkins, Richard, 14, 16, 58
deduction. *See* explanations: deductivist view of
de facto objections. *See* theistic explanations: *de facto* objections to

defences, and theodicies, 134–35
de Laplace, Pierre Simon. *See* LaPlace, Pierre Simon de.
Dembski, William A., 96–97, 104, 108
Dennett, Daniel C., 151–52. 188 n.54
design argument, 60, 79–81. *See also* intelligent design; fine-tuning argument.
design stance, 152
Dionysius the Areopagite. *See* Pseudo-Dionysius.
discovery, context of. *See* context: of discovery
Dover, Pennsylvania, 8
Draper, Paul R., 124, 134–35, 167 n.19, 168 n.35
Dray, William, 186 n.6
Ducasse, C. J., 54, 62
Duhem-Quine thesis, 164
dynamic consilience. *See* consilience, dynamic.

E
Earman, John, 13, 26, 75, 169 n.68
Einstein, Albert, 35, 120, 176 n.106, 182 n.11. *See also* physics: and general relativity.
electrons, 38, 109, 117, 120, 172 n.3, 185 n.101
empirical content: defined, 44; of the natural sciences, 138; and testability, 117–19, 174 n.73; of theistic explanations, 15, 44–46, 88, 169 n.71. *See also* spurious unification.
entailment condition. *See* Hempel, Carl G: on entailment.
Epicureans, 72
epistemic optimism, 172 n.6
events and states of affairs, 59–60
event-tokens and event-types, 61
evidentialism, 135
evil, argument from, 44, 98, 124, 137
evolution by natural selection: as alternative to theistic explanations, 11, 132, 180 n.15; and confirmationism, 26–27, 37; and creationism, 70, 79; and *vera causa* principle, 127.
ex contradictione quodlibet, 50, 51, 78. *See also* paraconsistent logic.
Exile, Babylonian. *See* Babylonian Exile
explaining the *explanans*, 16, 58, 155–57, 170 n.82, 175 n.103
explanatory redundancy. *See* theistic explanations: apparent redundancy of; natural explanations: apparent redundancy of.
explanations: accepting, 23–27, 37–38 (*see also* acceptance and belief); *ad hoc*, 136; and arguments, 27–29, 153–55; and auxiliary hypotheses, 133–34, 135–36, 165–66, 184 n.77, 184 n.89; best available (*see* inference to the best explanation); causal, 51–58 (*see also* causation; intentional explanations: causal thesis); and chance, 177 n.30, 183 n.35; complete, 175 n.102 (*see also* explaining the *explanans*); deductive-nomological model of, 170 n.11; deductivist view of, 28–29 ; intentional (*see* intentional explanations); and laws (*see* explanations: without laws; intentional explanations: and laws); lovely and likely, 138, 142; and miracles (*see* miracles); paradigmatic (*see* paradigmatic explanations); proposed, potential, and actual, 20–23, 31, 102, 105, 115; and religion, 7–8 religious (*see* theistic explanations); singular, 61–63, 189 n.73 (*see also* causation: singularist definitions of); solitary (*see* solitary proposed explanations); standards of adequacy (*see* explanatory virtues); as success term, 20–21; theistic and religious, 19–20; theoretical, 33, 34–36, 84; without laws, 161–62, 188 n.58
explanationism, 26–27, 111–12, 182 n.45. *See also* justificationism; confirmation theory.
explanations of religion. *See* theories of religion.
explaining under a description. *See* intentional explanations: explain under a description.
explanatory force, 90
explanatory success. *See* past explanatory success.
explanatory virtues, 112–14, 115, 116–42. *See also* testability; background knowledge; past explanatory success; simplicity; ontological economy; informativeness.
extraterrestrial beings, 81
fallacy: of affirming the consequent (*see* affirming the consequent); genetic

(*see* genetic fallacy); representational (*see* representational fallacy)
falsifiability, 174 n.73. See also theistic explanations: falsifiability of.
Farabi, al-. *See* al-Farabi, Abu Nasr.
Feuerbach, Ludwig, 64

F

fine-tuning argument, 70–71, 177 n.42. *See also* design argument.
feline psychology, 48, 49, 174 n.65
folk psychology, 46, 147, 188 n.62
folk theology, 46
Forrest, Barbara, 9–11
free will: conceptions of, 186 n.22; defence, 98

G

Gale, Barry G., 26
Galilei, Galileo, 138
Garcia, Laura L., 90–91
Genesis. *See* creation story.
genetic fallacy, 10
geology, nineteenth-century, 1, 12
Gerber, Paul, 182 n.11
Gey, Steven G., 9–11
Gillespie, Neal C., 168 n.42
Ginet, Carl, 186 n.8
God; analogical language regarding, 47–48, 139; concepts of, 19–20, 48–49 (*see also* theism: coherence of); direct experience of, 173 n.27; literal language regarding, 48, 139
Goodman, Alvin, 112
Gould, Stephen Jay, 83–84, 86
Grayling, A. C., 86.
gremlin hypothesis, 105–106
Grünbaum, Adolf, 52–53, 173 n.41

H

Haack, Susan, 2, 145
Hampshire, Stuart, 186 n.6
Hart, H. L. A., 186 n.6
Hempel, Carl G: on deductive-nomological model of explanation, 170 n.11; on entailment, 28–29, 171 n.47; on explanation as aim of science, 168 n.43; on Nicod's criterion, 182 n.14; on the raven paradox, 103, 121, 122, 182 n.16; on testability, 116
Herschel, J. F. W., 127, 136–37, 181 n.42
Higgs boson, 75

Himma, Kenneth Einar, 180 n.15
Himmler, Heinrich, 159
Hoffman, Joshua, 174 n.66
Holy Spirit, internal testimony of. *See* internal testimony of the Holy Spirit.
Honoré, A. M., 186 n.6
Horton, Robin, 7, 173 n.28
Huckleberry Finn, 159
Hughes, Gerard J., 46
Hume, David: on argument from evil, 97; on causation (*see* causation: Humean definitions of); on coherence of theism, 46–47, 174 n.66; on explaining the *explanans*, 170 n.82; on independent specification criterion, 77, 82, 97; on induction, 104; and Malebranche, 177 n.24; on miracles, 72, 74–75, 178 nn.45, 54; on proportioning cause to effect, 101, 179 n.33; scepticism of, 96, 172 n.10; and suboptimality arguments, 86; on theistic explanations, 169 n.73
Huxley, Thomas Henry, 14, 26–27, 169 n.71
hypotheses and theories, 23. *See also* explanations: proposed, potential, and actual.
hypothesis of indifference, 124, 134–35

I

ideal types, 147–48
incontinent action. *See* weakness of will.
independent specification criterion, 31, 77, 82, 97, 178 n.14
Indian Ocean tsunami. *See* tsunami, Boxing Day.
induction, 103–4. *See also* abduction and induction.
inference to the best explanation: as apparently fallacious reasoning, 109; theism best defended as, 31, 33, 170 n.6, 172 n.20; when only one proposed explanation on offer, 110–12, 122–25
informativeness, 138–42
in principle objection. *See* theistic explanations: in principle objections to.
instrumentalism. *See* realism and antirealism.
intellectualist theories of religion. *See* theories of religion: intellectualist.

intelligent design theory: arguments against, 79, 170 n.5; avoids identifying the designer, 20, 96–97; and inference to the best explanation, 107–8; and science, 8–9. *See also* creationism.
intentional explanations: of animal behaviour, 48, 174 n.65; as arguments, 28, 40, 124, 153–57 (*see also* practical syllogism); belief-desire thesis, 147–48, 149–51; and causal deviance, 149–51, 187 n.24; causal thesis, 51–52, 148–49, 186 nn.6, 8; and character of the agent, 89, 160–61, 179 n.31, 188 n.56; and differing reasons for action, 156–57, 187 nn.40, 43, 188 n.60; explain under a description, 41–42, 69; falsification of, 40, 166; and generalizations, 40, 161–62; and intentions (*see* intentions as *sui generis* mental states); and laws, 74; 161–64, 188 nn.58, 63; legitimacy of, 39–40, 147; and natural-scientific explanations, 69, 177 n.37; of our own behaviour, 160, 188 n.54; and pro-attitudes (*see* pro attitudes); and quantifiability, 138–39; and rationality principle (*see* rationality: principle of); as research programmes, 164–66; testability of, 32, 39, 159–66, 188 n.53; as theoretical explanations, 41
intentional specificity, 45, 118–19, 146
intentional stance, 151–52
intentions as *sui generis* mental states, 150–51, 158, 186 nn.17, 20
intercessory prayer, trials of. *See* prayer trials.
internal testimony of the Holy Spirit, 141, 185 nn.113, 115
INUS conditions, 186 n.22
Islamic philosophy, 8, 64

J

James, William, 38
Johnson, Phillip E., 4–6, 12
Jones, John E., 8–9
justification, context of. *See* context: of justification.
justificationism. 23–26, 111. *See also* explanationism; confirmation theory.

K

Kim, Jaegwon, 59, 164
Kitcher, Philip, 12, 27, 29, 43–44, 141. *See also* spurious unification.
Kvanvig, Jonathan L., 176 n.23
Kretzmann, Norman, 179 n.40

L

Lahav, Ran, 188 n.62
LaPlace, Pierre Simon de, 131–32
Large Hadron Collider, 75
Laudan, Larry, 168 n.48
Lawson, E. Thomas, 14–15
Leftow, Brian, 174 n.66
Lehrer, Keith, 27, 171 n.44
Leibniz, G. W., 45–46, 60
Lewis, David, 54–55
Lewontin, Richard C., 3, 6
light, wave theory of. *See* wave theory of light.
likelihood principle, 79, 105, 123, 181 n.22
Lipton, Peter, 16, 22, 138, 170 n.14
logical possibility, 180 n.48
lovely explanations. *See* explanations: lovely and likely.
Lycan, William G., 27, 112, 113, 115, 171 n.44
Lyell, Charles, 1, 132, 136–37, 167 n.5

M

Mach, Ernst, 35
Mackie, J. L: on background knowledge, 128, 131; on causation, 53, 54; on explaining under a description, 173 n.34; on the freewill defence, 98, 179 n.32; on INUS conditions, 186 n.22
Maclaurin, James, 167 n.18, 168 n.54
Malebranche, Nicolas, 64, 176 n.20, 177 nn.24, 25
Malle, B. F., 173 n.29
Martian hypothesis, 109
Maxwell, Grover, 172 n.5
McCann, Hugh J., 176 n.23
McCauley, Robert N., 14–15
McCausland, Ian, 182 n.11
McGrew, Timothy, 26, 171 n.35, 182 n.45
Medjugorje, 66–67.
Melden, A. I., 186 n.6
Mele, Alfred R., 186 n.20
methodological naturalism. *See* naturalism, methodological.

Meyer, Stephen C., 20, 107–8, 114, 170 n.6, 181 n.34
Michelson, Albert, 120
Mill, J. S., 103, 104, 180 n.16
miracles, 15, 30–31, 58, 71–75, 178 n.45
misconditionalization, 175 n.97
modal scepticism. *See* scepticism, modal.
modus tollens, no probabilistic equivalent of, 123
moral scepticism. *See* scepticism, moral.
Montero, Barbara, 167 n.23
Morgenbesser, Sidney, 174 n.42, 179 n.34
Morley, Edward, 120
Mormon, Book of, 185 n.115
Morris, Thomas V., 179 n.40
Moser, Paul, 177 n.37
multiverse hypothesis, 71
Muslim philosophy. *See* Islamic philosophy.
Musgrave, Alan: on inference to the best explanation, 109–10, 181 n.42; on intermediate causal mechanisms, 175 n.80; on justificationism, 170 n.18; on misconditionalization, 175 n.98; on natural kinds, 173 n.32; on solitary proposed explanations, 122; on theory choice, 112

N

Nadler, Steven, 64
natural explanations: accepted by theists, 67–68; apparent redundancy of, 57–58, 64; contested by theists, 70–71. *See also* theistic explanations: and natural explanations.
natural kinds, 41, 173 n.31
natural selection. *See* evolution by natural selection.
naturalism: as *a priori* commitment, 5–7; methodological, 4–5, 9–11, 17, 144–46, 167 n.12; ontological 4–5, 145; presumption of (*see* presumption of naturalism); Quinean, 2, 4, 144–45; scientific, 1–4, 144–45
nature, 2, 167 n.19
Nelson, Paul A., 87–88
Neurath, Otto, 168 n.43
Newton, Isaac, 131, 176 n.106. *See also* physics: Newtonian.

Newtonian physics. *See* physics: Newtonian.
Nicod's criterion, 121, 182 n.14
null hypothesis, 125
Numbers, Ronald L., 167 n.3.

O

occasionalism, 57, 63–65, 176 n.23, 177 n.28
Ockham's razor, 137. *See also* ontological economy.
ontological economy, 71, 136–37
ontological naturalism. *See* naturalism: ontological.
Oppy, Graham, 169 n.73
optimality condition, 31, 84–85, 88–97, 179 n.33. *See also* suboptimality arguments.
origin of religion, 7

P

panda's thumb, 83–84, 87–88
paradigmatic explanations, 140
paraconsistent logic, 174 n.72, 175 n.74. *See also ex contradictione quodlibet*.
past explanatory success, 131–32
Peacocke, Arthur, 114
Pears, David, 178 n.14
Peirce, C. S. *See* abduction: Peirce's schema for.
Pennock, Robert T., 4–5, 15, 73
Perrin, Jean, 120
Phillips, D. Z., 172 nn.18, 19
physical stance, 151–52
physicalism, 2–3
physics: and general relativity, 120, 176 n.106; 182 n.11; Newtonian, 120, 176 n.106, 182 n.11; and theology, 38–39
Plantinga, Alvin, 7–8, 47, 185 n.113
poltergeist, 42, 117, 128–29
Popper, Karl R., 25–26, 44, 120, 133, 171 n.33
positivism, 35. *See also* realism and antirealism.
potential explanations. *See* explanations: proposed, potential, and actual.
practical syllogism, 40, 73–74, 98, 154–55
prayer, petitionary, 62–63
prayer trials, 63
prediction: quantifiable, 138–39; and retrodiction, 119–22

preemption, causal. *See* causal preemption.
presumption of naturalism, 146. *See also* naturalism: methodological; theistic explanations: as explanations of last resort.
presumption of rationality, 151. *See also* rationality: principle of.
Priest, Graham, 175 n.74
primary causes. *See* causes, primary and secondary.
principle of charity, 152. *See also* rationality: principle of.
principle of credulity, 181 n.29
pro attitudes, 46, 149. *See also* intentional explanations: belief-desire thesis.
probability, conceptions of, 24–25, 171 n.33. *See also* confirmation theory; Bayes's theorem.
prophets, biblical, 68
proportioning cause to effect, 101, 179 n.33
proposed explanations. *See* explanations: proposed, potential, and actual.
Pseudo-Dionysius, 47
Psillos, Stathis, 172 n.6
psychology: feline (*see* feline psychology); folk (*see* folk psychology); social (*see* social psychology)
Ptolemaic astronomy, 11, 171 n.35

Q
quantum mechanics, 43
Quine, W. V., 2, 4–5, 27, 127, 144–45
Qur'an, 185 n.115

R
Ramanujan, Srinivasa, 10
Ratcliffe, Matthew, 140, 147–48
rationality principle. *See* rationality: principle of
rational reconstruction, 33
rationality: criteria of, 89–90, 153; presumption of (*see* presumption of rationality); principle of, 40, 51, 74, 82–84, 108, 151–53, 162, 187 n.34
raven paradox, 103, 121–22, 182 n.16
realism and antirealism, 34–38, 41, 172 n.18, 177 n.37
Reichenbach, Hans, 35, 172 n.9
religion: and explanation (*see* explanations, and religion); origin of (*see* origin of religion); theories of (*see* theories of religion)
religious explanations, 19–20. *See also* theistic explanations.
representational fallacy, 163
research programmes, 131–32, 166
retrodiction. *See* prediction: and retrodiction.
revelation, 9–11
Rosenbaum, Ron. 176 n.7
Rosenkrantz, Gary S., 174 n.66
Rowe, William L., 93–94
Rundle, Bede, 173 n.41
Ruse, Michael, 4
Russell's paradox. *See* barber paradox.
Ryle, Gilbert, 186 n.6

S
sacred scripture. *See* scripture, sacred; Qur'an; Mormon, Book of.
Salmon, Wesley C., 25
Scanlon, T. M., 186 n.10
scepticism: modal, 78–79, 94–96, 184 n.84; moral, 134; theological, 78–82, 95, 141
Schoen, Edward L., 47, 62–63
Schueler, G. F., 156–57, 187 n.34
Schutz, Alfred, 147–48, 185 n.1, 186 n.2
science, supernatural, 13
scripture, sacred, 140, 179 n.33, 185 n.115
Scriven, Michael, 188 n.61
secondary causes. *See* causes, primary and secondary.
Sedgwick, Adam, 12
semantically anomalous propositions, 14. *See also* theistic explanations: flexibility of; theistic explanations: danger of accommodation.
semantic realism, 172 n.6
Shanks, Niall, 12–13
silver bullet. *See* theistic explanations: silver bullet against.
singular causal explanations. *See* causation: singularist definitions of.
simplicity: divine, 46–47; explanatory virtue of, 71, 132–36
Smith, Morton, 72–73
Smith, Quentin, 53–57, 178 n.53
Sobel, Howard, 26
Sober, Elliott: on critics of theistic explanations, 169 n.80; on likelihood principle, 105, 123, 181

n.22; theological scepticism of 79–84, 94; and solitary proposed explanations, 121, 122–25
social norms, 140, 147–48
social psychology, 173 n.29
solitary proposed explanations, 31, 111, 121–25
spurious unification, 29–30, 43–44, 141. *See also* empirical content.
states of affairs. *See* events and states of affairs.
Steinhardt, Paul J., 175 n.87
Stoney, G. J., 172 n.3
Stove, D. C., 175 n.97
subdoxastic venture, 38. *See also* acceptance and belief.
suboptimality arguments, 83, 85–88, 88–97 *See also* optimality condition.
supernatural science. *See* science, supernatural.
Swinburne, Richard: on background knowledge, 128–31, 184 n.53; on coherence of theism, 49–50, 101–2; on complete explanations, 175 n.103 ; and confirmation theory, 23–26, 79, 111, 171 n.35, 183 n.33; design argument of, 60, 67, 70–71, 121, 124, 176 n.4; on divine eternity, 174 n.66; on divine immutability, 174 n.66; as evidentialist, 135; on fine-tuning argument, 70–71, 177 n.42; on God's purpose in creating, 174 n.43; inductive arguments of, 102–8; on intentional explanations, 9, 150–51, 177 n.33; and justificationism, 111, 182 n.45; on positing a poltergeist, 42–43, 45, 128–29; on principle of credulity, 181 n.29; on probability of theism, 106–7, 181 n.24; on religious experience, 107, 181 n.29; on simplicity, 71, 132–33, 136, 179 n.33
syllogism, practical. *See* practical syllogism

T

Taylor, Richard, 150
teleological argument. *See* design argument.
testability, 31, 63, 116–26, 182 n.1. *See also* theistic explanations: falsifiability of.

Thagard, Paul R., 133–34, 183 n.26, 183 n.39, 184 n.77
theism: coherence of, 46–51, 92; probability of, 106–7, 181 n.24; as research programme, 131–32
theistic explanations: apparent redundancy of, 64, 176 n.19; *a priori* rejection of, 5–7; and background knowledge (*see* background knowledge); danger of accommodation, 141–42 (*see also* theistic explanations: flexibility of); *de facto* objections to, 9–10, 11–13, 20–21, 29–30, 77, 81, 102; as explanations of last resort, 17, 146; falsifiability of, 15–16, 169 n.80 (*see also* testability); flexibility of, 14 (*see also* theistic explanations: danger of accommodation); informativeness of (*see* informativeness); in principle objections to, 10, 13–17, 20–21, 29–30, 77, 81, 102; and intermediate causal mechanisms, 52–53; as intentional explanations, 33, 40; and miracles (*see* miracles); and natural explanations, 57–58, 64, 66–71; no victory by default, 79–80, 111; ontological economy of (*see* ontological economy); optimality condition applied to (*see* optimality condition); and past explanatory success (*see* past explanatory success); silver bullet against, 13, 101–2, 143–44; simplicity of (*see* simplicity); suboptimality arguments against (*see* suboptimality arguments); testability of (*see* testability). *See also* basic actions; explanations: theistic and religious.
theodicies, and defences, 134–35
theological correctness, 20. *See also* God: concepts of
theological scepticism. *See* scepticism: theological.
theology: folk (*see* folk theology); twentieth-century, 10; and physics, 38–39
theoretical explanations. *See* explanations: theoretical.
theories and hypotheses, 23
theories of religion: intellectualist, 7; Wittgensteinian, 36, 168 n.47
Thomson, J. J, 34, 109, 117, 120, 172 n.3, 185 n.101

tsunami, Boxing Day, 60, 61, 68, 140, 176 n.7
Turok, Neil, 175 n.87
Tylor, E. B., 7

U

ubiquity of divine causation. *See* causation: ubiquity of divine.
Ullian, J. S., 127
unfalsifiability. *See* religious explanations: falsifiability of.
Ussher, Archbishop James, 169 n.81

V

van Fraassen, Bas C., 36–37, 110, 113
van Inwagen, Peter, 3, 95–96, 134–36, 180 n.48, 184 nn.83, 85
vera causa doctrine, 127, 136–37, 181 n.42

victory by default. *See* theistic explanations: no victory by default.
Vienna Circle, 35
Virgin Mary. *See* Medjugorje.
visions. *See* Medjugorje.
von Wright, Georg Henrik, 155, 173 n.35, 188 nn.53, 54

W

wave theory of light, 183 n.39
weakness of will, 85, 157–59, 160–61
Wilcox, Roger M., 183 n.38
will, weakness of. *See* weakness of will.
Wittgenstein, Ludwig, 36, 168 n.47, 172 n.18. *See also* theories of religion: Wittgensteinian.
Worrall, John, 120, 121
Wright, Georg Henrik von. *See* von Wright, Georg Henrik.